The Divine Unity of Scripture

By Adolph Saphir

PANTIANOS
CLASSICS

Published by Pantianos Classics

ISBN-13: 978-1-78987-495-2

First published in 1895

Contents

Preface

These lectures of Dr. Saphir were delivered in Kensington at the close of 1888 and beginning of 1889. They are, in some respects, the most important of all his writings, as they give, in connected form, his matured views of the relation of the two great divisions of the Bible. No preacher or writer of our day had such a clear insight into the spirit and connection of the sacred writings. This was the great charm of his preaching, which made it so attractive to many earnest-minded Christians of all Churches. It was full of instruction, because it brought out the deep meaning, quite apparent when indicated, — for his interpretations were not fanciful, but real, — of the symbols and prophecies of the Old Testament, as well as of the narratives and sayings of the New. The unity of teaching he most clearly proved and strikingly illustrated. His identification of Jehovah with Jesus can scarcely be disputed by any careful and prayerful student of Scripture. It is everywhere manifest in the claims and teachings of Jesus Himself. His distinction between monotheism and Jehovahism is vital, and clears away much of the vague mistiness of modern speculation. Dr. Saphir was a man of genius and commanding intellect, belonging to a family famed for literary ability throughout Germany and Hungary, His Jewish mind and training enabled him easily to apprehend the typology and eastern imagery of the Bible. He I.ad also the great advantage of understanding thoroughly both the philosophy and literature of Germany, having been brought into painful contact in his youth with Hegelianism (by which he was much attracted), as well as with the now prevalent materialism. He understood, therefore, much better than most English theologians, the sources from which many of the weapons are derived that are now used in the criticism of the Old Testament. These lectures are better than directly controversial. Indirectly, — as, for instance, in meeting the attempt to weaken the authority of Christ's testimony to the ancient scriptures, — they seriously affect the position of recent assailants of the antiquity and authenticity of the books of Moses and the prophets. They bring out also such an *organic connection* between the Pentateuch, as the basis, and the books which follow, and also between the histories, psalms, and prophecies themselves, as to render the attempt to revolutionise the times and order exceedingly difficult. I may state, in conclusion, that Dr. Saphir had these lectures carefully written out by a well-known reporter, which was his usual method, and was preparing them for the press when he was so suddenly and unexpectedly removed from the earthly scene. They are published — with, of course, corrections for the press — *just as he left them.*

G. CARLYLE.

London, 1892

iv

I - The Eternal Word and the Written Word

My subject this morning is – The Bible a Living Book in the Present Day.

Between Jesus Christ, the eternal Word of God, and Scripture, the written Word of God, there is an organic connection; and because there is this unity, there are a number of resemblances, which strike even the most superficial observer, between Jesus Christ and the Bible. I shall instance only three.

The first is that Jesus is the Son of God, the Lord from heaven — who came from above; and that Jesus at the same time is the Son of Man, who in all things became like unto His brethren. So we behold the Scripture — the Word of God and yet an intensely human book, written by men and for men, and breathing everywhere the atmosphere of human life and of human emotions.

The second parallel is this: that Jesus is not merely man born of a woman, but that He is the Son of David and the Son of Abraham. He came out of Bethlehem. He was brought up in Nazareth. He taught in Galilee and Judaea, and over His cross the words were written, "Jesus, King of the Jews"; and the special relation in which Jesus stands to the Jews was not merely for a certain period, but for all the ages, as long as this earth stands and the sun and moon endure. Likewise the Scripture is an intensely Jewish book. All the authors, both of the Old and New Testament writings, not even Luke the beloved physician excepted, were Hebrews of the Hebrews. Jewish is the history, Jewish is the tone in which it is written; even the Greek writings of the New Testament speak with the voice of Israel; and the full contents of Holy Scripture will never be thoroughly understood, until Israel is again brought back to the allegiance and faith of its Messiah.

But although Jesus came to His own, yet Jesus is the Light of the World, the Blessing of all Nations, and the name of Jesus is to be made known among all families and kindreds of the earth, for there is only one God and one Mediator between God and man — the man Christ Jesus. Likewise is this Jewish Bible the book for the whole world, and here there is neither Jew nor Greek, barbarian, Scythian, bond nor free. It is the book of humanity.

Third parallel: Jesus Christ spoke in the simplest possible language. He taught daily in the temple. He spoke in the streets and in the concourse of the multitudes. He said, "He that hath ears let him hear," and yet only they that were enlightened by the Spirit of God were able to understand His words. Only His sheep hear His voice. Likewise the Bible is the simplest book accessible to the most illiterate and to children, and yet it requires the illumination of the Holy Ghost in order that its simple words may be understood and its lucid and clear invitations and announcements may be accepted.

If there is this resemblance between Christ and the Scripture, there is also a resemblance between the effect of Christ's words and the effect of the Scriptures on the minds of men. The words of our blessed Saviour drew round Him various circles, more or less distant from Him. The outer circle is pictured in the officers who went to take Jesus, and who said, "Never man spake like this man." There was something so unique, so real, there was something so high above all human utterances in the words of this man, that this very peculiarity declared unto them His sacred right of authority. The world has never heard such a voice. The world has never heard such words and such wisdom.

Nearer to Christ is another circle. When the men who were in the synagogue of Nazareth, and who listened to the words of Jesus as He expounded His mission to them from the prophet Isaiah, bore witness to Him, and were astonished on account of the gracious words which flowed from His lips, their feelings were touched, their imagination was roused. Still nearer were those who, after the Sermon on the Mount, were astonished at His teaching, and said that He spoke with power and not as the scribes. Here the conscience and the heart were stirred. There is a message of God Himself to men in the words of this man.

Still nearer to Christ were the disciples who said, "Lord, to whom shall we go? Thou hast the words of eternal life"; and yet closer to Him were the apostles, and all Christians after the coming of the Spirit on the day of Pentecost, who, in the fulness of the assurance of understanding and of joy, were able to say, "The darkness is past, and the true light now shineth."

But to-day I wish to speak only of the very outermost circle round Christ — the world that says of the Scripture, "Never man spake like this man."

But before I speak of the Scriptures or Bible — "the Book" — I wish to remind you of the objections which have often been brought forward against our assertion that God has embodied His message unto mankind in a BOOK. That seems a strange and a mechanical thing to some men who are conversant chiefly with their own intuitions and with the speculations of the human mind. Let us think, then, for a moment why God has chosen a book to be the channel, the vehicle of His thoughts and of His purposes to mankind.

The gift of language is very wonderful, nay, it is divine. It is the Rubicon which none of the lower creation have ever crossed. Man alone upon earth *speaks,* and we are unable to separate thought and self-consciousness from words. Man is able to communicate his thoughts and his feelings to his fellow-man in words. Man is able to embody his experiences in words. As long as human beings attained such a long life as we read of in the book of Genesis, tradition was a safe vehicle for conveying important thoughts and events and facts to subsequent generations. But, very soon, man felt the need of securing and embodying his words in such a form that they would be steadfast and correct and easily accessible. And what a wonderful benefactor of the human race was he who invented writing! It seems as if, by writing, thoughts were imprisoned, stereotyped; but, rather, by means of writing, thoughts receive wings to fly abroad through all the ages and nations of the earth. Without writing, human progress would have been almost impossible, individual progress exceedingly slow, the progress of communities scarcely perceptible.

And here, again, there is a distinction to be made. Some of the ancient nations embodied their thoughts in writings which appealed to the eye, reminding the eye of objects and actions, by pictures, which were brought before it, whereas a far more perfect way of conveying our thoughts is by an alphabet which, through the eye, affects the inner ear, and in which every sign is representative of a sound; — this was the kind of writing which was known probably to the patriarchs, certainly to Moses and to the people of Israel in his day, so that we meet now with this extraordinary fact, that the Egyptians, the Babylonians, and the Assyrians, nations far greater and more powerful than the Jews, earnestly wishing to give immortality to themselves and to their history, embodied their past experiences in great and colossal monuments upon which there were inscribed mysterious figures. Notwithstanding, for centuries and centuries they remained unknown to the world, and within even the last century they exercised, and sometimes baffled, the sagacity of the most ingenious, whereas this poor despised nation — God's nation — was able [1] from the beginning, in an easy, correct, and accessible manner, to embody its history also in a compact and continuous method; and for ages all the educated nations of the earth have known that history. Your children and the children of most of the nations of Europe were familiar with that history before they were familiar with the history of their own country. When, therefore, God said to Moses, "Write in a book," and again, "Write in a book," and when we find that our Saviour and all the apostles laid such great emphasis upon that which is written, and when John in the Apocalypse received again the command, "Write in a book," do we not see that God acted, not merely with the most profound wisdom, but also with the most fatherly adaptation to the wants of humanity?

But I must advance a step further. By degrees the books of the Old Testament were written, as the history of the Old Testament developed. Israel after the captivity, having been, by the judgment of God, delivered from idolatry, now concentrated all its religious and intellectual energy upon the Scripture, the law, and the teaching which God had given them, — and with the utmost reverence and the most scrupulous fidelity they collected and they preserved the sacred writings. But the book was in Hebrew and it was in Palestine, in a corner of the world; and if this book is for the world, who is to publish it and give it unto the nations? Then there came that wonderful conqueror Alexander the Great, a bright meteor appearing for a brief time; and this was his great work, that he introduced the language and the culture of Greece into Asia. Thus there was formed a bridge between the Jews in Palestine and the whole outer world. The Greek language was destined to become the language of the whole inhabited earth, and thus in the providence of God, through the existence of multitudes of Jews in Alexandria and the surrounding countries, there was produced the translation of the Hebrew Bible into the Greek Septuagint, which served a double purpose: first, God's Scriptures were now translated into a language in which they could reach all the known nations of the earth; and secondly, that very language, the Greek language, was made plastic to express those ideas which no Greek, in fact no nation of the world, ever had before, and which were embodied in the New Testament — the ideas of humility, of grace, of God, — and afterwards the evangelists and the apostles found ready to their hand the Greek language in which they carried the tidings of salvation unto all the nations of the earth. When this book was thus formed — the Old Testament by the care of the Jews, the New Testament by the care of the early Church— then it began its history among the nations; and what I wish to impress upon you to-day is, that if we have the book at present as a living book amongst us, this is a wonderful fact, for the persecution of it has never ceased.

This book was in the first place persecuted by pagan Rome. There was a persecution of the Bible and of the people that possessed it One of the persecutions was in the year 303. The early Christians delighted in the Word of God. The early teachers of the Christian faith exhorted them to study the whole of the Word. Irenaeus says, "Read the whole Scripture, because it is written, 'Of every tree of the garden shalt thou eat.'" Origen says, "You must not neglect the Old Testament, but study it equally with the New, in order that you may be as a good householder, bringing forth out of his treasure things both old and new." And thus at the public assemblies of the Christians large portions of the Scriptures were read; and since copies of the Scriptures were expensive, [2] those Christians who were rich spent large sums of money in getting copies distributed among the poor members of the Church, So the Christians often met together in friendly and familiar intercourse, in order that the Scripture might be read aloud to them; and so intently did they listen to the reading of the Scriptures that Eusebius tells us that one John in Egypt, who conducted services, was able to repeat not merely chapters, but whole sections of the Word of God. The pagans saw that these Scriptures were the very strength of the hated doctrine, and therefore the edict of Diocletian went forth. Many copies of the Scriptures were burnt, and many of those who kept the Scriptures were put to most painful and agonising deaths, two bishops among them. Papal Rome also persecuted the Scriptures, but chiefly in this way: that instead of being the custodian of Scripture it became the jailer of Scripture, and for many centuries the Word of God was hidden from the people, and legends and traditions of men became the food of the human mind. When Martin Luther emancipated the Scriptures and sent them forth into the world, the discovery of printing, under the providence of God, having been made only a few years before, the teaching of Luther began and continued with the key which opened the Scriptures, namely, justification by faith in the Lord Jesus Christ. Then the nations of Europe came and listened gladly to the heavenly voice. Still the Book had not exhausted all the persecutions it was to endure, for after a while it was persecuted by Rationalism, —

and it is very important to note this fact; for some of those who call themselves advanced, but are in reality the most retrograde people we have among us, are, perhaps unconsciously to themselves, leading us back again to that dreary, sandy desert. A Rationalist does not believe in the divinity of Christ, does not believe in the direct interference of God in miracle, does not believe in prophecy as foretelling future events, does not believe in the expiatory atonement of our Saviour. What does he believe? He believes no more than he might know without the Bible, except that in Jesus there appears a beautiful and a grand character. This Rationalism, while treating the Bible outwardly with respect, leaves it like Samson shorn of his locks and his eyes blind when the cry went forth, "The Philistines are upon thee." Oh, no wonder that there is no strength and no energy in this emasculated Bible.

Then came the period of infidelity, bold, mocking, scornful, calling the Bible a liar, and predicting that in fifty years there would not be a trace or a vestige left of this book. Then, even in our own days, there came Pantheism, which said that miracle was impossible, that there was no personal God, that that which is God becomes conscious of itself only in the human mind, and that therefore all the narratives concerning Jesus Christ were only mythical garments by which to represent an idea. Pantheists derided the Bible as a thing that had long had influence, but had now disappeared from among living powers.

Then came the internal criticism, applying the resources of history, of physical science, of archaeology, to examining the Scriptures and the authenticity and integrity of its various books, which has precisely the same effect on the mass of people as tradition had under the influence of Rome, — namely, to make them think that the simple and unlearned man is not able to understand the Scripture, that there is a hedge of thorns and briars round about it, and that only those who devote themselves to the study of specific points can with any certainty ascertain what is true and what is spurious in the Bible. And yet notwithstanding these facts — that pagan Rome sought to kill the Bible, and papal Rome to imprison the Bible, Rationalism to emasculate the Bible, French infidelity to deride the Bible, Pantheism to bury the Bible, and this modern criticism to remove the Bible to an infinite distance from the generality of mankind — the Bible lives, like the Jews. Pharaoh tried to drown them, another great king tried to burn them, Haman tried to give them up to an ignominious death. But notwithstanding all this, they live, and so does the Bible live; and not merely does it live, but it has never shown so much vitality as in the present day.

Is not the Bible Society a wonderful fact? A great philosopher, many years ago, who was president at one of its meetings, gave a very remarkable address, in which he showed the importance of the Bible Society; he said that in the Bible Society the principles of the Reformation were, as it were, embodied before all nations — that this book is the property of all men, that in the Church of Christ all members are in direct communication with God Himself, and that it is easy for all to understand it. This Bible Society has published more than 312,000,000 copies of the Bible and translated it into 350 languages, and 70 of these — and this is a remarkable fact — languages which at the beginning of this century possessed no alphabet, and not the slightest vestige of a literature. We can scarcely measure the importance of giving to a people letters, the possibility of a literature, and, to begin that literature, the Book of books. To have done this seventy times is a wonderful achievement. While the Church of Rome boasts that among all nations of the earth she is continually repeating the Mass in the dead Latin language which appeals to no human heart, evangelical Christianity has gone forth, renewing the Pentecostal miracle, and showing the all-embracing philanthropy of our great God and Saviour.

This book is full of interest, whether to enemy or friend. Never has the Bible been so minutely studied, never has it occupied so much the attention of men generally, and never has the desire of Christians to be made acquainted with the whole counsel of God as embodied in it, been so strong as at this day. It is indeed a living book.

And yet I have only touched, as it were, the outside of this great subject So familiar are we with the facts, that it is necessary for us to look them more fully in the face in order to impress them on our minds. No other book can be compared with this, simply as a book. It is an Oriental book, but as Sir William Jones pointed out long ago, all the other Oriental books, be they ever so poetical, or be they ever so wise, in order to be made intelligible and palatable to the western mind, require to be transfused. Many omissions are necessary, and many modifications are requisite. How is it that this Oriental book has taken possession chiefly of Japhet, of the western nations — of England, of Germany, of America? How is it that this Oriental book, whether taken to Greenland, or to Madagascar, or to South Africa, or to the interior of India, is a book that appeals to the mind and heart of those that hear it Only last week I read an account of a missionary who was reading the 1st chapter of the epistle to the Romans, in which heathenism is described in its effects; and when the chapter was finished, a Brahmin who was present went up and said, "That describes us." He recognised in the words the condition of his own nation. To this book there is no limitation of race or nationality. It has become in all nations a household book, a home book, a heart book. Look at the history that it has had in the past. We can measure the universality of a book by the power it has of being translated into other languages. Look at the German Bible. The German Bible is the standard of German literature. All Germans, whether they be believers or unbelievers, Romanists or Protestants, acknowledge that Martin Luther, in translating the Bible into German, transformed and fixed the German language. The German language, as it were, renewed its youth, nay, more than that, it imbibed vivifying and transfiguring elements which it never possessed before. Every turn of Luther's Bible, every mode of expression is intensely German, out of the very depth of the heart of the German nation. Is it not so with your English Bible also? How is it that this Hebrew book becomes the most German and the most English of all books? Because it speaks to the heart of humanity. Consider all the minds which in the past this book has influenced. Unless you examine with this special purpose, — thanks to the writings of Milton and Shakespeare and other great authors, — you cannot imagine how the Bible narratives, the Bible truths, the Bible similes, the Bible expressions, have entered into the very marrow of English literature. You continually find terms and expressions which they owe to the Bible.

And I am sure that all will bear me witness that I tell what they themselves have experienced when I say that if you have a speech of the most brilliant eloquence, or a piece of the most subtle and acute reasoning, and if a Bible passage be quoted, that passage in the midst of all that is brilliant will shine forth more brilliant still, and will appear deeper than all that is profound, and will take hold of men and of the affections of men, as nothing else can.

Consider again the minds which have bowed in admiration of this book, as Leibnitz, Milton, Lord Bacon, Pascal, Faraday, Newton Locke, metaphysicians, men of natural science, poets and philosophers — not that I wish to adduce this as an argument for the truth of the Bible, It was not because these men were wise and learned, but because the Holy Ghost enlightened them, that they saw the truth as it is in the Scriptures; but this fact proves that although there are many wise men who reject the Bible, it is not their wisdom that forces them to reject it, neither is it the wisdom and learning of others that incline them to receive it. This book is high above all human wisdom or genius, coming from above with its own light and with its own power.

But I would remind you of another and far larger class to whom the Bible has thus endeared itself and been its own witness. It is a very strange thing that there is no other book in the world for children like the Bible. There is a remarkable passage in one of the addresses of Huxley, in which he says that although he is entirely in favour of secular education, yet he is completely at a loss what substitute to have for the Bible, for there is no other book in which the highest, the most sublime and purifying thoughts are made so accessible and so attractive to the child's mind as the Bible. Professor St. Hilaire writes: "I have travelled north and south, and cast and west, and have been much struck with the fact that in all the countries in which the Bible is read there is a literature for children and for working men, but in those countries in which the Bible is not read, as in Italy, or even in France, there is no literature for the children or for the poor. Where do you find history? where do you find narratives? where do you find characters? where do you find doctrine? where do you find poetry — such as the Bible presents? Universal is its language. It is like the sun which enlightens all lands."

Poets especially have acknowledged the supremacy of the Bible. Goethe, that great representative of modern thought, has said, "Let the world progress as much as it likes, let all branches of human research develop to the

11

very utmost, nothing will take the place of the Bible — that foundation of all culture and of all education."

Look at the style of the Bible, for every book has its style. What is the style of the Bible? The style of the Bible is difficult to describe, but every one has a distinct idea of it The simplicity, the perfect objective calmness of its narratives, its power, its lucidity, its attractiveness, its terseness, every one has felt, whether he believes it or not. Where is there in the whole realm of literature a narrative like that of Abraham taking up Isaac to Mount Moriah, or of the raising of Lazarus, or of Joseph making himself known to his brethren? Or take the whole gospels, in which not for a single moment does the enthusiasm or feeling of the writers betray itself. Did you ever think of the 23rd Psalm, — six short verses a compendium of all human life, — a little nightingale that has gone through all the countries of the earth pouring forth its inimitable melody, thrilling the heart and bringing peace and consolation to the soul? Do you think that all the poets in the world, if they were working for ever so many years, could produce such six verses? How wonderful is that style of the Bible!

I will read you what a great artist, one of the greatest lyrical poets, has said about the Bible. He being a true artist saw what was beautiful in the Bible, and because he was a true artist he saw that there was an infinite distance between anything that art could produce and this book. These are the words of Heine, for many years a pantheist, a frivolous and pernicious writer, but a man of great genius: "What a book! great and wide as the world, rooted in the depths of creation and mounting into the mysterious azure of the heavens. Indeed it is God's Word, while all other books evince only human skill. In the Bible is not a vestige of art. It is impossible to criticise its style." This man came very near seeing what was the secret of the style of the Bible. As nature is above art, so is the Bible above other literature. When you see an artificial rose, you say, "How clever!" When you see a real rose, you say, "How beautiful! how fragrant!" As nature is above art, so is inspiration above nature. The man of genius is above the commonplace man. He is a law to himself. His words, his pictures, his sculpture are, as it were, a creation. But although the difference between the man of genius and the ordinary man is exceedingly great, it is nothing compared with the difference between a man in whom the Holy Ghost has kindled His light, and by whom the Spirit of the Most High is speaking, and the greatest and most brilliant genius. It is the voice of God, but yet a human voice, which speaks to us in this Word; and all, whether they believe or not, must say, "Never man spake like this man"; "Never book was written like this book."

Let us pass now from the form to the substance of the Bible. There is no other book in the world so interesting to man as man, as the Bible. What is new? What is old? People often make great mistakes in not distinguishing between modern and new, for there are many modern things which have been buried thousands of times already, and are only walking about like ghosts, having no blood and life in them; whereas there are old things that are full of life, because they are eternal. In many branches of knowledge there is progress. Fact is discovered after fact, and experience comes after experience; and so by degrees stone is laid upon stone, and the great edifice is reared. But in the things which interest us most deeply there is no progress. The questions which were asked in the days of Job are the same questions which are asked now, and, apart from revelation, man has not advanced one single step towards answering these questions. We know with the utmost certainty that the three angles of a triangle are together equal to two right angles, and there can be no doubt about the calculations of astronomy as to the heavenly bodies; but of what use is such knowledge to man, woman, and child, in affliction and in death? But the Bible contains those things which concern our inmost spiritual and everlasting life; and therefore, no matter what turn history may take, no matter what development science may have, the intense interest and youth of the Bible will remain throughout all ages the same. There is a story told of one of the generals of Frederick the Great. This general was a true believer in Scripture, and Frederick the Great often addressed questions to him, partly to annoy him and partly to elicit some answer. He said to him one day, "Now tell me, why do you always revert to the Bible?" and General Schmidtt gave him this answer, which I think a most beautiful answer: "Because the Bible reveals to me a Father who numbers the very hairs of my head; because the Bible reveals to me a Saviour who by His blood expiates every one of my sins; and because the Bible shows unto me a heaven where I am to spend an everlasting and blessed existence."

And now I shall read you the testimony of a German pantheist, the celebrated Strauss, who did not believe in a personal God, and who during his last illness said to his friends: "I am just going out like a flickering candle that is burned down." In one of his latest books he said, in order to account for the power of Christianity: "The misery caused by the consciousness of our faults and the reproaches of conscience is relieved by Christianity. Through its doctrine of an expiatory atonement, the desolate feeling that we are the victims of blind chance vanishes before the sheltering arms of Providence, and the darkness of the gloomy night of our earthly life is illuminated by the prospect of an immortal and heavenly blessedness." Just what the Christian had said from his experience, and stated as a fact derived from the Bible, this man sees to be just that which meets the requirements of the human heart and conscience, and sees that it is provided by Christianity. There is no peace without a Father who loves us and cares for us, a Saviour who has taken away the burden from our conscience, and a hope of everlasting blessedness, which is a hope that "maketh not ashamed."

I shall conclude by saying a few words about Jesus; and while I speak of Jesus, think of the Bible parallel. Jesus — born at Bethlehem, brought up at Nazareth, never at the colleges of the learned, rejected by the Pharisees derided by the Sadducees, crucified, dead, and buried — lives. The mothers bring their little babes to Him. Children sing to Him, "Hosanna!" An innumerable multitude of weary and heavy-laden ones hear His voice, "Come unto Me." And the chosen of God confess, "Thou art the Christ, the Son of the living God. Unto whom shall we go? Thou hast the words of eternal life.' Amen.

[1] In a paper on the great discovery of the cuneiform inscriptions of Tel-el-Amarna by Professor Sayce, the discoverer, read at the Victoria Institute in 1889, it is said, "How highly educated this old world was we are but just beginning to learn. But we have already learnt enough to discover how important a bearing it has on the criticism of the Old Testament. It has long been tacitly assumed by the critical school that writing was not only a rare art in Palestine before the age of David, but was practically unknown. Little historical credence can be placed, it has been urged, in the earlier records of the Hebrew people, because they could not have been committed to writing until, a period when the history of the past had become traditional and mythical. But this assumption can no longer be maintained. Long before the Exodus, Canaan had its libraries and its scribes, its schools and literary men. The annals of the country, it is true, were not inscribed in the letters of the Phoenician alphabet on perishable papyrus; the writing material was the imperishable clay; the characters those of the cuneiform syllabary."
[2] Writings were, however, much cheaper at this period of the early Church than many suppose. There were great numbers of copyists of the Greek and Latin writers, so that copies could be got for very moderate sums. There were many copyists or scribes, doubtless, also in the Church.

II - A Book Revelation - An Intrinsic Necessity

The subject which is to occupy us this morning, and if it please God also on the next occasion, is the following: The Bible is the Word of God.

I wish to dwell more specially to-day on the Bible as a revelation from God, and to consider in my next lecture the human, historical, and progressive aspect of Scripture in relation to Christ and the Spirit of God.

A divine revelation embodied in a book is not unworthy of God, and it is according to divine wisdom and love that God, who revealed Himself in acts and in words to the fathers by prophets and apostles, should have caused the whole revelation to be committed to writing in order that all future generations might possess it in a form secure, complete, correct, and easy of access.

A book revelation is an intrinsic necessity. In no other way could the divine purposes of love have been secured, and, as we have already shown, this book has made a deep impression upon mankind, so that among all the books of the world it stands out pre-eminent, even as Jesus Christ stands out pre-eminent among all the children of men.

A few days before his death, when Sir Walter Scott was in his library, he said to his son-in-law, "Will you read something to me?" and when asked what book, his immediate reply was, "You need not ask. There is only one book." A few years ago, as a French pastor tells us, there was a meeting of a number of literary and scientific men, some of whom were sceptics and materialists, and in the course of conversation the question arose: If we were banished to a lonely island, or if we had to suffer imprisonment for a lifetime, what book, from among all the books of which human literature consists, would be chosen to be our sole companion? and the unanimous answer was, "The Bible."

This book, which in the wonderful providence of God arose gradually, the art of writing being known to the children of Israel at least as early as the days of Moses, and which afterwards, through its translation into the Greek language, found its way to all nations, is, now as ever, after having contended against all persecution and opposition, a book unique in its vitality, in its attractiveness, in its interest, and in its power. Greek literature stands out above the literature of all other nations, and all agree in acknowledging its brilliancy and power; but it does not reach the heart of man, for it does not breathe the atmosphere of eternity; it does not reach the deep things of the human soul; whereas Hebrew, a much poorer and barer language, planting itself before the very sanctuary of human consciousness, has taken hold of the hearts and souls of all races and families of the earth. Yet, while dwelling on this, and on the peculiar, powerful, and attractive style of Scripture, we were after all only in the outer court It is as when standing before a beautiful and glorious cathedral where, at the very outset, the gates attract our attention and offer to us many interesting points of observation, but the real beauty and glory can only be seen when we pass on, — within. Or, it is like standing before a garden where there is a hedge which does not altogether prevent us from seeing what is beyond. Through the gaps in the hedge you can get glimpses of some of the lovely flowers and perceive the fragrance of others, yet you cannot really see the beauty of the garden till you enter it and stand within.

Yet the attractiveness of the Bible, its unique style, the hold it takes upon the human heart — none of these would have existed if the Bible had been only human. It is because it stands above mankind that it dwells within mankind; and who is He that inhabits the high and holy place, and yet dwells in the human heart, but God the Lord; and as God is, so is His Word.

I shall speak now of Scripture as it is regarded by the friends of Scripture. As I reminded you that, whilst, in regard to Jesus, it was acknowledged that no man ever spake like this man by those that were strangers to His grace, there was also an inmost circle of His disciples who believed and were sure that He was the Son of God, so is it also in regard to the Scriptures. The Scriptures might say to those who persecute them, "Many good works have I done among you. For which of these good works do ye persecute me?" And the answer of men would be "For a good work we persecute thee not, but because thou, being a book like other books, claimest to be a divine book." But the testimony of the intimate friends of the Bible is that Scripture is the Word of God.

It may be said that the testimony of friends is not of decisive value; and yet, after all, who but a friend can witness effectively? The witness of enemies is negative. So it was in the case of Jesus. Judas said, "I have shed innocent blood." Pilate said, "I find no fault in Him." The Pharisees were unable to bring any accusation against Him, or to convince Him of sin; but it was only the apostles who were able to testify of the person of Jesus; and remarkable it is, that that disciple who 'was most intimately acquainted with the humanity of our blessed Saviour — he who leant on the bosom of Jesus — was the disciple who most emphatically testified that they had beheld the glory as of the only begotten of the Father. And the testimony of the friends of the Bible is of great importance when we remember this: that the friends of the Bible were not born friends of the Bible — were once strangers to the Word, and enemies of the Word; but that there was given to them light from above, and a conviction which nothing in this world can shake. Another peculiarity about the friends of the Bible is this, that every one of them is an independent witness. Every one of them can say, like the men of Samaria, "Now we believe the Bible, not because we have been so taught from our infancy...nor because of the testimony of the Church and its ministers; but because we have seen it ourselves, and heard its voice, and are convinced that it is the Word of God. For that light, which shines into every one that believes, is the same light which shone in those who knew Him, and now shines in the original testimony of those who bore witness unto Him, — that we may believe that this is indeed the Christ, the Son of God, and that believing we may have life through His name."

Thus, when the whole world acknowledges the peculiarity of the book, and when we know the reason of that peculiarity, we contrast it with all other books. All other books are ephemeral, simply pamphlets which come and go. This is for all ages. Others address themselves to a limited sphere of mankind, whether of race, or of learning, or of class. This speaks to all mankind. Others, in the course of centuries, are exhausted, and all that is valuable in them is absorbed. This book is inexhaustible. The mine is deep; the more we search, the more are there brought out treasures of gold and silver from its hidden depths. Other books contain errors which have to be refuted, and imperfections which have to be supplemented. This book is like gold tried in the fire. And not merely is it free from error, but it contains in itself a rectifying power which is able to cope with every error and heresy, as it arises in the history of mankind; and this, because it is God's book.

A revelation from God. Do we require a revelation from God? The wonderful gift of reason, that beautiful light and noble instrument with which God Himself has endowed us, is indeed most precious, but it is the lesser light. It is to shine in the realm of this world, and has to do with the things of time. It is capable of receiving light from above. It is not light creative, but light receptive. Two very powerful testimonies have been given to this by men who are acknowledged in modern times to be stars of the first magnitude in the horizon of philosophy. The one was Kant, a man of the most subtle analysis. He wrote thus to a friend. The extract has not been published in any of his biographies, but was mentioned recently in an Augsburg paper. He said, "You do well in that you base your peace and piety on the gospels, for in the gospels, and in the gospels alone, is the source of deep spiritual truths, after reason has measured out its whole territory in vain." And another great leader of thought, the pantheistic metaphysician Hegel, on his death-bed, would have no book read to him but the Bible; and said that if God were to prolong his life he would make this book his study, for in it he found what mere reason could not discover. His favourite hymn during those dying days was a German hymn of which the bearing is, "Jesus, draw me entirely unto thyself."

From above there comes revelation. "Eye hath not seen" — observation cannot discover — "ear hath not heard" — tradition and the learning of the past ages cannot transmit — "neither hath entered the heart of man" — genius and intuition cannot find out — "what God hath prepared for them that love Him, but unto us He hath revealed it by His Spirit."

Now, of those things that are revealed to us by the Spirit of God, and which are contained in the Scriptures, from Genesis even to the culminating book of the Apocalypse, I wish now to speak to you; and I single out six great things — I do not like to call them ideas, because they are realities — which have been revealed to us in the Bible.

The first is God. The world in its ignorance and folly knows not God. The world in its wisdom knows not God. The world in its sinfulness knows not God. The world in its virtue, Pharisaic and stoical, knows not God. Nature does not reveal God. Nature, when it pleases God through it to speak to the heart, reveals the existence, the power, the goodness, and the wisdom of God; but nature does not reveal God Himself. Polytheism did not know the one God, but only an abstract, a supreme force or reason. Atheism denies God. Pantheism degrades God. Positivism ignores God. Scripture reveals God. The idea of God that Scripture gives to us is so majestic and yet so heart-winning, is so sublime and yet so simple, is so full of variety and apparent contradictions and yet so united, that all those who, by the grace of God, have learnt from the Scripture, feel and are convinced that God has revealed Himself to them. Infinite and incomprehensible, dwelling in light that is unapproachable, He yet condescends to make Himself known to the children of men, even to babes. Eternal and omnipresent. He lives with us from day to day, and is the home and sanctuary of His people, in all generations; holy, so that He chargeth even the angels with folly, and yet the Redeemer and Saviour of sinners; just, and the justifier of the guilty; terrible in His majesty and in His judgment, tender and compassionate, merciful, patient, and long-suffering, infinitely blessed in Himself, and needing nothing external for His life and for His joy, — and yet weeping over Jerusalem and sighing over His sinful nation; stretching forth His hands against a gainsaying people, and, again, calling heaven and earth to sympathise with Him, all fields and all trees to rejoice with Him, because He has found the one that was lost, and has quickened him that was dead; revealing Himself to us, and making known to us His secret thoughts; and yet after all His revelations, we say, "Who is like unto God? Oh, the depth of the riches." He tells Israel that they must make themselves no image of God, for they have at no time seen any form or similitude of Him. But He Himself speaks to Israel in such a concrete way. He has eyes, and He sees; He has ears, and He listens to the voice of our supplication. The sacrifice of Noah ascends unto Him, and He smells a sweet savour. He has hands, and they are stretched forth to rescue the perishing people, He arises and awakes, and rouses Himself out of His sleep and hastens to deliver the godly. He remembers His promises of old. He sometimes forgets to be gracious and to hear. It repents Him that He has ever created man; and then He rejoices as if there were no joy for Him except in the salvation and in the blessedness of His people. Who would ever venture to speak thus of God? But, Scripture speaking thus of God, there is no danger of the simplest human being misunderstanding it. The spirituality of our human God far transcends all the ethereal speculation of human wisdom. He compares Himself to a father: "As a father pitieth his children." He compares Himself to a mother that is not able to forget her child. He compares Himself to a bridegroom that rejoices over his bride. He speaks of Himself as a friend who cannot do anything, unless He communicates it first to His chosen ones. Oh, when the Bible brings us God revealing Himself, it is no abstraction; it is no philosophy: it is full of life and full of love, and enters into the very inmost heart of man. There is nothing so sublime, and there is nothing so pathetic.

But we must go still deeper into this subject. God reveals Himself Knowledge of God in the sense in which metaphysicians take it, God denies to be possible for human beings. As metaphysicians speak of the being of God, of the essence of God, of the substance of God, and the necessity of God's existence, it is impossible for us to understand such things. Neither man nor angel can comprehend God, or possess an intellectual knowledge of God, as of something that he is able to estimate. There was no light in the Holy of Holies for, "I the Lord dwell in darkness;" and none can know God. But God reveals Himself as He wishes to reveal Himself, not to the intellect only, but to the whole man. Where mind and will meet, in their central unity in the heart, there it is that God makes Himself known by the Scriptures. "The fool hath said in his heart, There is no God," and only the fool thinks that he can know God as a philosophical study. Both reason and will combine in the heart; and the children of God with the heart believe that God has spoken to them. And therefore you will never find in the Scripture the idea of God or the substance of God — none of those metaphysical, high-flown abstractions and impossibilities; but the Scripture speaks of the dear face of God. That is all we want. We want to see His face. That is all we want of father and mother, and wife and child. And the Scripture speaks of the name of God. That is the aspect of God manwards, and therefore you must never, when you read the Bible and when you read God, think that the God that is mentioned there is the God of whom the world speaks — that abstraction, that idea, that power, that heaven, that "providence." Oh no, it is Jehovah; it is Christ; it is God in His aspect towards us. This, He has revealed to us. Therefore it is a great mistake to say that the religion of the Old Testament is monotheism. The religion of the Turks is monotheism. The religion of the Old Testament is Jehovahism. We are taught that this Jehovah, God of Abraham, Isaac and Jacob, who brought us out of Egypt and led us into the land of Canaan, is *the* God, and also that Jesus Christ is the true God, and everlasting *life*. For God (as we have no better name for it) is person. Do you know what is implied in being a person? We are but of yesterday. A few years ago we had no existence. By degrees we become self-conscious and distinguish ourselves from all other human beings, and from all the things that are around us. Only by degrees and imperfectly do we find out what we are, what is within us, our thoughts, our will, our character, our reason, our emotions; but never, at any given moment of our earthly life, are we in full consciousness of our own individuality. Never in any given moment of our life do we see all that is within us and all the thoughts and experiences of our past; and continually do we feel that there are influences from without, and that there are dark things within, which interfere with our individuality, and do not belong to us. But now rise for a moment to a different and eternal sphere. Think of Him who is from everlasting to everlasting, who, before any of the worlds were created by His will, said, "I," who is always conscious of His thoughts, and of His purposes, and of the perfections and attributes which are in Him. Therefore does God continually call Himself, "I." "I am." "I am the Lord." "Then shall ye know that I am he;" and in the New Testament, "Be not afraid; it is I;" "Unless you believe that I am he;" down to the last chapter of the book of Revelation, where He says, "I, Jesus." Now of this one — that is "I" the only one of whom we can say in perfection that He is a person — will you not admit of Him what you have to admit of the youngest child and of the most limited human being, that, unless He chooses to tell you His thoughts and His will, you cannot know them? You may guess them, but you cannot know them. He speaks. And if God is person, will you not allow to that person the right which you claim for yourself? There are some to whom you open yourself, and there are others to whom you cannot open yourself. "How is it that thou wilt manifest thyself unto us, and not unto the world?" "The secret of the Lord is with them that fear him." "The father and I will come." God as a person, in His sovereignty and of His abundant love, reveals Himself.

But I must pass on now to the second fact — Man. Apart from Scripture we do not know that the world was created by God. The wisest Greeks and Romans did not know it. No cosmography has ever been discovered in which there is the slightest trace of the idea that God created the heavens and the

19

earth. Matter was considered to have existed from eternity. A speculation, which has been again revived in our own days, spoke of atoms out of which by degrees the present cosmos was shaped. If God had wished to state at the beginning of Scripture, "Now I begin to speak, and here ends all human wisdom, and where human wisdom ends revelation begins," — if God had wished, as it were, to place a barrier to separate His book from all the books of the world. He could not have done it better and more effectively than He has done it, by declaring, "In the beginning God created the heavens and the earth." That single sentence separates Scripture from all the rest of human wisdom and productions; and the creation of man in the image of God, with majesty and solemnity, the whole Godhead as it were retreating into the depth of its wisdom, and of its love, and saying, as it had never said before, "Let us make man in our image," — only Scripture reveals. And the fall and sinfulness of man Scripture reveals. It shows man his guilt, without degrading him, like the cynics. It shows man his misery, without driving him to despair. It shows man his exaltation, and yet ascribes all the glory and honour to God. Instead of dwelling on speculations as to the pre-Adamite man, why will not the men of science tell us what the post-Adamite man will be — the future man? Scripture tells us what the deutero-Adamites will be — the future of humanity, when Christ shall appear, and when they who are Christ's shall be made manifest; and as we have borne the image of the earthly Adam, so we shall bear the image of the heavenly, not through any evolution, but by the renewing of the Holy Ghost, and by the resurrection power of the great Son of God. Scripture reveals to us — man.

The third thing that the Bible reveals is — Grace. The world does not know what grace is. Grace is not pity; grace is not indulgence or leniency; grace is not long-suffering. Grace is as infinite an attribute of God as is His power, and as is His wisdom. Grace manifests itself in righteousness. Grace has a righteousness which is based upon atonement or substitution, and through the whole Scripture there run the golden thread of grace and the scarlet thread of atonement, which together reveal to us for man a righteousness that comes down from heaven.

Here is the great difference between the Bible and all religions of the world: that, whereas man tries to make himself more worthy of the Deity, the Bible declares to us that we begin with perfection of righteousness, even the best robe descending down to us through the love of the Father, and the atoning death of our Saviour Jesus Christ.

I pass on to the fourth idea — Incarnation! Some people have spoken as if the Hindoos and the Buddhists have also the idea of incarnation. Very few words are required to completely demolish this assertion. In the Hindoo theology we read of avatars or gods assuming monstrous and multiform appearances for a definite purpose, as of rewarding a favourite, or of bringing justice and vengeance on an enemy. But to the fact of incarnation, as it is revealed to us in Christ, these grotesque fancies have not the slightest resemblance; and as for Buddhism, it cannot teach incarnation, because it is atheism, and does not believe in God at all, and therefore those Buddhas that appear from time to time are simply men of great wisdom and virtue who, after teaching for a certain number of years, vanish again into what they consider to be the greatest blessedness — nonexistence. But what is revealed to us in Scripture? That the Word was made flesh, and dwelt among us, that God was manifest in the flesh, that the Son of God took upon Him our nature, and was born of a woman, and that this wonderful person — eternal, and appearing in time, infinite, and clothing Himself with humanity — is Son of God and yet true man, two natures in one person, and that He is to be such for ever and for ever. And that as truly as the Son of God lived here, and died upon the cross, so truly is the Son of Man now sitting at the right hand of the Majesty; and that such a glorious being is now the Mediator rooted in the very centre of humanity, and rooted in the very centre of the Godhead — oh, what a wonderful revelation is this. And in Scripture this is asserted not merely in the gospels and in the epistles; but from the beginning of Genesis, through the whole of the Old Testament, there runs the announcement, there runs the preparation — there is the instalment, so to speak, of this great fact, there is the angel of His presence in whom is the name of God, as in the marvellous vision that appeared to Isaiah when he saw also the glory of Christ, as he beheld the Lord sitting on a throne high and lifted up.

I come to the fifth point. Nowadays people are always talking about morality, about ethics. Oh, they do not want dogma, they want ethics. Even into our pulpits this unscriptural word has forced its way. Let me assure you that if an idea cannot be clothed in Scripture words, you may be sure that this idea has departed from Scripture truth and fulness. What is there so great and noble in the words "morality," "ethics," or, as the Germans call it, *sittlichkeit?* They all mean the same thing — custom. *Ethos,* customs; *mores,* manners. Sittlichkeit is that which is become the habit, or, in other words, the highest idea that man has of rectitude, character, and conduct. It is very noble, it is very good, it is very great, but after all it does not rise above the level of humanity. Not so with the Bible. An ancient Jewish teacher made this remark: "There are several hundreds of precepts, there are several hundreds of prohibitions in the Scripture, but all these hundreds (I think about six hundred) may be reduced to ten — the ten words which God spoke; and these ten words may be reduced to two — love to God, and in God, love to your neighbour; and these two may be reduced to one, 'the just shall live by faith.'" He was not far from the kingdom of God. The Bible speaks not of morality, but the Bible says, "Enoch walked with God." God appeared to Abraham and said, "I am thy God. Walk thou before me and be perfect"

And what are the ten commandments? They are not founded on an abstract idea, not upon what the Greek calls the good, the true, the beautiful. "God spoke these words and said, I am the Lord thy God which brought thee out of the land of Egypt, out of the house of bondage. Thou shalt have no other gods beside me." And in each of the first five commandments it is, "The Lord thy God."

The Bible enters into all the details of human life. The Bible goes into small minutiae of our conduct and of our circumstances; but upon each of the Bible commands is written, "I am the Lord." "Thou shalt put no stumbling-block in the way of the blind." I am the Lord — identified with this blind man. And Jesus says to us in that Sermon on the Mount that is so much admired for its morality — but morality is not there — something much higher than morality and inclusive of morality, "As your Father which is in heaven is perfect;" and then He says not merely that, but "Abide in me and I in you, for without me ye can do nothing." And then a man like the apostle Paul says, "To me to live is Christ." Where are the ethics now? That person the object of my life, the joy of my life, the source of my life, nay, the very life of my communion with God, our Wisdom says, "I am man" — "Homo sum" — and everything that is human interests me. The Bible wants to make us men of God.

And, lastly, the Bible gives to us a revelation of God's kingdom, and by "kingdom" do not understand an abstraction of principles, the prevalence of ideas, not even the acceptance of Christianity. That is not meant by the kingdom of God. The kingdom of God means the kingdom of God — God the King, Christ His Vicegerent, Satan His adversary, mankind the centre, the earth the territory, Israel the centre of the nations, the transfigured Church with Christ the Son of Man come down to reign on the earth. We are waiting for the kingdom when He who first came out of Bethlehem shall come down from heaven, His saints with Him, and Israel converted unto Him, and all the nations of the earth walking in the light of God, when His will shall be done on earth as it is in heaven. This promise, this hope, is traceable from the very first promise about the seed of the woman that should bruise the head of the serpent, to the 20th chapter of the book of Revelation, when that very serpent is mentioned again — how he shall be bound, and Christ shall gain the victory.

And now when I bring before you these things which no human reason could ever have invented, which no human ingenuity could ever have discovered, and which, even after they are revealed to us, must be made clear to us by the Holy Ghost, remember that they are not stated in Scripture in a systematic and methodical form; but in a method far more wonderful and convincing. Just as in nature there is the most harmonious irregularity— not like a systematic and botanical garden — just as in nature all the different powers co-exist and work together in a way which we are not able to understand, light and gravitation and electricity and all that God has caused to exist in order to uphold the universe — so is it in the Scriptures that from beginning to end, at sundry times and in divers manners, by gradual manifestations, acts, miracles, words, commandments, institutions, God has unfolded His whole counsel.

Now in conclusion I will say only this. The Bible from beginning to end ascribes glory to God. He is the first and He is the last. He is the beginning and He is the ending. "Glory to God in the highest." That is written upon every page of Scripture. Of Him and through Him and to Him are all things. It is the Word of God.

I do not say that the Bible *contains* the Word of God. I say that the Bible *is* the Word of God. I think it a most erroneous and dangerous thing to say that the Bible contains the Word of God. The Bible, with its history, with its laws, with its poetry, with its maxims, with its biographies, with its epistles, with everything that is in it, is the Word of God. I wish to notice the human element, the individuality of the men who wrote, the gradual growth, the progressive manifestations of Scripture, in connection with the person of Christ and the work of the Holy Ghost. May the children of God remember me in prayer that the Lord's blessing may be with us.

III - The Relation of the Human, Historical, etc., Elements to the Divine

I continue my subject this morning — Scripture is the Word of God. In my last address I spoke to you chiefly of Scripture as a divine revelation. Revelation descends from above. It speaks to us out of the fulness of divine omniscience. It reveals to us spiritual and heavenly realities. It unveils to us a world which we never could have discovered by our own research. Here there is not a steep and laborious ascent which reason attempts. Here there is not the bold flight of genius, intuition, or imagination. Here the things which eye hath not seen, nor ear heard, neither have entered the heart of man, the things of God which God freely gives to those that believe, are unveiled to us by the Spirit of God who searcheth the deep things of God. It is on account of the things which are revealed to us in the Holy Scriptures that the children of God recognise in Scripture the Word of the Most High. Here, as we saw, there is revealed to us the true and living God, as Pascal wrote upon the memorial that he always carried about with him — not the God of the philosophers, of the wise, but the God of Abraham, Isaac, and Jacob, whom Athens did not know, whom Samaria did not understand, the true and living God Jehovah. He reveals Himself in this Word, and we know Him — that God is light, that God is love, that God is Father, Son, and Spirit. Here is revealed to us what no human wisdom could discover — creation, and, without the knowledge of creation, man not merely walks in ignorance and in blindness, but he walks also in bondage and in servitude, as if there was a blind force and fate surrounding him on every side. Here is revealed to us the origin of man, the condition of man, and the glorious prospect which God in His wonderful love has put before us. Here the great mystery is disclosed as we find it in no other nation, and in no other book of literature — divine grace through righteousness, by a sacrifice bringing to us the salvation of God in all fulness, not as the heathen nations dreamt of a sacrifice by which they had to appease the gods, but a sacrifice which God makes, suffering in the person of His own Son; not as the heathen imagined sacrifices, services, self-denials, which gradually and slowly may lead to the goal of the acceptance of the Deity, but, beginning from the very beginning, with the love of God and our full acceptance in Christ. Here is that wonderful mystery of godliness, the incarnation, of which there is no trace to be found anywhere else — that God was manifest in the flesh, and that the Son of God became man, to be man for ever and ever, the true Mediator between God and man. We have here the new life of God having communion with us, and here the idea of the kingdom of God, inward and spiritual, outward and manifested, having for its two agents the nation of Israel and the Church of Christ, and waiting yet to be revealed at the second appearing of our great God and Saviour. It is because we have found these things in the Holy Scriptures, and because the Spirit of God has made these things clear to our minds and our hearts, that we find in the whole Scripture, large, capacious, varied as it is, one spirit which pervades it, one light which illumines it, one hope which animates it, and that we hear in it the voice of one, even of that Eternal One who, having in His own mind purposed in Himself the great plan of our salvation and of His glory, has spoken to us and caused it to be written for our instruction.

But now I must look more particularly at the book in its various parts, and see the relation which the human, historical, and progressive elements of that book have to the fact that it is the Word of God.

The truths of which I have spoken are not put before us in the Scripture in a systematic and methodical form, so that doctrine succeeds doctrine, and that the facts and the promises of God are arranged for our learning. There is in Scripture, as I said before, the same harmonious irregularity as there is in nature. Above all, Scripture shows to us a history in which God Himself was the great agent. He takes the initiative. His acts have priority not merely in time but also in causality. After the fall of man, God begins by giving His promise, and after the three great catastrophes or judgments — the expulsion from the Garden of Eden, the judgment of the Flood in the days of Noah, and the dispersion of the human race at the Tower of Babel — there begins, in the call of Abraham, the golden history of election and grace, which does not end until the appearing of Jesus Christ and the outpouring of the Holy Ghost, and concludes when the apostle Paul had become preacher of the Gospel, not in Jerusalem only, but in Rome also. God chooses Abraham and delivers Israel out of Egypt. God guides Israel through the wilderness, and brings them into the promised land, and raises up unto them judge after judge, and chooses David from the sheepfold, and allows Israel to go into captivity, and brings them back again through the instrumentality of His servant Cyrus, and sends the angel to Zachariah and to Joseph. God sends His own Son. God sends the Spirit. A series of acts direct from God Himself, As

God acts, so He speaks. There is interference of God in action, interference of God in revelation and oracle. He gives His message to His servants the prophets. He gives His law and embodies His thoughts and His purposes in institutions. Through Moses His servant He gives promise after promise, through a long series of history, for Christ did not come immediately after the fall, or immediately after the birth of Isaac — Christ came "in the fulness of time." Century upon century had elapsed; and in this history the great thing that God did was that He prepared a nation, Israel, out of which Jesus was to come. "Out of Egypt have I called my Son." He prepared this nation, which was not better than any other nation, but which He had chosen in His sovereignty, first by creating within them, through the law, the feeling of the need of a Saviour; secondly, by showing to them through that very law, with its types and appointments and institutions, the way of expiation, and the way of approach to God. But not merely did He prepare the nation by the law for the coming of Christ, both negatively and positively, but He pre-figured Christ by living men — by Abel, by Isaac, by Moses, by David; and not merely by living men, but also by things, like the brazen serpent, and the various types which we behold in the tabernacle. And those men whom He sent to Israel pre-figured Christ by that in which they resembled Christ; and they also pre-figured Christ by that which it was impossible for them to give to Israel — which only Christ could give, so that both their excellences and their deficiencies are like arms stretched forth in intense longing for the Advent of Him who was the Only One — that was to come.

And not only was this done in the history of Israel and in the words which God had sent to Israel from time to time, but the nation itself had to be prepared not merely for the first advent of Christ, but also for the second advent of Christ; so that everything that is told us of the nation of Israel, which to many of us appears to be uninteresting and unimportant, the genealogies of Israel, the different statements that are made about the different localities, and all the minute prophesy which speaks of their restoration to their own land and their condition in those days, are a necessary part of the Word of God, which will be seen in all its clearness and in all its fulness, when that blessed time arrives.

But some one may think, "Here all is divine. God acts mostly in miracles. God speaks by visions, and by direct revelation. God gives a pattern of the tabernacle which Moses was to rear, showing it to him on the Mount. All is of God, divine, supernatural, miraculous." But if we thus concluded, we should have an altogether erroneous impression. It is a drama, and not a monologue. Israel responds. Israel replies either in faith or in unbelief, either in obedience or in disobedience, either by going the path that God appoints, or, by self-will, going circuitous routes; God overruling all their unbelief and all their unfaithfulness, for the election of God standeth sure. Yet is Israel an agent, personal, spontaneous.

And do not imagine that miracle upon miracle, oracle upon oracle, succeeded in such rapid succession that there were no intervals, so to speak, of quiet natural development. Why, even during the forty years in the wilderness, the miraculous element was not so overpowering that it excluded unbelief. It did not force faith. There were, even in those days, men who acknowledged the hand of God, and men who explained all things in such a way that God was not acknowledged. And not merely were there long pauses in the period of the Judges, and afterwards in the period of the Kings, even as there were 400 years between the end of Genesis and the beginning of Exodus, and 400 years between the end of Malachi and the beginning of the New Covenant, but during the whole period of God's dealings with Israel there was always the divine initiative — there were always periods in which the divine interference paused, so to speak, to see the effect which it had upon the people, and to allow a peaceful development of the nation in all its varied private, family, and public life.

The books of Moses, which laid the foundation, do, indeed, mostly contain the divine beginnings of things; and here we have chiefly, although not exclusively, divine acts, divine initiation, divine speech, divine law and institutions. But when we come to the historical books, from Joshua to the book of Chronicles, we enter as it were upon a new phase. And as to these historical books, many portions of which seem to us to be so entirely natural and human, describing much that is imperfect and much that is even sinful, I wish now to show you what is their position in the Scripture.

I begin by reminding you, or perhaps telling some of you for the first time, that the ancient Hebrews who collected the Scriptures called the historical books beginning with Joshua "The Former Prophets," and in this they showed their wisdom, for the history of the Jews, as you find it in Scripture, is not like an ordinary secular history which simply aims at the enumeration of events, in order to fill up as fully and completely as possible the chronology of the nation's existence. In this history many events are passed over, either silently or very briefly, which to a worldly historian would appear important; and others, which to the eye of sense and reason appear insignificant, are treated with the greatest fulness and circumstantiality. The history of Israel that is given to us in the Scriptures has reference to one point; that is, the kingdom of God. It hastens to one consummation; that is, the advent of the Messiah; and everything recorded must stand in relation, more or less, direct, to this. Therefore they who wrote those histories required to be of the prophetic mind — that is, men of the theocratic spirit; but it required more than their theocratic spirit, for only He who knew the end from the beginning could sec these events and personages in their proper relation to Christ and to the kingdom. Moreover, in these histories there is shown to us the very heart of man, the inner motives out of which actions spring. And these historians pronounce a definite judgment upon men. This man was good, and walked in the ways of the Lord and pleased the Lord, and the other man was wicked, and did not walk in the ways of the Lord.

Another requisite these historians had to fulfil. Whatsoever is written aforetime is written for our instruction; and therefore the events and characters which they describe must have an everlasting significance. They must be symbolical of those truths and experiences which always repeat themselves in the history of God's children. And now who could be the real author of those books? Whether they be written by Samuel, or by Joshua, or by some anonymous writer, who could have been the real author of those books? Who knows the counsel of God? Who beholds the image of Christ? Who searches the depths of the human mind, and who provides for all generations of God's saints instructive, edifying, guiding, and correcting history? Therefore the historical books, the books of the earlier prophets, are "Word of God" in all that they contain. If it be said, "Oh, there are so many things in the historical parts of Scripture — sins, vices, crimes, wickedness," — certainly; God wants us to know all this. God wants to show us what the world is in which we live, and the anatomy of our own heart; and there is no wickedness and villainy in the world, secret, private, or public, that is not fully described in the Word of God, — but as God alone can describe it, in its real nature and depth, and in such a way that the poison is, as it were, hermetically sealed — not like the wicked and filthy literature of the world which tries to make evil appear seductive and guilt excusable. God, like a father when he is sending forth his child into the wicked world, gives us instruction as to what we are to find in the world.

Or it is said, and it has often been said, "You call this the Word of God, and it contains the very words of the devil." Certainly it contains the words of the devil. It is most important for us to know what the devil says. One of the truths revealed to us in Scripture, of which this age has no hold, and of which believers have little hold, is the important doctrine that is revealed to us concerning the devil, and concerning his kingdom and his influence over men. In the 3rd chapter of Genesis we have the methods of Satan: "Hath God said?" In the 1st chapter of the book of Job we have the tactics of Satan, the accuser of the brethren. In the 4th chapter of the gospel of Matthew we have the most subtle stratagem of Satan when he tested even our Lord Jesus Christ. We are not ignorant of Satan's devices, and why? Because God has revealed to us the depths of Satan in His own word. And the sayings of wicked men are reported, from that first question of Cain, "Am I my brother's keeper?" unto that last one recorded in the 2nd epistle of Peter, which you hear nowadays constantly. Things have remained the same from the beginning of the world. The course of nature and history is uniform, while you speak of the second advent of Christ, and of supernatural manifestations.

There is another section of Scripture of which it is sometimes thought that we can scarcely say of it that it is the Word of God; and that is the response of Israel to God's acts and to God's words — the Psalms, the Proverbs, the book of Ecclesiastes, the book of Job, and the Song of Songs. Suffice it to say of these also that in them we see the purpose of God, that this echo of Israel to His revelation should be known to all generations; and not merely do we read the wisdom of Solomon which was very great, but in the book of Proverbs we read of that other Wisdom which Solomon describes in the 8th chapter, and which *was* before the foundations of the world were laid, and of which James says in his epistle, "The wisdom that is from above."

But let us look at this human element in a more direct manner. Do not imagine that, when we emphasize the divine authorship, we do not wish to lay full emphasis upon the human authorship. On the contrary, everything that is in the Christian meets this great fact with exultation and thanksgiving. The Bible is written by men for men. "Do not let God speak to us," said the children of Israel to Moses, "but speak thou unto us." The great promise which God gave unto Israel was this, "A prophet like Moses will I raise up unto you from among your brethren;" and, although he was possessed of final authority, yet he was of their own brethren. An angel came to Cornelius, but the angel did not preach to him the gospel with the Holy Ghost sent down from heaven; but Peter the apostle preached to him the glad tidings of salvation. How could it be otherwise when the only mediator between God and man is the man Christ Jesus? And in that simple fact, that it is the man Christ Jesus who is the Son of the Most High who mediates between God and us, there is already granted the true, real humanity of all the channels through which the Scriptures were written.

Let us look at the men. We like to see them, each with his own face. There was Moses, brought up in all the wisdom of the Egyptians. There was Amos, taken from the simple scenes of shepherd life. There was Daniel, who was a statesman at the court of the great world-monarchy Babylon, and of the succeeding monarchies. There was Matthew, who was a publican; there was Luke, who was a physician; there were the apostles, who were fishermen. There was Saul, who had been a disciple of Gamaliel. They lived in different ages of the world's history, in different countries; and their different surrounding circumstances are reflected by their individuality and their styles of writing. But that is nothing when we come to their own personal character. Oh, there are no characters like the characters in the Bible. There is nobody described in history, and there is no one that you know at the present moment, whom you know as well as you know Moses and David and the apostle Paul. It does not matter that Moses was eighty years old when God appeared to him in the fiery bush, and that Saul of Tarsus was a Pharisee who had long resisted Christ when Jesus came and converted him. These men God had chosen from their mother's womb and separated unto Himself, and all their birth and natural conformation, their childhood, their youth, all their influences, their sins and errors — everything was part and parcel of God's chiselling and preparing of that instrument by which He was to speak and to write. Moses — we see what he is; his zeal for God, his love to his nation, his impatience, his impetuosity, his indignation; on the other side, his meekness, his self-sacrifice, his boldness in asking God to change His mind, lest the nations of the world should say that He was not able to carry out His purpose, his wonderful humility, his wonderful faith, and yet his human weakness, so that he was not able to rise to the height of the divine argument, and so that he smote the rock instead of merely speaking to it, for which sin, because he did not sanctify the Lord God, he was not allowed to enter into the land of promise. Or again, David, his fragrant childhood, his chivalrous youth, his manhood with its manifold wanderings and dangers, tears, sorrows and joys, his spirit of affection and loyalty to his nation, by which he gathered to himself all the noble and the meek of the earth who feared Jehovah, his petitions, his cries of anguish, his thanksgiving, his rejoicing and jubilation: we know it all, — we can see into his very heart. As for the apostle Paul, sent by Christ, enlightened by Christ, inspired by the Spirit, he communicates to us the whole counsel of God in his epistles, but he passes all through his own experience. There is no doctrine he states, no experience he describes, but we see it vibrating through all the nerves and fibres of his being. Thus when he describes in the 7th of Romans, "I lived once without the law, but when the law came it killed me," when he says to us in the 8th of Romans, "I am persuaded that nothing shall separate us from the love of God," or when in the 9th to the nth of Romans, he lays bare to us his heart, and we see it a weeping heart having sorrow and heaviness continually on account of Israel, God's nation; or if you read the Corinthians, where you can see Paul's conflict, or the Philippians, where you can see Paul's peace, or the epistles to Timothy and Titus, where you can see the paternal apostle looking forward unto the coming ages, — it is Paul who speaks — this man Paul and all that is within him; but God has used him not merely to be a pattern to us, but that through him the teaching should be given.

But you say, "Oh, that is very true, but how can we imagine and how can we conceive human beings receiving teaching and disclosures from above? Why, they have nothing to do but just to receive them and to send them forth again." Oh, it is not so. The Scripture shows us the humanity of these men in the very act of their being inspired and receiving the Word of God from above. And the first piece of humanity which we can all understand is this: that they will not, — they are not willing. When God appeared to Moses and said, "Go now with My message," Moses said, "No. Send some one else, I am not fit." He resists. The apostles were the witnesses of the resurrection, but they would not believe it themselves for a long time. They doubted. How did they become the witnesses of the resurrection? Look at Jeremiah. Jeremiah was a man of feminine temperament, gentle, sensitive, — and God sent him with nothing but messages of rebuke and judgment; and whereas there were a great number of flutes, and harps, and viols that were most poetically playing to the nation cheerful and sanguine melodies, God sent Jeremiah to destroy and to pull down and to rebuke and to announce the judgment of God;

and Jeremiah expostulated, "What a selection you have made! You choose the very thing that lacerates me. *I* am to do this? I will not do this. I am distracted by reason of thy terrors day and night." He expostulated with God. He says, "Am I to weep away all my soul in rivers of tears?" He cursed the day of his birth; he kept silence; but it burned within his bones as a fire, and God's Word he must speak, and he did speak. There you see God and the man.

Look at Daniel. God gave to him a vision. In the 2nd chapter of Daniel there is an image represented. In the 7th chapter there is the revelation given of the four monarchies, and of the descent of the Son of Man from heaven; but in the book of Daniel we can see the effect that it had upon him. He fainted. For days he was not able to eat. It was as if his soul had gone away from him. And then he asks the question, "What shall the end of these things be?" Or again, Isaiah, when he saw the glory and heard the "Holy, holy, holy," said, "Woe is me;" and again, when the great revelations were given to him he burst forth in the exclamation. "Who hath believed our report?" or "Oh that thou wouldst rend the heavens and come down." And John in the book of the Apocalypse! Now notice this. Of no book of Scripture can we say so emphatically that it is God's Word, for it is the book of the revelation which God gave of His Son Jesus Christ. Certainly here is a divine objective authority, but the person of John the beloved disciple we can see throughout the whole book. And do you not remember in the 1st chapter he fell down at his feet as dead, and Jesus comforts him? And do you not remember afterwards that no one was able to open the book: "I wept much. I wept much"? Do we who believe the Bible ever think of the men by whom the Bible was written as mere instruments and pens?

But now I must emphasize the other side. Let us take, then, the most subjective part of Scripture, the Psalms. A man says to me, "Surely you do not mean to say that the Psalms are God's Word! Are not they David's word, his faith, his doubt, his impatience, his thanksgiving, his experience?" Of course they are. But what if the whole David was God's Word? What if God had prepared and made and guided this David that in him as a pattern, and an instalment in a finite, imperfect and sin-mixed way there should, by the Spirit, be shown forth the experience of Christ in an infinite, perfect, and altogether sinless and divine way? Is not the Psalter the prayer book of the Messiah? Is not the 22nd Psalm, although it does refer to David, and was uttered out of David's own depth of heart, really far beyond David's depth of heart, and did he not by the Spirit say, "The Lord saith unto my Lord"? And in the 2nd Psalm, in which he says, "Thou art my son; this day have I begotten thee," and in all the Psalms in which the events of Christ's life are predicted, and the events of the lives of those who are identified with Christ, is it David who speaks, or is that true which David himself said on his deathbed — the last words of David the King of Israel, the sweet psalmist, — *The Spirit of the Lord spake in me?* The Psalms of David are the most subjective part of the Bible, and it is most evident that all the Psalms of David are God's Word.

Take Jeremiah. Certainly the message that he delivered to Israel was none of his seeking, neither was it to his taste, but does not Jeremiah know perfectly that God has sent him, and that he is not one of the false prophets? In no other prophet is the contrast given with so much emphasis as in this prophet between false prophets who also spoke what they called "word of the Lord" — very beautiful, poetical, religious, and pious. But God had not sent them. In our days some men have the ignorance and the audacity to compare the inspiration of Scripture with the inspiration of Shakespeare and poets and sculptors, for man has intuitions and imaginations and ideas and may express them, — but what is the chaff to the wheat? "My word," saith the Lord, "is like a hammer that breaketh in pieces the rocks," and also "like the rain which comes down from heaven." And did not all the apostles know with the greatest certainty and conviction that the things that they spoke and wrote, they spoke and wrote with the words, not which human wisdom teaches, but which the Spirit of God teaches?

And I wish yet to lead you still farther into the human element of the Scripture. God reveals to us His mysteries, but not like a magician or thaumaturgist, in as bewildering and mysterious a manner as possible, but in as simple and unostentatious a manner as possible, just as our blessed Jesus concealed what other men would have pronounced publicly. His birth in Bethlehem after thirty years was completely forgotten, and people thought that He belonged to Nazareth. And during the thirty years that He was in Nazareth, He did not go about with a divine halo round His countenance.

We have the five books of Moses. As for their composition, that belongs to another subject. These five books of Moses, in some form or other, were in the hands of Joshua and in the hands of the rulers and kings, for them continually to meditate on; and the promise was given to them that, if they meditated on these books, God would bless them. I do not know of any promise that God gives to us for reading any other book. He is father to this book, and will stand by it. Then what is revealed in Moses we see traces of in all the other writings which follow. Moses is constantly quoted by the later historians and by the prophets. If it was only the name which God pronounced to Moses, "The Lord God, merciful and gracious, long suffering," and so on, it forms as it were the foundation of the Psalms and the prophets, with the benediction of Aaron: "The Lord bless thee and keep thee." Then we find in the days of David and the other psalmists that they are studying the Word of God. Then we find that Isaiah quotes the prophet Micah. Then Daniel studies the books of Jeremiah. Then we find that the apostles are always referring to the books of Moses and the prophets. Then we find in the 2nd epistle of Peter a reference to the epistles of the apostle Paul. So you see how it grows. No evolution. It is not as if that which was started first by Moses, by itself, in the mind of man, developed and became better and clearer and fuller. They did meditate on it; they did think about it; they did pray over it; but it did not develop by itself. God had to interfere again and again with new revelations, creative beginnings direct from above. And this fact is of the greatest importance for this reason. Our blessed Saviour did not come to Israel after David and Solomon, when one might have said, "You see now what is the result of the development of the Jewish nation. At last they have produced David, and then they have produced Solomon, and now they produce the real man, who is the Messiah." From Abraham to David, fourteen generations; from David down to the Babylonish captivity, fourteen generations; and from the Babylonish captivity through a still drearier territory to Joseph, fourteen generations. And when of the tree of David there was nothing left but what Isaiah calls a stump, when the tabernacle of David was fallen low and the representative of the house of David was the blessed and dear Virgin Mary who brought a pair of turtle doves because of her poverty, then Jesus came; for this is the motto of Israel, "With man it is impossible, but with God all things are possible."

Now whereunto shall I compare this growth of the Scriptures? Shall I say that it is like a building? But what building have you ever seen that begins in this way — that there is a house of small dimensions — it has a firm foundation; it has good walls; it is covered in by a roof of safety and shelter; but it is small, and after a number of years you see it larger, and after a number of years you see it still larger? There is no such building; but the Scripture is like that. The five books of Moses contain a house for God's people. And then the Scriptures were enlarged, and still further enlarged, until they became complete. Or shall I say that it is like the growth of a plant? That is better, because the seed contains everything. And what is the seed? The word of God is the seed, and contains everything; and out of this seed the Scripture came, and in every part of the growth there is the life of the seed, and there is the form of life that is also in the seed. Or shall I compare it to the human being — the infant, the child, the youth, the man? Yes. Well, let us look at the infant. Genesis — that would be the infant Oh, but the apostle Paul in the epistle to the Galatians, writing in the fulness of time and after the Pentecostal disclosures, cries out, "This infant Genesis knows everything. This scripture Genesis has foreseen that the Gentiles apart from the law shall be justified through faith in the promised seed." Is Genesis then omniscient? Genesis is not omniscient, and the men that wrote Genesis were not omniscient; but God who caused Genesis to be written was omniscient. The first three chapters of Genesis find their explanation in the last three of the book of Revelation, Melchisedek is explained in the epistle to the Hebrews, — the patriarchal life in the doctrine of justification by faith and the ingathering of the Jews, What a wonderful book! So compact did it become at last in the days of our blessed Saviour that there was no doubt about the books which constituted the Scripture — the things that are written.

And now I can only touch on another subject; but I must mention it, as it confirms all that I have said. You believe in Jesus, the Son of God and the Son of Man, the Messiah, He has a two-fold relation to Scripture as God; and as man He has a two-fold relation to the law of God and to everything. As Messiah He is under the Scripture, As Son of God He is above the Scripture, as He is above the law. All that Moses and the prophets wrote pointed to Christ. All was fulfilled in Him, Now, when Christ was upon earth, what was His attitude to the Scripture? Our blessed Saviour never speaks of the principle of the Scripture, of the idea of the Scripture, of the teaching of Scripture, of the promises of the Scripture, of this or that in the Scripture, of "the divine element" in the Scripture, as our moderns would say, or of the Word of God contained in the Scripture. He always speaks of the Scripture, that body, that written thing, that collection of books. And of that Scripture He says, "I do not receive testimony from man," but "Search the Scriptures, They testify of me." Therefore it is a divine testimony. But what in the Scriptures testifies of Him? Everything, the whole Scriptures, the Scriptures themselves. So He says, "Think not that I am come to destroy Moses and the prophets Not till heaven and earth pass away shall one jot or tittle" (that is, one of these little letters) "be removed," When he argues with the Jews, and quotes incidentally a passage from the Psalms, He says, in parenthesis, "And the Scripture cannot be broken." He does not say, "This verse cannot be denied," or, "The teaching of the Psalms cannot be gainsaid"; but simply, "Because this verse is in the Scripture, *ipso facto,* the Scripture stands good for it, and the Scripture cannot be broken." What does He say to the Sadducees, in the narrative of the rich man and Lazarus? "They have Moses and the prophets. Let them hear them." What is the hearing? "It is written." It is God's Word written. Therefore let them hear them. "Have you not read what God said?" Therefore God's Word is to be read.

But not merely this. Our blessed Saviour found in the Scripture His own portrait. When He preached in the synagogue of Nazareth, He opened the book of the prophet Isaiah, and said, "The Scripture is fulfilled to-day in your hearing." When He showed mercy to the publicans and sinners, He described His own mind by that which was written, "I will have mercy, and not sacrifice." His whole work. His whole suffering, His whole death. His whole resurrection. He found in what was written. The Scripture must be fulfilled. All that is written concerning Him has now an end. Was it not Word of God to Jesus? Was it not the portraiture of Christ Himself? Was not it the revelation of God's secret counsel and will concerning our salvation? When Jesus argues with Satan, He says, "It is written." When Jesus prays to the Father, He says, "The son of perdition is lost, that the Scripture may be fulfilled"; and when He authorises the disciples, and prepares them for their apostolic mission. He tells them that He entered through sufferings into glory, because it was so written. As it was written, so it happened; and as it is written, and as it happened, so it must be preached unto the world. So the testimony of Jesus concerning the whole Scripture is that it is the Word of God.

To say, "The Bible contains the Word of God," instead of saying, "The Bible is the Word of God," is inadequate and misleading. Everything that is in

Scripture would authenticate itself to us as Word of God if we understood it in its right connection with the centre; but we must not say merely that the Scripture contains the Word of God; and we had better not say it at all, because, in the first place, what else does Scripture contain besides the Word of God? Nothing is in Scripture that does not belong to it, and nothing is outside of Scripture that ought to be introduced into it. It is perfectly true that there are some parts of Scripture more vital, more noble than others, like the book of Genesis, which is like the head; like the gospel of John, which is like the heart; but as the apostle explains to us in his splendid comparison of the body with the Church, all the members are members of the body, according to their various positions, importance, and significance. Life goes through them all, and it is not for us to separate anything that belongs to the living and sacred body of Scripture. And if Scripture only contains Scripture, who is to judge what is Word of God, and what is not Word of God? There are many things in the Scripture which perhaps are not interesting to this one or to that one; but Scripture is not given for an individual, but for the whole Church; not for the Church of one age, but for the Church of all ages. There are many people who take no interest in the Jews, but God takes the most intense and everlasting interest in the Jews; and that of itself will place a very large portion of Scripture in another light.

Is our Christian consciousness what men have called the "verifying faculty" to be set up, as a judge, over the disclosures which are to be found in the Scriptures? Is the very creation of the Scripture, the very child which owes its existence to the teaching of Scripture, to assume the position of a superior? When I read the Bible, am I to hear the voice at every page, "Hath God indeed said this? Hath God indeed said this? Is this merely contained in the Word of God, or is it Word of God? "It is said that Scripture is the rule of faith. So the Church of England, so the Church of Scotland, so every Protestant evangelical Church, has declared that nothing is to be demanded of God's people to believe and obey, unless it be founded on the Word of God. Scripture is the rule of faith; but who is to rule the rule, or to correct the rule? Scripture could never be the rule of faith unless it was the foundation of faith and the source of faith. "Faith cometh by hearing, and hearing cometh by the Word of God." And where does the Word of God come from, but from God Himself? And so let us believe it as it is declared to us in the Epistle to the Hebrews, "At sundry times and in divers manners, unto the fathers by the prophets," but in them all, and through them all, God spake.

I hope to finish what I have to remark on this subject especially about the New Testament, and the work of the Holy Ghost in the formation of Scripture. The subject of my next lecture will be the certainty which believers have concerning Scripture, and the testimony to it of Christ.

IV - The Testimony of Jesus Considered and Decisive

The subjects to-day are: the testimony of Jesus Christ concerning the Old Testament Scriptures decisive; the relation in which Jesus stands to the New Testament; the Spirit of God and His relation to the Scripture.

It is most important that all Christians should be fully convinced in their own minds that the testimony which Jesus bears concerning Moses and the prophets is decisive. It leaves not a vestige of doubt in the mind of any one who acknowledges that Jesus is the Son of God. It gives us a perfect and incontrovertible conviction that the Scriptures of the Old Testament are the Word of God. Many doubts, many objections, have been brought against this view, and I can only remind you in a few words of the tactics of the rationalists who do not believe in the divinity of Christ, who attempt to show that our Saviour accommodated Himself to the prejudices of His contemporaries, and that, although He Himself did not believe in the inspiration of the Old Testament, or in the existence of Satan, or in those who were possessed of devils as really possessed by them, still adapting Himself to the ignorance and weakness of the Jews, and wishing to lead them, as it were, into a higher and nobler sphere of thought, He argued with them from the things which they admitted. Thus a course of action is suggested unworthy of the character of an honest man, unworthy of the dignity of a prophet, blasphemous as applied to Jesus, who is God over all blessed for ever. Jesus, who never for a single moment accommodated Himself to the prejudices of the Pharisees and scribes, who with all the energy of His character protested against the traditions of the elders, who not merely in secret, but in the presence of all people, declared that every plant which His Heavenly Father had not planted, however venerable and pious it might seem, must be rooted up, — how could He for a single moment teach what He knew to be untrue?

Another explanation has been attempted. It has been stated, and that in the most recent times, that when the Son of God emptied Himself, and laid aside the glory of His divine state of existence, and became man, His human knowledge became limited, and that this limitation must be taken into account when we consider His declarations about Moses and the prophets. A few sentences will suffice to show that this whole mysterious subject, of the self-limitation of the Son of God in becoming man, does not in any manner touch the subject that is before us.

Let me remind you of the facts that are brought before us in the gospels, which show the range of Christ's vision as man upon earth. He saw into the depths of Nathanael's heart when Nathanael was under the fig-tree; He saw into the depths of the sea, and beheld the coin in the mouth of the fish; He read the whole past life of the woman of Samaria, whom He had never seen before during His earthly pilgrimage. He knew that Judas was going to betray Him. He saw the man waiting on the road with the ass and the foal of the ass, and the other man who had prepared the guest chamber for Him to eat the passover with His disciples. Many more instances I might quote, but what I wish to bring before you is this — that Jesus, when He was on earth, was the Searcher of Hearts. This is God's prerogative. "*I only* search the heart." Jesus knew what was in man, and did not require any one to tell Him. Secondly, He saw the whole invisible realm of angels and of devils. "I beheld Satan fall like lightning from heaven." "Satan hath desired to have thee, that he may sift thee as wheat." And in all the possessed — and possessed they were as surely as we have a gospel record — the Lord Jesus Christ saw the powers of the evil one. But more than that, Jesus saw the Father. Jesus said, "No man knoweth the Father but the Son." He who saw the depths of the human heart, He who saw the whole of the invisible world of spirits, He who knew God absolutely, He it is who says unto us, "The Scripture cannot be broken."

I wish to establish this point still more firmly. Let us look, then, upon Jesus as a prophet. None of the old Socinians would ever have dared or wished to say the things that are now said by people who are in evangelical Churches. Much mistaken as they were about the person of Christ, they all held clearly that He was the truth, that He was the Light of the World, that He was the perfect prophet whose testimony is to be received implicitly.

Let us first look upon Jesus merely as a prophet. What is a prophet according to the Old Testament? A man who runs not, before he is sent, who is sent by God, who is entrusted with a divine message, who delivers not his own thoughts, but the things which God has committed unto him; who preaches repentance, and at the same time preaches the coming of the Messiah, even of Jehovah Himself, in His glory. Such a prophet was Jesus, sent by the Father in the fulness of the Holy Ghost, preaching repentance and the advent of the kingdom of God. But all the Old Testament prophets were only precursors of the real prophet that was promised, and therefore the great promise given unto the people by God through Moses is this: "A prophet like unto thee I will raise up unto them from among thy brethren." And what was then the resemblance of the prophet that was to come to Moses? As the first Adam points to the Lord from heaven, so Moses points to Christ. God spoke with Moses face to face. Moses was not merely a prophet, but he was the mediator, and he Weis faithful in all God's house; and thus, after all the prophets that God sent unto Israel, there was to come at last a prophet like unto Moses at the beginning of the new dispensation — the mediator between God and the people who should speak to God face to face. And this promise which God gave through Moses was afterwards expanded in the subsequent prophets. Let me remind you of the features of the prophet which was to come. He was to know the whole mind of God. He was to possess the Spirit in His sevenfold plenitude. He was to be entrusted with the whole message of God, and not merely with fragments. But more than that. He was Himself to be the fulfilment of the promise; for not merely was He to be a prophet, raised up from among His brethren, but He was also to come down from heaven, and in Him the fulness of divine light and divine life was to be manifested upon earth. Such a one was Jesus.

Other prophets were not always in the Spirit. The Spirit came upon them from time to time: but Jesus, every moment of His existence, and in every utterance that proceeded from Him, was filled with the Holy Ghost. He said, "My doctrine is not mine, but my Father's who sent me. All I have heard of the Father, I have given unto you. I speak not of myself, but whatsoever I see the Father do, I do likewise." Therefore this blessed Jesus, always in communion with the Father, always receiving from the Father the words which He was to give unto the people, and always in communion with the Holy Ghost, is that perfect prophet who speaks nothing but what is in accordance with the divine mind and the divine will.

But to show this still more emphatically, Jesus was not able to tell the disciples everything, because they could not have borne it. Therefore the Holy Ghost was to come afterwards; but that Holy Ghost was not to reveal any other thing than that which Jesus had revealed. "He shall bring to your remembrance the words that I have spoken unto you." He was only to show in fuller light and development what Jesus had already taught. If, then, the words of Jesus are fallible, we have no infallible God — neither Father nor Holy Ghost. When Jesus was on the Mount of Transfiguration, there were Moses and Elijah as the representatives of the Old Testament history, but they disappeared. God the Father from the excellent glory spake and said, "This is my beloved Son, in whom I am well pleased"; but He added something that He had not said on the day of Christ's baptism, for then the prophetic office of Christ was only beginning — now it had come to its conclusion — "Hear him." God visible is Jesus. God audible is Jesus. This is that prophet like unto Moses and greater than Moses of whom God the Father says, "He is my representative and my mouth.. Whatever he speaks unto you, believe and accept."

Were I to stop here, I think I would have proved my point; but I cannot do so, because I believe that Jesus is the Son of God. We can never understand the relation of the divinity, in its omniscience and omnipotence, unto Jesus of Nazareth. Whether it was in abeyance, or whatever theory we may form on this mysterious subject, has nothing to do with what is revealed to us in the gospels. As it is with the omnipotence of Christ, so it is with the omniscience. Christ performed His miracles by faith in the Father. Christ, every evening that He went to His rest, commended Himself to the Father. Christ was true man. His prayers were reality. Therefore the glory of His miracles Christ afterwards attributed to the Father; and when He raised Lazarus, He ascribed this to the Father, and thanked the Father who always heard Him. But not like any other prophet, relying upon the omnipotence of God, did Jesus perform miracles, but by His own omnipotence. How did He raise Lazarus from the dead? "I am the resurrection and the life." In Him there was the resurrection power, and to raise the dead implies omnipotence. And thus also it is with the omniscience of Jesus. It is true that Jesus says of that hour when the Father shall send again the Son, He knoweth not. Here there was a limitation of knowledge, but Jesus knew that He did not know it, and said that this was kept from Him during that time, throwing all the more light on all the other declarations that He made. As He says to Nicodemus, "We know that we speak." "The Son of Man who is in heaven is the only one who, having come down from heaven, shall ascend again." "I am the truth," He says; and like God Himself, He says, "Verily, verily, I say unto you."

In the Sermon on the Mount, Jesus speaks as a prophet, but He speaks as the Son of God, as God manifest in the flesh. "Verily, verily, I say unto you." He contrasts Himself with the Jehovah of the Old Testament, and if I may use that expression He shows that Jehovah is now revealing Himself in a more glorious manner than He did before. When Jesus as a prophet speaks of the last day, how does He speak? "Many shall say unto *me*; and I shall say unto them, 'Depart from me.'" Therefore Jesus in His humanity beholds Himself as the judge of the quick and the dead. The secrets of the future are before Him. And when He privately instructs His disciples about the destruction of Jerusalem and the second advent, He refers to the prophet Daniel; but He says, "When the Son of Man shall come in his glory."

Another point — for there is not a single loophole of escape. When Jesus rose again from the dead, where was then the limitation of His human knowledge? why did He lead back His disciples, on all the occasions when He appeared unto them, to Moses and the prophets, as if this was the only way in which He could reveal Himself and manifest Himself to the children of men? "Ought not the Christ to have passed through sufferings unto glory?" "And beginning with Moses and the prophets, he expounded unto them all the things concerning himself." And this was His last commission — that they must preach as it was written, and as it was fulfilled. No, my beloved friends, whatever stage of conviction you may be in now, and whatever influences may surround you, examine the question, test it, search it, sift it; this is my testimony, that as true as God the Father is the Father of all truth^ and the Spirit of God is the Spirit of truth, and Jesus Christ is the Son of God, so true is the testimony of Jesus concerning Moses and the prophets — the whole Old Testament scripture as it was embodied in that book which the Jews called Scripture, — that it is infallible, that it is authoritative, that it reveals Himself in all His glorious person, and in the perfections of His work.

And so did the apostles preach. Where have you got your Christianity from? Who has converted you, pagans, into worshippers of God and Christ? Have you not derived everything from the apostles? Are you not built upon the foundation of the apostles? And how did the apostles preach? "That Christ died according to the Scriptures." Not a single syllabic of the New Testament was written then. And they preached that Christ rose again, "According to the Scriptures." And when people came to believe in Jesus, how did the apostles teach them? They taught them from Daniel about the man of sin, the

Antichrist that was to come. They taught them from the history of the Jews in the wilderness, that all these things had happened to us for an example. They referred them to the whole of prophecy that had gone before, saying that by the consolation which the Scriptures give us, and by patiently waiting for the fulfilment of the Scripture, we should have the hope, namely, of Christ's second advent. By Scripture they instructed the unbelievers; by Scripture they instructed those who had already become Christians; and the apostle Peter, shortly before he laid aside his tabernacle and finished his course, knowing the great errors and the false prophets which were already beginning their pernicious work, reminded the Christians of the testimony of the transfiguration of Christ, reminded them also of the sure word of prophecy. To this they were to attend; by this they were to be cheered; and by this they were to be defended against all the assaults of the wicked One. And the apostle Paul, when he had reached the end of his earthly journey, and after he had declared to Timothy that perilous times were coming, had only one counsel to give him: "From a child thou hast known the Holy Scriptures, which are able to make thee wise unto salvation through faith which is in Christ Jesus." "All Scripture is given by inspiration of God."

But I must come now to the New Testament. Jesus Christ is Jehovah. Only Jehovah can say "I, even I, am he that forgiveth thy sins." Jesus says, "Be of good cheer; thy sins are forgiven thee." Only Jehovah can say, "They have forsaken me, the fountain of living water." Jesus says, "If any man thirst, let him come unto me, and drink." Only Jehovah can say, "As a bridegroom rejoiceth over his bride, so will I rejoice, O Zion, over thee." Jesus says, "I am the bridegroom, and how can the children of the bride-chamber fast while I am with them?" Only Jehovah can say, "Thou shalt love the Lord thy God with all thy heart"; and Jesus says, "If any man loves father or mother or wife, or child more than me, he is not worthy of me." Who is Jesus? He is Jehovah, and Jehovah promised that He would come, and Jehovah has come according to His promise. Because Jesus is Jehovah, He is the centre to gather Israel. "How often would I have gathered thy children together." Could any prophet ever have said that, or any angel? Could the angel Michael come down and say, "Israel, come to me"? Jesus is the centre of Israel. Jesus says, "I will build my Church" — "*my* Church." The ecclesia belongs only to Jehovah. When Jesus says to Peter, "Feed my sheep," how are they His sheep, unless He be Jehovah, who is the shepherd of the flock? Therefore said Jesus to Jerusalem, when He foretold the destruction of that city, "Behold, I sent unto you prophets and wise men and scribes." Who sent the Old Testament prophets? Jehovah; and if a man was not sent by Jehovah, he was a false prophet. Who sends the apostles? Jesus, who is Jehovah. And what is the authority that Jesus gives to the apostles? "He that heareth you heareth me." Notice that. Not "*As it were* me." He that heareth you heareth me. And therefore it is that Jesus promised to the apostles the Spirit that was to lead them into all truth. Jesus did not say, "I have been three years with Peter and James and John and Philip and

Thomas. They love me; they believe in me. They are loyal men. They remember what I have told them; I rely now upon them to spread Christianity." That is what you read in these silly boastful nineteenth-century books; but no. Jesus knew that without the Holy Ghost, and without His special presence and authority, the apostles were altogether unable for the high task which He had assigned to them. And therefore are the writings of the evangelists and of the apostles the very words of Jesus, the teaching of Jesus. We are built upon the foundation of the apostles. They require no successors, because, up to this very day, they are in the midst of us and teach us. And, like the disciples in the days of the first Pentecost, we continue steadfastly in the teaching of the apostles, which is none other than the teaching of Jesus.

Therefore the apostle Paul in the epistle to the Romans, in a passage which is very little considered, says that the mystery which had been hidden for ages was made known unto all nations by the prophetical writings, in which he does not refer to the Old Testament prophets, but to himself and to the other writers of the New Testament. And these writings of the apostles have this peculiar characteristic. All is in them more fully revealed than in the Old Testament, and yet God uses more the individuality of the writer than He ever did before. And therefore all the New Testament writings, with a few exceptions, are in the form of letters, the personal testimony and experience of the apostles, and yet the very Word of God and revelation of Jesus Christ.

Now to sum up, Jesus says; If you believe Moses, *ipso facto,* you believe Me. If you do not believe the writings of Moses, of course you do not believe My sayings. Moses wrote of Me. Each word is weighty. Moses himself wrote — committed to writing — and Jesus is the sum and substance of what he wrote. That is. He is the foundation of the whole history of the Old Testament, and of its prophetic teaching. And not merely this passage or that passage, but the whole collection of books as they were among the Jews, is the Scripture which cannot be broken, and in which Christ Himself is delineated.

Now I come to the next point — the relation of the Spirit of God to the Scripture. There are many pepple who ask questions about the inspiration of Scripture to whom the best answer would be this: "Have you received the Holy Ghost? Is there anything that you believe because the Holy Ghost has taught you? Do you know that a man cannot believe in Jesus, unless the Holy Ghost teaches him and enables him? What do you know about the Holy Ghost at all, that you ask this question whether the Scripture is inspired?" Father, Son, and Holy Ghost, — one God. The Father gives; the Son is the channel; the Holy Ghost imparts. The grace of the Lord Jesus, the love of the Father, come to us in the communion of the Holy Ghost. God the Father created. By the Word He created and the Spirit of God moved upon the face of the waters The Father sent Jesus; Jesus came of His own accord; and by the Holy Ghost was He conceived in the womb of the Virgin Mary.

Jesus died. The Father gave Him up to death, and by the everlasting Spirit He gave Himself as a sacrifice for our sins. The Father can do nothing except by Jesus and through the Spirit. Christ can do nothing except by the Father and by the power of the Spirit. The Spirit knows nothing, says nothing, docs nothing, but according to the Father's will, and through and in Christ Jesus. And so every man that has been converted says, as that little boy said to Mr. M'Cheyne, when he was dying, "I love the Father, who loved me and gave Jesus to die for me. I love Jesus, who shed His precious blood for me; and I love the Holy Ghost, who made me know the love of the Father and the love of the Son."

Now, with people who know this it is possible to speak. What is the use of speaking to the others on this point? Oh yes, on many other points, but not on this point. As Scripture is the whole counsel of God unto salvation, as Scripture is the perfect portraiture of Christ, both in His first and His second advent, so Scripture could not have come into existence without the Holy Ghost I say to the people every Sunday: "Let us read the Word of God"; and then I say "The 19th Psalm of David." What is the connecting link? The Spirit spake by David. The Spirit speaks. What the Spirit spoke by the mouth of David had to be fulfilled in the history of Jesus. The Spirit speaks and testifies. "Your sins I will remember no more." "Holy men spake as they were moved by the Holy Ghost." What is that moving of the Holy Ghost? It is a very strange thing that even the heathen poets, when they had some great subject that they wished to describe, invoked the muse. As Homer says, "Tell me, O muse, the man in all his wanderings" — speaking of Ulysses. Or, "O goddess, I wish to sing the wrath of the son of Peleus, Achilles," — feeling that the human spirit, as it were, was not sufficient to describe things worthy of their grandeur. The prophets spake, not by their own imagination, nor by their own impulse, as I showed to you before. They spake as they were moved by the Holy Ghost, carried along by the Holy Ghost, the Holy Ghost bearing them along, not destroying their individuality, but upholding them continually. So does the apostle Paul say that all Scripture is God-spirited, breathed by the Spirit of God. What a wonderful truth is revealed to us here! We are not able to understand it We are not able to describe how it is that the Spirit of God worked in these men. We know one thing, that they themselves did not fully understand what they wrote, "searching diligently what the Spirit that was in them did signify"; and we know that all the narratives which are contained in the Old Testament could not have been fully understood at the time, because they are for our instruction, upon whom the latter days have come. Yet this is the truth, that they themselves, men of God, holy men, wrote as they were moved by the Spirit of God.

And if this is true, let me note, in passing, one of the peculiarities of the present day — what is called "advanced" preaching. "Advanced" preaching means this, to make Moses and the prophets say as little as possible, and, if possible, no more than we could know without them; and the great question is always, "Oh, you think this Psalm refers to Christ? How could David know this? David could not have an understanding of this. We must remember the time of David, the circumstances of David." Oh yes, there is a different exposition of Scripture which is not Scripture itself The New Testament exposition of the Old Testament is the only true exposition, for it explains not merely what David and the prophets could understand, and tried to understand, but what the Holy Ghost understood, and deposited with them, distinctly, in this way. Supposing that there is a little plant before me, I can examine it. But supposing that I have a powerful microscope; I look at it, and now I can see a number of things which before were entirely non-existent to me. Have I put anything into that plant that was not there before? Have I changed the plant? Have I introduced my pet ideas into that plant? So, when we read Leviticus with the light of the epistle to the Hebrews; when we read the whole Old Testament with the light of the evangelists and the epistles, that is exposition, not imposition. We do not put anything into it. The Holy Spirit enlarges our vision to see what is there. There are many questions in connection with this to be answered, and difficulties to be solved; but I do not enter into these. I have shown you what the Word of God, as the basis of the doctrines which are essential and vital teaches us; and any one of you who believes in God the Father, Son, and Holy Ghost, and in Jesus Christ, that He is both the Son of Mary and the Son of the Most High, must necessarily grant what I have said. Upon such broad basis let the thing rest at first, because it is for all Christian people.

And now I pass on to the last point. How am I sure that the Scripture is the Word of God? Oh! people are so anxious nowadays. This man will not believe in the miracle of Jonah, and this man will not believe in the extermination of the Canaanites being by God's commandment, and another cannot believe the Psalms, because David speaks of the vengeance which is to overtake God's enemies. This thing arises, that thing, this difficulty, that difficulty, all little isolated fragments and bits; they do not regard the whole. We may go on arguing in this way for thousands of years, and not bring a person any nearer to the truth. This Bible is not a book in the way in which there are other books. God the living one is testified of there. Worship not the book. Never think of the Bible as separate from God the Father and Jesus the Saviour, and the agency and work of the Holy Ghost. We are sure that Scripture is the Word of God, because the Spirit of God testifies of it as the only ground of our absolute certainty. There are many arguments, there are many evidences, there are many things to predispose you to listen to the Scripture. As I have already pointed out, the sublimity of its doctrine, the beauty and attractiveness of its language, the grandeur of its commands, the unity of all its component parts, the power which it has exerted in the world and in the Church — all these things are difficult to gainsay. There is enough evidence to make every person guilty in the sight of God who does not acknowledge the Scripture; but tell me how you are sure that Jesus is the Son of God, or that Jesus died for your sin, or that you are a child of God? It is the Spirit that witnesses, and the Spirit is truth.

And all Christians and all Christian ministers ought to have the fulness of conviction that the Spirit is truth. There are certain portions of Scripture in which, as it were, you are not at home. You have not felt their power. But other people have felt their power. Some generations of the Church of Christ are led into one portion of God's Word and some into another. The Scripture beareth witness unto the whole Church of Christ — the Spirit, with the Scripture, is truth, for as is the Holy Ghost, so is the Scripture. The object of the Holy Ghost is to glorify Christ. The object of the Scripture is to glorify Christ. The method of the Holy Ghost is to convince, to save, to comfort with the assurance of God's favour, to enlighten, instruct, warn, guide, cleanse, establish those that come to Christ. The object of the Scripture is to be profitable for doctrine, for correction, for instruction in righteousness, that the man of God may be perfect, furnished thoroughly unto every good work. As is the Scripture, so is the Spirit — one aim, one method. The two go together. The power of the Bible when the Holy Ghost is with it is the power of the Word of God. Oh, how many there have been opposed to God! but the Word of God has been to them like the hammer that breaks in pieces the rock. Oh, how many there have been in sadness when they heard the voice, "Come unto me, all ye that labour and are heavy laden, and I will give you rest." A poor man, as he was led to the scaffold because he had committed murder, on being asked whether he was afraid to die, gave this answer: "I rely on one verse of Scripture, 'God so loved the world, that he gave his only begotten Son,' when I heard this I saw the arms of God wide open, 'that whosoever believeth in him shall not perish but have eternal life.' When I read this, I felt the arms tightly close in upon me, and I am saved." Do you remember how Martin Luther by the reading of the Psalms, by the reading of the epistle to the Galatians, by the reading of the epistle to the Romans, was, out of the depth of despair, transplanted into a heaven of thanksgiving and jubilation? What was it that was the instrument of the conversion of Augustine but that, opening the Scriptures, he saw the verse in the 13th chapter of Romans which called him to rise out of darkness and out of night. How many Jews have been converted simply by the reading of the 53rd chapter of the prophet Isaiah — as Luther calls it, the clearest Gospel in all the Bible; and after a man has been converted, is there anything el.sc in the whole world, arc there any sermons, are there any words of God's witnesses that can feed him, that can strengthen him, that can encourage him, that can rebuke him, and that can give him light and assurance in the hour of death? God has taken great care in the Bible that we should know what the Bible is. There are many passages in Scripture describing the excellence of Scripture. Such a passage is the 119th Psalm. There are no vain repetitions. There is always something fresh and something new. And what is the testimony concerning the Word of God? Here is a picture of all life. We see the young man who has a great ideal of perfection before him. We sec a man who is in affliction and in sorrow, and we see a man who is despised and mocked by the people around him. We see a man who is surrounded by adversaries, and by enemies who are continually wresting his words. We see a man who is often disheartened, whose soul is cleaving to the dust, but in every circumstance of life it is the Word of God to which he looks, not to the maxims which prevail among Israel, not to the traditions of men as preached among them, not to the ideas that are held by the people with whom he is associated, but to God's Word only. God speaks to him, and this Word of God is all-sufficient to him. He knows of no other piety, he knows of no other devoutness, he knows of no other diligence in God's service, he knows of no other carefulness to do the thing which is right apart from the Word of God, for "all Scripture is given by inspiration of God, and therefore it is profitable for doctrine, for reproof, for correction, for instruction in right-eousness, that the man of God may be perfect thoroughly furnished unto eve-ry good work." The Holy Ghost accompanies the Word, and the power of the Holy Ghost is in the Word. Be not deceived, the Word of God in the highest sense means the Son of God. He is the Word. Word of God in the sense next to that means the Gospel message, "And this is the Word which by the Gospel is preached unto you." And the Bible never for a single moment should be sepa-rated from Christ, the living Word, and from the message of God, which is the treasure of the Word; and the work and agency of the Holy Ghost is the em-bodiment and incorporation of that Word.

Separate it is from all other books. As Augustine says of the Bible, "What is the Bible else but a letter of God Almighty addressed to His creatures, in which letter we hear the voice of God, and behold the heart of our heavenly Father?" Be established in the truth.

The Bible needs no defence. The Bible defends itself; the Bible explains it-self I do not dread the pagans, I do not dread the infidels, I do not dread scep-tics. I dread the false, compromising and conciliatory modern teaching in our Churches. That is the only thing that is to be dreaded. Let the Bible only be kept separate. As it is, it needs no defence. Britannia needs no bulwarks, and why? Because God has separated her by the sea. That is her strength and her defence. The Scripture needs no bulwarks. The Word of God is the sword of the Spirit, and who ever heard of defending a sword? It is the enemy who will advise you to put the sword into the sheath, a beautiful sheath with all kinds of metaphysical and artistic ornamentations. The sword must be unsheathed, for the sword is aggressive. Oh that we may know the Scripture not merely as the sword of the Spirit, for that sword, although it may inflict pain, is meant for healing. Oh that we may know it as the gentle dew and rain that comes down from heaven and returneth not thither, but prospereth in the things which please God. My wish for each one of you, and for myself, is this — that when the time comes that we must part even from this dear book, we may be able to say, this has been God's message to me, in the Scripture. "I have loved thee with an everlasting love, therefore with loving kindness have I drawn thee." Amen.

V - The Jews — As Custodians and Witnesses

The subject this morning is the following: The Jews the custodians of the Old Testament Scriptures, and witnesses to the truth of Bible history and prophecy.

You remember that in the epistle to the Romans, which is the most comprehensive and systematic exposition of the gospel of Christ which the apostle Paul preached for the obedience of faith among all the nations of the world, the question is asked by the apostle, "What advantage, then, hath the Jew?" He had proved in the previous chapters that both Jews and Gentiles were guilty before God, and that the Jew, having received far greater privileges, was under greater condemnation; and now the question at the very outset of the epistle bursts forth, "What advantage, then, hath the Jew?" And the answer which he gives is in every respect instructive and striking: "Much, every way, but chiefly that unto them were committed the oracles of God"; a very important expression which the apostle uses with regard to all the communications which God had made to Israel; the revelations which He had given to them, and which He had afterwards caused to be written and to be transmitted to future generations. He uses the very strongest expression to convince us that these are the very words of God, authoritative and everlasting. And he also used another expression, which is very striking: that these oracles, as the very Word itself also teaches us, came down from heaven, and that they were merely entrusted to the guardianship of Israel. The Israelites did not produce them. They only received them. And the third thing he shows in these short words is, that in this consisted the sum and substance of all their privileges and advantages, that these holy Scriptures, if they are received by faith and by the blessing of the Holy Ghost, are the summary of all the blessings and privileges which it is the purpose of God to bestow upon His chosen ones.

From the very outset let me remind you of this fact, which all of you who are familiar with Scripture must have often considered, that with the exception of the first eleven chapters of the book of Genesis, the book of Job, the book of Proverbs, and the book of Ecclesiastes, the rest of the Old Testament is occupied entirely with the Jews, — God's dealings with them, their experiences, the promises which were made to them. The whole Old Testament, with the exception of the very few sections which I have enumerated, deals exclusively with the Jews. When we come to the books of the New Covenant, we find that the four gospels have to do exclusively with the Jews, and with the manifestation of Jehovah in the person of Jesus in the midst of them. The book of Acts, in the first chapters, has to do exclusively with the Jews when the Gospel was first preached in Jerusalem and in Judaea. And afterwards, although it goes to the Gentiles, yet never for a single moment does it leave out of sight Israel; and the very concluding chapter of the book of Acts shows us the apostle Paul in Rome testifying to the Jews that he alleged none other things than those which Moses and the prophets had testified. And even in the epistles we never lose sight of the Jews, for as I have already referred to the epistle to the Romans, I beg you to notice the significance and importance of this instance. Here, if anywhere, you might have expected that the apostle Paul, speaking to the whole world before the dispensation of the times of the Gentiles, would leave out of sight Israel, and that if he did produce Israel, it would only be as a preparation, as a scaffolding that was to be removed as soon as the building could be exhibited. But in this world-wide epistle, in this, the epistle of the Gentiles, the apostle devotes three chapters to the subject of the Jews, for it was an integral part of the whole counsel of God which he had to give to the Church, and his great anxiety was lest the Gentile Church should be ignorant concerning this mystery. And therefore we find that in the book of the Apocalypse we return again to the Jews. So all Scripture brings before you the Jews embodied in everything that is important and essential for our salvation, connected with the holy purposes of God which have not yet been fully realised. And this fact alone shows to us that an exposition of Scripture in which the Jews do not form an integral part is not a correct transcript of the mind of the Spirit. It is perfectly true that everything that happened to the Jews was typical and illustrative of their spiritual truths and experiences, and for your edification that through their examples and encouragements you might be helped upon your way heavenward; but the symbolical and typical character of that history does not in the slightest degree interfere with the actual historical reality of it, and with its being the beginning of the future which is yet before us. You are perfectly right, dear Gentile Christians, when you apply to yourselves all the promises that God gave to His people Israel, that He would never leave them or forsake them, and that, through all their chastisements, He would bring them in safety and give them glory. But only think for a moment that if God did not keep these promises to the people to whom He had given them in the first instance, what encouragement would there be for you to believe that He would keep them to you who, only by inference, are able to take them unto yourselves.

And the second point about the Scriptures is this. These oracles of God refer to such a large extent to the Jews that they were all written by Jews. Pharaoh had a dream. Joseph alone could interpret it. Nebuchadnezzar had a vision. Daniel alone could interpret it. Israel is the prophetic nation chosen by God for that purpose, and therefore all the writers of Scripture, not even Luke, the beloved physician, excepted, belonged to the chosen people. "What advantage, then, hath the Jew?" Much, every way, chiefly because unto them were committed the oracles of God.

But think not that I am going to praise the Jews. I only wish to glorify God, and I only wish to show, that by sovereign election God appointed them to be the recipients and the vehicles of divine treasures. The oracles were entrusted to them. Some modern writers have tried to account for the peculiarity of the Old Testament by the peculiarities of the Shemitic race, and have taught us that there was something in the Shemitic race which peculiarly fitted them to think of eternal, sublime, and great subjects. The election of Shem was before the election of Abraham, and if there were any peculiarities in the Shemitic race, which in any way were in accordance or in harmony with what was afterwards to be entrusted to them, I know not. He who is the Creator and the God of nature is also the Redeemer, and if there were any such peculiarities, this is not contrary to what is taught us in Scripture; but much better is it for us to look at facts and not at speculations. Israel did not find God. God found Israel. Monotheism made the Jews; the Jews did not make it. This is the great peculiarity of the Scriptures and of the Jewish nation — that in them we find something entirely different from what we see in other nations. There is an influence from above. Yes, with regard to all other nations you can account for their religion by their peculiarities.

In the Greeks, conscience was entirely subordinated to the sense of the beautiful; as Ruskin says, "The poets and the philosophers of Greece made the religion of Greece." In the Romans, the state was everything, and their whole religion had only one purpose — was subservient to the strength and interest of the commonwealth. In the east, in India and Persia, religion was nothing but metaphysical speculation of a pantheistic kind, clothed in ceremonies and forms. It had no God; it had no eternity. As was the nation, so was the religion. But we cannot say that as was Israel so was the religion, because Israel's religion came down from God.

And what did it find? It found a stubborn and a stiff-necked nation. Idolatry was in their heart, as it is in the heart of all human beings. No sooner had they been brought out of the land of Egypt than they worshipped the golden calf. Centuries after, when the apostasy of Israel came, there was a calf again. "These be thy gods which brought thee out of Egypt." In the wilderness, as the prophet says, they sacrificed unto Remphan and other gods. During the period of the Judges and of the kings, their tendency was continually to idolatry, and the testimony of the prophets was against this idolatrous inclination which manifested itself in two ways: either that they worshipped other gods, or that they worshipped Jehovah in a heathenish form which God had forbidden.

How did Israel meet this religion, then? It was only through the great and sad experiences of the captivity that the tendency to idolatry was driven out of the nation. God entrusted the oracles to Israel, and therefore Moses and the prophets wrote by inspiration. They were not the product of their age. They were not the exponents of their nation. They were the exponents of the chosen among the nation who had been taught by the Spirit of God, and these chosen ones of the nation, as well as the prophets, received all from above, from the Lord God Most High.

Therefore is the Scripture such a wonderful book, and therefore are all those fanciful theories, about the books of Moses having been fabricated after the exile, utterly void of common sense, as will appear still further from the next point. There is no other nation on the face of the earth that could have been induced to preserve books which so pictured their unthankfulness, their constant apostasies, comparing them with the other nations of the world, and saying in effect, "You are worse than any other nation, less loyal to me than the other nations are to their false gods." If we read the five books of Moses from beginning to end, how do they furnish a continuous picture of the wickedness and ingratitude of Israel? and so with the other historical books. What does the prophet Isaiah say? "We should have been like Sodom and Gomorrah if the Lord had not left a small remnant in the midst of us." And what do all the prophets say to Israel? "Be not as your fathers." Where is the nation which would have preserved for centuries such a record testifying against themselves?" There is nothing good in Israel. Do not imagine that I have chosen you because you are better than the other nations. It was my sovereign love, and my love for Abraham, Isaac, and Jacob." That is the work of God's grace in them. Had such a record been artificially made, centuries upon centuries after the histories had taken place, it would not have been received. What an extraordinary thing it is that the Jews who killed the prophets and stoned them that were sent unto them, did not dare to touch the written records of their lives and all their testimonies! nay, they reverenced those records, and they looked upon them as the testimony sent to them by the Most High. The lively oracles were entrusted to them. Pascal says most truly, as well as most pithily: "The sincerity with which the Jews have preserved their Scriptures is without parallel among the nations, and has its root not in nature," for Pascal knew the doctrine of election and of grace, and saw that it was God and God only who had so ordered it.

But let us look now at the Scriptures, for, as I have often said to you before, it is not merely the words that were spoken; it is not merely the events that happened; it is all these, selected and arranged by the guidance of the Holy Ghost, and incorporated in a book. Let me remind you briefly of how often God commanded the things to be written. In the book of Exodus, after the victory of Amalek, Moses was commanded to write it in the book, and in that same book of Exodus he tells us that he wrote the words that the Lord had spoken in the book. In the book of Numbers we are told that he wrote the wanderings of Israel in a book. In Deuteronomy we are told that the future king was to keep the book of the law, and that he was to read and meditate on it; and in that same book of Deuteronomy, when God gives a song to Moses for the children of Israel, in which their whole future down to the coming of the great Deliverer is described, Moses was commanded to write it in the book. This book was to be kept by the priest, and every seven years it was to be read to the people. Joshua was to write his experiences in a book, adding it to the books which already existed. So was Samuel commanded to write, and he laid it before the Lord. That shows that it was not a mere human book, an ordinary literary production, but that it was holy unto the Lord. Then we find that the first seventy-two psalms have been collected together, and we read afterwards "the prayers of David the son of Jesse are ended," and afterwards we find that there were further collections of psalms in the days of Hezekiah. All these commandments which are given for writing of the books show us the purpose of God, The prophet Isaiah refers to the book of the law in which the people were to read; and to the prophet Isaiah God said that he was to write upon tables, and then to put the writing into a book, in order that it might continue from generation to generation. You remember how Jeremiah, after the roll, which by the command of the Lord he had written, had been destroyed by King Jehoiakim, was commanded by God to write another roll, and to put all the former prophecies in it, and others which were added, showing the special punishment of Jehoiakim. And you remember how the prophet Habakkuk was told by God that he was to write distinctly upon tables; so distinctly, that he who ran might be able to read.

There is one fact that I must refer to here, namely, that in the reign of King Josiah there was found the roll of the book that had been neglected for a long time, and some critics from this draw the inference, that this law could not have existed all these centuries and then gone into oblivion. It is very strange that modern writers tell us so emphatically what could not possibly have been. Surely it is much better to ask historians to tell us what could have been, because it has actually happened. What must occur to every one immediately as perfectly parallel to this, is the history of Scripture for many centuries, during the Middle Ages. When Martin Luther first began to think on the subject, he imagined that the whole Scripture was contained in the gospels and epistles and other extracts which were in use in the devotional books of the priesthood. And so it happened in the history of Israel. Israel was a disobedient nation, and there were ages in which there was no fear of God, and no earnest desire for God, except among very few. When we come to the days of Ezra and of Nehemiah, we see that a great effort was made to collect all the books which up to that period were in existence, and to form them into one collection. Thus we find the testimony of the books of the Maccabees to this collection as containing the five books of Moses and the historical books to the end of the books of Kings, and parts of the Psalms and Proverbs, and afterwards the rest of the books which, after the return of Israel from the captivity to their own land, were gathered together, as we also read in the book of the Maccabees. This remains certain — that, according to the commandment of God, all the books that we possess were gradually added and afterwards collected, and, 300 years before our era, existed among the Jews as the only authoritative sacred collection of books; and it is a very remarkable thing that the Jews had never any doubt about these books. The Jews possessed literature of every kind. You know the books of the wars and other books are mentioned in the course of our Scriptures — historical and poetical records of battles and of events that took place. You know also that Solomon wrote thousands of proverbs, and also books on natural science, as we would call it, and songs; and in the book of Ecclesiastes there occurs the expression that there is no end of making books. But out of a very large or comparatively large literature they selected the.sc books in regard to which the apostle Paul uses the expression in the epistle to Timothy, "Holy books," that is to say, books which belonged to God and were separated unto Him. And as for the Apocrypha, the Apocrypha never pretends to be on a level with the other Scripture. On the contrary, it speaks of all the other Scriptures with the greatest reverence, as a great treasure which God had given to Israel, and it speaks of itself with great moderation. And, besides, the Apocryphal books contain many stories which are evidently legends, the character of which is entirely different from those miraculous records that we have in Holy Scripture. The Apocrypha is not of the slightest interest as a link between the Old Testament and the New Testament, either historically or theologically, for where the Old Testament ends, there, and nowhere else, docs the New Testament begin. The Old Testament ends in the book of Malachi — "I will send a forerunner before my face." And the New Testament history virtually begins, "There was a man sent from God, whose name was John." Neither was there any development in doctrine or in prophecy. These books are interesting indeed, but they are not at all an organic part of the Scripture; nay, they contain things which are contrary to the Scripture. They are entirely on a human or lower level. And therefore the Jews *never for a single moment* acknowledged them as belonging to the canon.

One thing is interesting to notice in the Apocryphal books. They mourn that there has been no prophet in Israel for a long time. One wonderful thing is this — not merely that God protected His faithful people against the temptations to lose their nationality and to accommodate themselves to the Greeks, and that He protected them in the hour of danger, but that during all this period when Israel was full of valour and courage, when the heroic spirit was strong in Israel, there is not a single instance of a false Messiah, because, according to the prophecy of Daniel, during these 400 years Messiah was not to appear; and no sooner was the prophecy at an end as to the time^ than the Jews were all in expectation of the Messiah, and the Messiah appeared in Jesus.

But now I must say a few words about the state of the Jews in the days of our Saviour. They had the Scriptures. The testimony of Josephus is well known to all. I shall not read it to you, because you can easily refer to it. He says that the Jews possessed twenty-two books of Scripture, the five books of Moses, historical books, four books of hymns to God, and proverbs teaching about the conduct of life, and the prophetic books, and he says that none has ever dared to add to them, or to take away anything from them, and that the Apocryphal books, although interesting, were never added to them, and that they looked upon the Scriptures as divine. After the Babylonish captivity the whole energy of Israel went into the Scriptures — the law which God had given them by Moses to preserve, to keep, to defend. But, alas! this veneration for the Scriptures became a false veneration. Here, indeed, we may speak of bibliolatry, of the worship of the book apart from the living God. They imagined that the whole five books of Moses had come down from heaven to Moses, some said on one day, some said at different periods.

Now they confused the written Word of God, who was with them from all eternity, and they spoke with the utmost blasphemy of God so delighting in the five books of Moses as to read them every day. They identified that which was to be a channel through which God speaks to them with the living God. And then there came necessarily the misunderstanding of the law. The Bible, when it becomes a dead book apart from the living God, is converted into a mere spell. It is frittered away by petty ingenuities, as by the scribes in the time of Christ. It is now the reign of casuists. The spiritual meaning of the law evaporates, the whole system of self-righteousness is wrought out.

The prophets had a twofold object. First, they showed the nation that the law is spiritual, and that outward observance did not satisfy God, and that therefore the object of the law was that people should repent and should long after a Saviour, and then the prophets pointed out to them the Saviour; but when people are self-righteous, they do not want God's righteousness, and when they are whole they need not a physician, and when they keep the law, and, like the old Jews and many other people, imagine they can keep even more than the law, so that they have works of supererogation, the voice of prophecy with its beautiful consolation and announcement of the atonement has no charms. And therefore there was a strange thing when our blessed Jesus came. The Jews believed Scripture to be God's Word; Jesus believed the Scripture to be the Word of God; but between those two there was enmity. The Jews rejected Jesus. Jesus testified against the Jews. The testimony of Jesus against the Jews was this: "You have not the Word of God in you, and therefore you are not able to believe who I am; I am sent unto you from God the Father. If the Scriptures lived within you, you would recognise my countenance, and you would hear my voice." But what a strange tragedy happened here — a warning to professing Christians who may reverence the Bible and fight about the Bible, and yet to whom the Bible, instead of being a thing to help them to God, becomes an obstacle that keeps them from God. Just as they misrepresented the Sabbath, in regard to which their tradition made void the commandments of God.

But even the traditions, which were not committed to paper for eight centuries, were intended only to reverence the Bible, and the reason why, from the time of the great synagogue, it was forbidden to write any other tradition, was lest the commentary and the tradition should be confused with the written Word of God, the oracles that were committed to them. So even in their sin and in their tradition, which was contrary to the mind of God, God kept them faithful and loyal as conservators of the Word. A poor nation indeed to guard the treasure that He had entrusted to their care!

But there were Israelites who did hear the voice of God in the Scriptures, First of all there was John the Baptist, who reverberated Isaiah and Malachi and the 1st Psalm, and all the declarations of Moses and the prophets. There was the Blessed Virgin Mary, who had imbibed the songs of David and the predictions of the fathers. There was the priest Zacharias, who was waiting for the horn of salvation to rise in the house of God's servant David. There were aged Simeon and Anna, and what were they feeding on? The Word of God was in them. And what was that Word of God? "Comfort ye, comfort ye my people," saith your God, "and speak to the heart of Jerusalem, and say to the cities of Judah, 'Behold your God.'" They were waiting for the consolation of Israel.

And when the blessed Jesus came, those to whom the Scripture was a living Word, although they may have been comparatively ignorant, understood His voice. It was the same voice again. "Blessed are the poor in spirit, blessed are they that mourn, blessed are the meek." Why was it that those first disciples, when they first saw Jesus, said immediately, "We have found the Messiah of whom Moses and the prophets did write"? Very few prophecies had been fulfilled all that time. Perhaps they did not know of any that had as yet been fulfilled. The Word was in them through the Scripture, and the Word which was before them appealed unto their minds. Jesus Himself did not go to their schools. They were astonished at His exposition of Scripture because He had not been taught in their letters, their comments, and their traditions, just as people nowadays think that unless people are great in philology and in criticism and in history, they cannot understand the Bible. But Jesus was the only one who ever understood the whole of the Old Testament. People that are ignorant are excluded from these learned investigations, but Jesus gave understanding to the simple. To Him belonged the key of David, and He opened unto them the Scriptures. But poor Israel? Do not think that the Pharisees were all hypocrites. They were all in danger of becoming hypocrites, and some of them were hypocrites but many of them were godly, religious, earnest men, and they truly reverenced the Scriptures, and had a zeal for God, but no great knowledge, and went about establishing their own righteousness. When Jesus told them in the parable that the kingdom would be taken away from them and given to others, they said, "God forbid," and it came out of their deep soul. "God forbid." And they fulfilled the prophecies by rejecting Jesus. So it had been predicted, as in the 118th Psalm: "The stone which the builders rejected"; 53rd chapter of Isaiah: "He was despised and rejected of men"; nth chapter of Zechariah: "Thirty pieces of silver they weighed for my hire." All that was fulfilled in Jesus. As the apostle Paul says in the book of Acts, the Jews, thinking that in doing their own will and purpose they were doing according to God's will, were only fulfilling the prophecies.

And now perhaps some one will say, "But what becomes of the Old Testament scriptures? What becomes of that whole preparation which for thousands of years God has given to His nation?" The Scripture was fulfilled in Jesus, and let me say that all that was predicted of the Jews in the future was also fulfilled in Jesus, for the promises were all made unto Him, and the rights that the Jews have in the land of Canaan arise from the covenant which God made with Abraham; but Christ is the actual instalment of the possession. And the Old Testament scriptures were, by the apostles, planted not merely among the believing Jews where they already were in existence, but among all the Gentiles who embraced the faith which is in Christ Jesus. But Israel as a nation is preserved. If all Jews had accepted Jesus as the Messiah, their testimony would have been regarded as partial; but because the Scriptures which contain the picture of Jesus remain in the hands of the Jews who have rejected Jesus, none can gainsay their witness; and if all the Jews had been destroyed, the witnesses for Jesus would have been absent. So God has ordered it in His infinite wisdom.

But look for a moment at Israel according to the flesh. You know the grief and sorrow which the apostle Paul felt on account of Israel. Jerusalem was *dark,* and all the different parties were intriguing and scheming and thinking that they would be able by statesmanship, and by conciliation, to steer calmly and quietly. Services went on as usual in the temple, but the word of judgment had already gone forth, and the destruction of Jerusalem and of the temple had already been predicted by the Lord; and to a spiritually-minded man like the apostle Paul, although the judgment had not yet taken place outwardly, the judgment had already taken place in reality. They hardened themselves against Stephen; they hardened themselves against the declaration of the apostles. They continued in their unbelief. The judgment was surely coming. The guilt was upon them— greater guilt than any they had previously incurred. And not merely was that guilt upon them, that guilt which alone can account for their eighteen hundred years' dispersion, but their spiritual condition was ripening fast into that state in which it has remained ever since. And not only so, but the political complications were also maturing; for although Israel committed this great sin against God and against Jesus Christ, they did not fall away from God. They still had a zeal for God. They still preferred to die rather than to worship idols. They were still waiting with all sincerity, and praying with all fervour. It was not like a nation that had become frivolous and idolatrous. When the nations of Europe fall away, most likely they may fall away into bottomless infidelity, but Israel never fell into this, great as their guilt was, Therefore did the apostle Paul weep for Israel, God's people, to whom pertained the adoption. He made them His children, and as His people He brought them out of Egypt and instructed them, as a father dealeth with his child. And to them belonged the glory, not the glory of weapons or the glory of science, but the glory that Jehovah had chosen them, and that He would be in the midst of them. And to them belonged the covenants made with Abraham, Isaac, and Jacob, and afterwards. And to them belonged the law, the ten commandments written by God Himself upon the tables of stone. And to them belonged the beautiful worship, the tabernacle with its Holy and Holy of Holies; and to them belonged the fathers. Oh, think only for a moment of the fathers. Think of Abraham, who was called the Friend of God, who received the promise in faith, nothing doubting, who was ready to give up Isaac, knowing that he would receive him back again from the dead; and of Jacob, who wrestled with God and was called a prince; and of Moses, by whom Israel went out of Egypt, and to whom there were given the ordinances of the law, and who was a mediator between God and the Jews. And think of all the warriors and judges, strong men and fervent, who did not yield to the masses, but were loyal to the Most High, and were contented with three hundred who chose to obey God, rather than with vast numbers. The stars in the heavens were fighting in their favour — the sword of Jehovah and of Gideon; they kept the people in discipline by the Word of the Most High.

And think of all those sweet singers and psalmists that poured out their souls in songs and melodies, and thanksgivings and praises; or of those prophets, pillars of light who were in communion with the omniscient mind, to whom a thousand years are but as one day. They heard the distant thunder of God's judgments, and they were afraid. They saw the beautiful countenance of Immanuel, and they poured forth words of consolation. And think of the martyrs that were not afraid of the lion or of the edge of the sword, or of the violence of the fiery furnace, of devoted children and loving mothers, and fathers of whom concerning the flesh Christ came, who is God over all, blessed for ever! And this is the nation whom God had to chasten in His sore displeasure. Jerusalem was destroyed. The temple, which was the very breath of their nostrils, was laid bare in the dust, and Israel itself became cursed among all the nations.

Here I must conclude with but one remark. See, then, this nation. How many have wept over Israel; for, whose sorrow can be compared, as it says in the book of Lamentations, with the sorrow of Jerusalem? Your poet has said, "The wild dove hath a nest, the fox its cave, mankind its country: Israel but the grave." Oh, no, and a thousand times no. Israel has the Scripture, and this Scripture it is which has kept Israel alive up to this day. Different from all other nations Israel has the Scripture, and whenever the Holy Ghost breathes upon them, they shall behold Jesus to whom Moses and the prophets have testified. For the future is still before them, and that future which is spoken of by the mouth of all the holy prophets, even from the beginning.

I have often thought of that triumphal arch of Titus which was erected after the destruction of Jerusalem. There it still stands in Rome, and on that arch you can see represented the captive Jews and the seven-branched candlestick of the temple and the table of shewbread, and in front the great emperor and conqueror Titus. There is another triumphal arch which the apostle Paul has also erected right among the Romans — the epistle to the Romans, from the 9th chapter to the 11th and on this arch it is written, "All Israel shall be saved." And in all this the Scripture partly fulfilled unto us already, will show forth its truth and its steadfastness unto the ages to come; for as the prophet said that there will be yet in the streets of Jerusalem children playing and making merry, so all the chapters of the Old Testament will shine forth with renewed vitality and beauty when the Lord shall visit His children and shall fulfil His word, and when all ends of the earth shall see together the salvation of our God. Blessed be the Lord God of Israel, who alone doth great wonders, and blessed be His glorious name, and let all the earth be filled with His glory. Amen.

VI - Israel Since The Dispersion - An Evidence of the Truth of Prophecy

My subject this morning is: Israel since the dispersion a witness for the truth of the history and prophecy of Holy Scripture.

With the captivity in Babylon begins a period of the history of the kingdom of God which still continues, and which shall only end at the second coming of our Lord. Why is the evangelist Luke so anxious to impress upon us that the birth of Jesus took place under the reign of Caesar Augustus, emperor of Rome? Why is Pontius Pilate mentioned in the creed? In order that it may be impressed upon us that the sceptre had indeed departed from Judah, and that it was under the fourth world-monarchy that Jesus the new-born King of the Jews appeared. But the times of the Gentiles appeared more clearly after the destruction of Jerusalem and the dispersion of Israel among all nations. This is the expression that our blessed Saviour Himself used, that during the times of the Gentiles Jerusalem was to be trodden under foot. And during this period we behold Israel under the displeasure of God, spiritually blind, scattered among all nations of the earth, and yet still in allegiance to God, and God still regarding them and watching over them with favour; whereas, on the other hand, we see the Church consisting both of Jews and Gentiles, knowing the name of the Triune, and going forth in the name of Jesus among all the nations of the world, yet themselves a little flock. And as Israel was opposed to and separated from all the nations, the Church is a witness against the world — a witnessing body and a suffering body, until it at last shall please God to give it the kingdom.

Israel is a witness for the truth in a negative way. The Church of Christ is a witness for the truth in a positive way. Only omniscience could have foreseen and foretold the wonderful and complicated methods which Divine providence was to take in carrying out the counsel of the Most High. That the Messiah, after many centuries of preparation, should come to Israel to be rejected, and that their rejection of the Messiah should not end their history, but only retard it for a number of centuries, while it gave opportunity and time of working to another portion of the Divine counsel, if it be possible still more sublime and more mysterious, none but prophets sent by God Himself could ever have foretold.

Very clear, indeed, is the prediction, as, for instance, in the 53rd chapter of Isaiah, that the time was coming when Israel would have their eyes open to see that the Man whom they rejected, and whom they thought to be an enemy of God and afflicted by God, was an innocent and spotless Lamb, and that His death was an atonement and expiation for their sins. Equally clear is the testimony of Zechariah that the final conversion, repentance, and glorification of Israel would be connected, not with the acceptance of the Messiah at the first advent, but with the acceptance of a rejected Messiah, when they shall look upon Him whom they had pierced. And how mysterious and inexplicable was the prediction of Daniel, that the founder of the fifth monarchy which was to last for ever was the Son of Man, who would come, not out of Bethlehem as Micah had predicted, but from the throne above, and with the clouds of heaven! How remarkable is it, and quite different from any imagination of man, that God, when He sent Jesus the first time, fulfilled most clearly the predictions which had been given by the prophets, and yet in such a way that the fulfilment by no means compelled faith, but remained a test and trial to Israel whether, so to speak, the kingdom of God was congenial to them; and therefore, although they fully believed in the whole of Scripture, they did not feel themselves shut up to the reception of Jesus. "Verily thou art a God that hidest Thyself." In all revelations of God there is still an element of darkness, in order that faith may be tested. And so Jesus Himself predicted to Jerusalem, summing up their whole past history, that they who had killed the prophets, and stoned them that were sent to them, were now at last to receive the recompense of their evil deeds, that their house should be left to them desolate because they had not understood the time of their visitation. But yet not for ever did He part with them. He held out the bright and glorious hope that they would see Him again, and not merely with the eyes of the body, but also with the eyes of faith, welcoming Him as the Blessed One in the name of the Lord.

See, then, the Old Testament predictions and the New Testament predictions tested most clearly, in the light of fact, by the history of the last eighteen centuries, that Israel rejected Jesus; that God gave up Israel to banishment and punishment, yet loving them and being faithful to the covenant which He had made; that this nation is preserved in a most wonderful way both physically and spiritually for the fulfilment of those predictions which are inwoven, in the Old Testament, with the predictions of the first advent. The apostle Paul, long before Jerusalem was destroyed, like all spiritual men, saw that the end had already set in, and therefore he uses the expression with regard to the Jews that the wrath had come upon them to the uttermost, — for, in reality, when Jesus died upon the cross, and when the veil of the temple was rent in twain, there was already spiritually decided what was to be the history of Israel. The guilt of rejecting Christ, the guilt of rejecting the testimony of the apostles, remained upon the nation. The spiritual self-righteousness and blindness only increased, and still as they were loyal to God, and abhorred all idolatry, and wished to obey the commandments of God, the conflict with Rome could not in any way be modified, and so the destruction of Jerusalem was only the outward and historical manifestation of the inward and spiritual facts which had already taken place.

But what a wonderful thing it is that Israel, God's people, should be scattered among all the nations of the earth! Let me speak plainly on this subject. What a strange thing it is, that after God for centuries and centuries had (to speak foolishly) done His utmost to separate Israel, in one corner of the world, from all the nations of the earth, — for that was the whole system of God with Israel, — He should then take this nation and scatter them among all the peoples of the world! It is quite true that for 400 years He. allowed them to be in Egypt, and there, when they were in Egypt being brought into contact with the most civilized nation of antiquity, they in many respects matured most rapidly in the things pertaining to this life. But during those four centuries they in no wise amalgamated with Egypt, for they, being shepherds, were an abomination to the Egyptians; and the Egyptians, who in every respect were exactly the opposite of what God had taught Abraham, Isaac, and Jacob, were also an abomination unto Israel; so there they were in Egypt, and yet separated from Egypt. Forty years He insulated them in the wilderness to keep them all to Himself, and, as it were, to show them that they were a nation entirely separated unto God. When He brought them into their own land. He gave them every possible instruction that they were not to adopt the customs of the nations that they still found there, and that they were to be very resolute in exterminating those nations; and He gave them a law which in every respect separated them from the rest of the world, for the strict prohibition of idolatry in every form and shape was like a wall of fire round Israel. All their regulations about their food and their vestments and their daily life showed them, and impressed upon them day by day, that they were a nation set apart unto the Lord. And the very country into which He brought them was altogether sufficient for itself. It was separated from all the rest of the world by the mountain ranges, by the Mediterranean Sea, by the large deserts on the south and south-east. It possessed everything that they required for their sustenance, for it was an exceedingly fertile land, so that there was no inducement for them to go out in the way of commerce, and commerce God discouraged in every possible way among the Jews. They were to take no interest upon money, which at once paralysed the idea of commercial speculation; nor was it according to the idea of God that people were to amass large capitals, so that neither by commerce were they to have intercourse with other nations, nor was there to be in them any desire of aggrandizement or of warfare. When afterwards God gave them David their king, and Jerusalem their centre, and the temple where was His habitation, it was said to Israel, "Oh, happy people, be content: here I have planted you. You are a nation of twelve tribes, descendants of twelve brothers. There never was a nation so compact together as you are. Love one another and walk before Me, and Jerusalem shall be your centre, and David the man after My heart, and the sons of David shall be your kings and your leaders."

But I have not said everything yet. When prophecy looks forward to the days of the future, even then it regards Israel as being settled in their own country not to leave it, and as having Jerusalem as their centre and Mount Zion as their centre; and the influence that they are to exert upon the rest of the world is not by aggressiveness, but by attractiveness. As long as the world stands, Zion and Jerusalem are to remain Zion and Jerusalem, and are the centre. The nations are to go up there. The Jews are not to go from Zion and Jerusalem to the nations. God's great idea for all times is not that Israel should be scattered, but that Israel should be concentrated in their own land, and that Jerusalem should be a centre of all religious and national life throughout the whole earth. And then He takes them, destroys Jerusalem and the temple, and scatters them among all the nations of the earth.

Now is there not here something wonderful? No human wisdom could have foreseen such a paradox. It is so paradoxical that it is astonishing that people are not more struck and perplexed by this problem, but it is simply because they do not believe the Bible literally; and in no other way can it be believed.

But there is another aspect of this which makes it still more complicated. God had not said to the Jews, "I have chosen you, and you only, and I have given you this country, and I have given you the temple. Now walk before Me." But He said to them, "I have chosen you only as my first-born; I want to bless the nations of the earth. You must not think that I have chosen you for your sake alone. You must be interested in all the idolaters of the world. You must pray that My light may visit the distant islands. You must have a world-wide heart You must sing:

'All people that on earth do dwell,
Sing to the Lord with cheerful voice.'

You must look forward to this as the great glory — My great glory and your great glory too — that all ends of the earth shall have the same privileges, and shall have the same joy which I have given to you."

Therefore God never allowed the Jews to think for a moment that He was only the God of the Jews. The prophets are interested in all the nations by whom Israel was surrounded; and now comes the preparation for the dispersion. The first preparation I spoke about in my first lecture — the adaptation of the Greek language through the empire of Alexander the Great — how it was brought to the Jews, and how the Jews were brought into the Graeco-Macedonian empire and adopted the Greek language; and owing to this there arose a new kind of Jewish population, the Hellenistic population, who, though they were loyal to the God of their fathers, yet were acquainted with the language and the culture of Greece, and thus became accustomed to think of the spread of the knowledge of Jehovah among all nations.

And, besides, there was another preparation. There could only be one temple in Palestine, which is a very important fact, and contains a very important doctrine; but although there was only one temple in Palestine, there could be as many synagogues as it pleased the Jews to erect, for wherever a few Israelites chose to gather together to worship God, to read the Scriptures, and to converse about the Scriptures, there was nothing to prevent them from forming a synagogue. And therefore those synagogues were all over the country, and as you read in the gospels and in the book of Acts, they met for worship, and chiefly for the reading of the Scriptures, and for conversation on what God had taught them. And along with this was what I tried to explain before — the concentration of the whole Jewish religious and intellectual power upon the Scripture, and above all, upon the law of Moses.

Now, when the destruction of Jerusalem came, and when thousands and tens of thousands lost their lives, and thousands were led into captivity, and calamity came upon Israel such as no nation ever witnessed, still this nation, notwithstanding all their calamity, remained loyal to God, although the blood-guiltiness was still upon them; and nothing ever induced them to give up the worship of the one true God, or to adapt themselves in any way to the idolatry and to the customs of the nations; and there they were, as if nothing had happened, wherever God in His providence had brought them, studying the Scriptures, rabbis having their disciples round them, whom they instructed in the wisdom and in the ways of God, meeting for worship every Sabbath Day, and holding their synagogue service, observing the law of Moses with the greatest loyalty and disinterestedness. They did not apostatise from God, they did not fall into infidelity. They were not swallowed up by despair, and they did not say, "Why should we serve God any longer after He has thus dealt with us?" They felt it was on account of their sins that God had thus dealt with them, but with a heroism and faith which does remain a marvel throughout all history they continued in the old ways. They had the Word of God, and that it was that preserved them. Although they did not understand it spiritually, although there was a veil upon their hearts, still God's Word was with them. The ten commandments were heard every Sabbath day. The life-giving Word of God sounded in their ears. The beautiful narratives of their forefathers were familiar to their memory and dear to their heart, for the Word of God, even possessed outwardly without the spiritual teaching unto salvation, is a great power, and there is no power in the world equal to it.

And so Israel, during all this time, has been a witness for God, All their past history is embodied in them now. Monuments made of marble and of stone are nothing compared with the nation of millions for eighteen centuries under the greatest persecutions, and in the most diverse circumstances, commemorating continually the great facts, that had been wrought out for them in the days of old. There is the Sabbath Day. Israel up to this hour, every seventh day, keeps the day which God had commanded their fathers to keep. What a marvellous idea is that observance of the Sabbath! Do not think now of the relation of the Sabbath to the Lord's Day. Do not think now of the Pharisaical Sabbath, which is often called the Jewish Sabbath by a great confusion of ideas. It was a caricature of the Old Testament Sabbath. But think of what you read in God's Word — that God, who created all things in six days, on the seventh day, on which He rested, having gone out from Himself into the outward, returns into Himself, and takes the whole world with Him, that it may rest in His own love. Therefore He hallowed the seventh day. To Israel, time was not like a wide ocean in which there are no divisions, and which is measureless and restless, as Milton speaks of Sabbathless Satan. But to Israel, time is articulated. God lives with His people. He lives with them, while they work for six days. He lives and rejoices with them when, on the seventh day, they rest before Him. In these days, when people are beginning to doubt the first article of the creed, what a marvellous testimony is Israel with its Sabbath Day, because God created the heavens and the earth!

Look at all the festivals that they keep. Look at the passover kept in every Jewish family. There you will see what happened in the upper chamber where Jesus was with His twelve apostles. They commemorate the wonderful dealing of God with their fathers when He sent ten plagues upon Egypt, and when, by the blood of the Lamb, He brought them out of the house of bondage. They read those chapters of Exodus. They sing hymns of praise. They break the unleavened bread, and all the members of the family partake of it. They bless four cups with benedictions; and one of these cups was the cup that Jesus set apart for the Lord's Supper. What a marvellous thing is this passover! and the little children among the Jews are very excited when the passover draws near. The unleavened bread is brought in, but along with that there is also to be a purification, and every vestige of leaven wherever it is found, even with childish scrupulosity, has to be removed from their vestments and from their rooms. You remember what the apostle says, "Keep the festival not with the old leaven of malice and of wickedness"? There is a commentary on that every year in the houses of the Jews. Or shall I remind you of the day of atonement when the Jews fast, and humble themselves before God, confessing their sins and believing that on that day God absolves them from their sins, so that they are able to go on for another year, in worship-communion with Him? Or the festival of the weeks and of the New Year? — what wonderful mementoes all these are of the facts which took place. What else could have made them observe them year after year, and century after century? And as they observe the festivals, so they observe the law of Moses; and it is owing to that law of Moses that they are still in existence, for Israel is not like any of the other nations. Other nations, when they have reached, as it were, their highest point, and when they have been living in great civilization and luxury, become effete, on account of their immorality and on account of their wickedness; but Israel has never become effete. The sanctities of family life endure in Israel up to this day, owing to the law of Moses, owing to the ten commandments, owing to the ordinances which God gave to His people, and to God Himself watching over them. They are physically, as they ever were, distinguished by their longevity, distinguished by their tenacity and vigour of purpose, distinguished by their mental freshness, so that they are able to enter into any branch of study or into any occupation of life. It is the Word of God that has done this. There is nothing so degrading as to be persecuted, as to be mocked, as to be banished into one corner of a town, as to be excluded from social life. If a nation ever might have become altogether degraded, and might have dwindled down into non-existence, it would have been the Jews; but God in the prophets said that they were never to cease as a nation before Him, and He says. Even when I shall punish you and banish you, I will not abhor you. I will never forget the covenant I have made with your fathers. I will still regard you with favour, and preserve you for the time when there shall be given unto you repentance. There is no analogous fact in history. Nations have migrated and, from stress of circumstances, sought other countries in which to settle. There has been colonization on large plans. There have been other movements which have brought nations into different countries; but then they have become amalgamated with the nations among whom they have settled, as the French refugees in England. There have been also the nomadic tribes of Egyptians who are wandering about over the world. But a nation like Israel, dispersed over the whole face of the earth, keeping their law and separated as a community, yet taking an interest, whenever they are allowed, in every development of history and of mental culture, has never existed. Some of them have attempted to forget that they are Jews, but have never been allowed in Gods providence to do so. As a Spanish rabbi said once some centuries ago, "There is a blessing on us, and there is a curse on us. You are trying now to exterminate us, and you will not succeed, because there is a blessing on us. And the time is coming when you will try to favour us and you will not succeed, because there is a curse on us." Mysterious nation! read the old Testament, read the New Testament, and you will see that what no historian can explain is explained by the omniscient mind of God. Therefore the great German metaphysician Hegel said that the history of the Jews was an enigma to him; he understood the philosophy of the history of other nations, but here was a problem that he could not solve. No man can solve it, because they are the nation which God has set apart — the paradox of the world's history, that paradox which finds its solution only in Jesus Christ, for as the prophet Hosea said, Many days — a long period — the children of Israel shall be without king, without priest, without ephod, but at the same time without idolatry either public or private. Formerly they fell into idolatry. Since their dispersion they have not fallen into idolatry.

But I must point out to you the spiritual deterioration of Israel. I have shown you the good points of Israel; I want to show you also the spiritual deterioration of Israel, and how this had been likewise predicted.

The first is this — and here Israel is a witness not merely for the Old Testament but for the New Testament, for there is no separation between those two, — the Jews cling to the Old Testament, and refuse the interpretation of the New. The Gentiles fancy that they can understand the New Testament without the Old Testament. Oh, it is perfectly impossible. The apostle Paul expounds the Jews to us out of his own experience. "They have a zeal for God, but without knowledge. They go about establishing a righteousness of their own, not submitting themselves unto the righteousness of God." Their attention has become concentrated on the law. This is an important point. Both Genesis and the prophets are comparatively neglected by the Jews for the sake of the law of Moses, and yet the law of Moses was only a parenthesis, and it is comparatively of less importance than either the book of Genesis or the prophets. Therefore having an outward view of the law, and thinking that they can fulfil the law, the very purpose of the law has not been fulfilled in them. That is, they have no true consciousness of sin, and no longing for a Saviour. This is the difficulty of all ministers with the Jews, as it is the difficulty also with the unconverted Gentiles. There is no difference. If people do not know that they are under the curse of the law, and that they are guilty in the sight of God, they will have no longing for a Saviour.

The second deterioration is as regards the Messiah. The Jews had many false Messiahs. One of their greatest men, a renowned rabbi, and a man in whom there is much to admire and even to reverence, was a follower of the false Messiah. But after the destruction of Jerusalem, when they had no certain genealogies, they thought that the only way of finding out when the Messiah was coming was to examine the dates and times of the prophecies; and when they examined these, and the people were often disappointed, then the Jewish rabbis gave a commandment that there was to be no more investigation of the Messianic times, because the people were only disappointed. In fact, the less they thought about the Messiah the better. And then there came a time when all those passages, like the 22nd Psalm and the 53rd chapter of Isaiah, and many others, which the ancient Jewish interpreters had referred to the Messiah, were explained away by the Jewish rabbis, because all Christians applied them to Jesus, and they were referred to the Jewish nation or to some righteous man, exactly as the rationalists have been trying to explain away the direct and indirect Mosaic testimony of the Old Testament. And then the idea of the Messiah was lowered by the Jews; and whereas formerly in the Old Testament it was not an exclusively national idea, but the Messiah was to be a light to lighten the Gentiles as well as the glory of the people of Israel, now the Messiah became to them, so to speak, a provincial idea — not a spiritual national idea.

Last of all — and this is the most important — why does the prophet Hosea say, "In the latter days Israel shall seek the Lord"? If I say that of heathen nations, "They shall seek the Lord," it is intelligible; but to say it of the Jews, who are constantly worshipping God, that they shall seek Jehovah, seems indeed very strange. And this is the thing that most offends the Jews when we tell them this. Instead of knowing the living God as He revealed Himself to

Abraham, Isaac, and Jacob, — the fulness of light and love, — the Jews have now come to think that their great religion is monotheism. I tried to explain in one of my lectures that monotheism is not the religion of the Old Testament, but that Jehovahism is the religion of the Old Testament. Now they lay all the stress upon the unity, of which the Bible never speaks. The Bible says that there is only one God, but the Bible says that in this God there is God, and God as He reveals Himself, and the Spirit of God. But instead of that, the Jews have this abstract idea of a unity: and in that abstract idea there is no warming for the heart, nor is there any peace for the conscience, and therefore is it said that in the latter days they shall seek Jehovah; and this accounts for the most extraordinary fact that the father of modern pantheism, Spinoza, was a Jew. This bare abstract idea of unity is not able to satisfy the intellect, and leads more or less to the departure even from monotheism.

And then can we be astonished, that along with this there is among the Jews a great deal of worldliness and indifference and unbelief, and of every kind of sin even down to infidelity? That is the state of the nation up to this day. While there is a remnant of those Israelites who, by the grace of God, have come to the faith in Jesus Christ according to the prophetic word that there must always be, even during the time of their dispersion, a remnant from Israel, according to the election of grace; and while the godly Israelites who are going on in Talmudic darkness are still clinging to the Word of God, there are great numbers of worldly, indifferent, unbelieving, rationalistic, and infidel Jews. What will become of them? But the actual condition of the nation during these eighteen centuries, physically, spiritually, morally, and the predictions of prophecy run perfectly parallel. And now to one who believes Scripture, it makes no difference whether a thing has been actually accomplished in history or is merely written in the Bible. One is as sure to us as the other. We have not the slightest doubt that Jerusalem was destroyed, not only because the Roman historians tell us, but because Christ said that it would be destroyed. Neither have we the slightest doubt that Israel shall be restored, converted, and reinstated in their own land, because God has said so. The Word of God standeth sure for ever.

Now prophecy is a stereotyped miracle. A man may say, "If I had been on the Red Sea and seen the Jews pass through it, or if I had been present when the Lord raised Lazarus from the dead, I should have believed; but these great facts took place in a day, in a moment, and then they disappeared." But prophecy is miracle stereotyped, continued miracle. It has been going on now from century to century. People speak about "realising" the Bible, What do you mean by "realising" the Bible, and the things that are spoken in the Bible? When people speak about realising things — an expression which is exceedingly dangerous and misleading — what they mean is that they want to get their imagination into such a heated condition, and their feelings so roused, that they may have something better than faith. So when they sec the Ammergau play, they think that that is realising the crucifixion of Jesus. It may be realising the crucifixion, but it is not realising Christ crucified. Read the 53rd chapter of Isaiah, and you will realise the crucifixion — that is to say, believe it. But if you wish to see the Word of God, study the Jews as they live in the present day, and there you will see how true it all is. I remember when I was a child, one evening, as I felt the air of the room oppressive, I went out; and there I saw the beautiful stars shining brightly, and the thought flashed across my mind, "These are the stars that God showed to our father Abraham, and we are here: the stars are here. Mow much more is God still in the world." And so all the history of the Jews — their father Abraham, their rabbi Moses, their prophet Elijah, the shield of David, the wisdom of Solomon— all these are national possessions which live within them. And all the history of the Gospels and of the Acts — and the very condition of the Jews themselves at the time of Christ, the way they talked, the way they argued, the way they rejected Him, and the way that some of them believed in Him — behold all these things you may now see with your eyes, and hear with your ears, over all the countries of Europe and most of the countries of Asia. God has given them to be a witness.

The Jews themselves do not understand their history, for they do not understand the reason of their dispersion. They confess their sins; they weep, as only Jews can weep; they fast on the anniversary of the destruction of Jerusalem. This very year in which I am speaking to you there have been collected poems written by Jews in Gallicia in the peculiar dialect of mixed Hebrew and German, in which there is as intense a national feeling and as mournful a spirit as can be shown by any nation, as if Jerusalem had only been destroyed last year; but the reason they do not know. That is again according to the Scriptures. It is only according to prophecy. In no other way can you account for it Eighteen hundred years, they have seen that they are in banishment. They ask themselves the reason why, and they are not able to answer it. Israel has never yet confessed the blood-guiltiness that is upon them because they crucified Jesus. The Athenians, after putting Socrates to death, very soon regretted the judicial murder which they had committed; but Israel has never acknowledged or regretted the crucifixion of Christ up to this day The insipid admissions of rationalistic Jews that those were the days of barbarism and of religious intolerance, which are greatly to be regretted, is no confession of the unparalleled, national, blood-red sin which Israel committed against the Just and Holy One. But the Old Testament tells you that it would be so. In the latter days they would say, "We thought Him as one smitten of God, and we hid as it were, our faces from Him." And Zechariah says, "There will be given repentance to Israel, and they shall mourn over him as over a son, an only son." *And He is their only son*. We have got nothing else: no power, no wisdom, no honour. The only thing that we have produced — and not we, but the grace of God and the Holy Ghost — is Jesus. He is their only son: but for many centuries they have not known it. But then shall they mourn over Him, as over an only son. As with the sons of Jacob, after they had sold Joseph into Egypt, returned to their father and their conduct afterwards was better than it had been before; but the blood of Joseph was still upon their consciences and hearts, and afterwards they were driven to Egypt, and there Joseph revealed himself to them — "I am Joseph your brother, whom ye sold into Egypt" — thus will it be with Israel. That they do not know Jesus up to this time has always been predicted; and this is what the apostle Paul says: "There is a veil on their hearts," so that they do not understand the whole covenant. And it is what Jesus says, "Ye shall see me no more till ye shall say, Blessed is He that cometh in the name of the Lord." Israel is a witness for the truth of the Old and the New Testament scriptures.

God is coming — God Himself in the person of His Son. Great judgments will be against the anti-Christian nations. Great power and majesty shall be made manifest upon His chosen people Israel. The Church of Christ has her position, and the Church of Christ is associated with the blessed Lord, and with the blessed Lord takes the deepest interest in the manifestation of His kingdom here upon earth. Oh that we may know the living God! Israel commemorating the passover every year says, "Next year in Jerusalem." The Church of Christ commemorating the passover on the Lord's Day, or whenever it is, even by partaking of that bread and of that cup, says, "Till He come": both together witnesses for the Scripture. The Scripture is God's Word, and this conviction we have the more strongly, the more we are filled with faith in the living God, and realise that there is a history going on, and know that He who was, and who is, is also He that is to come.

May the Lord grant unto us that His Word may thus be living to us. Amen.

VII - The Church of Christ Based on the Old Testament — the New Testament

I have endeavoured to show in my last addresses how the Jews were the custodians of the Old Testament Scriptures. I now wi.sh to direct your attention to the Church of Christ and her relation to the books of the New Testament as well as to those of Moses and the prophets.

It has often been remarked that the Church of Christ originated without the Scriptures, only by the preached word of the Gospel, and that as it thus originated, it also existed before the Scriptures. This assertion is very superficial, and, in fact, it is not true, because the preaching of our Lord Jesus Christ and the preaching of the apostles were always connected with the Scriptures of the Old Testament, yea, founded upon them, so that from the very beginning the Church owed its origin not merely to the preaching of the Word, but to the preaching of the Word as being the explanation of the Word which was written, and which God had given to the fathers. We can see this not merely concerning the Church, which was founded among Israel — for what was the preaching of the apostle Peter on the day of Pentecost, and of the apostle Paul in the synagogue at Antioch, but the explanation of that which was written, because that which was written was not now superseded, nor merely supplemented, but it was fulfilled; it was illumined and transfigured, and it was to remain for ever as the authoritative announcement of the Most High.

And when the apostles went to the idolaters, how remarkable is it that unto them also they preached the Scriptures, so that we find that in all the epistles which afterwards they directed to the congregations which had been formed from among the heathen, they proved every doctrine from the Old Testament Scriptures. Justification by faith was proved from the prophet Habakkuk, from the example of Abraham, and from the experience of David. And the apostle Paul was so anxious that in that worldwide epistle to the Romans there should be given light to the Gentiles, as to the true position of the Old Testament, that he shows in it how Jesus Christ was the minister of the circumcision to fulfil the promises which were given to the fathers, and how the Gentiles were brought in, in accordance with the prophetic word. He was afraid of that congregation in Rome, and of all the Gentile congregations, falling into what I may call Gentilising error, just as he was afraid of the Galatians falling into Judaising error; and all the practical exhortations that he gave to the Churches were based upon the Word of God — "as it is written." So he writes to the Corinthians that the experience of Israel in the wilderness was to be a guide and a warning unto them. And when the apostles were near the end of their earthly course, and saw the dangers to which the Church of Christ would be exposed, they with all emphasis directed men again to the Scriptures, which were to be a light shining to them in darkness, and which were profitable to them, and able to make them perfect, furnishing them to every good work.

The glory of the Old Testament is great. The glory of the New Testament is still greater. But it is not by depreciating the one that we shall be able to see the true magnitude and excellence of the other. The Old Testament in its humility compares itself to the night, although it is illuminated by the moon and the stars; and the very last word of the Old Testament in the prophet Malachi is, that unto them that fear God the sun of righteousness shall rise with healing in its wings. Therefore, although the night is solemn and beautiful, the day with the sun is still more glorious.

Think for a moment of what we have in the New Testament Scriptures. Think of the grandeur of the New Testament. Here God Himself is revealed Father, Son, and Holy Ghost, and for this reason it is that in the New Testament you find so often the expression used, "Before the foundation of the world," because the. New Testament, in this differing from the Old Testament, goes back to the eternal counsel of God, and shows us what was in the depth of God's mind when, in Christ Jesus as the Lamb, He chose the Church in order to show forth all His glory and all His praise. God is light, God is love, God Himself is made manifest to us in the New Testament.

And as this New Testament possesses such a wonderful grandeur and majesty, it possesses also a marvellous simplicity. What can be more simple than the words of Jesus and the exposition of the apostles? The very word "Jesus" is a summing up in the simplest form of all God's announcements and promises in the Old Testament. That name, which was never mentioned as the name of the Messiah in the Old Testament, sums up everything that God has promised to His people. Or take that expression, "The Lamb in the midst of the throne." Here you have all the sacrifices; here you have the predictions of Isaiah; here you have the still clearer and more condensed explanation of the prophet Zechariah when he speaks about the priest being set on the throne, and it is all summed up in the most lucid and sweet manner, "The Lamb in the midst of the throne." Greater is the majesty of the New Testament, and still greater is its simplicity.

Think again how compact it is. After all it is in a very small compass. The New Testament is not a large book, and the period of history which it has to sum up only comprises a few years. In three years Jesus finished His earthly ministry, and only twenty years sum up the history of the book of Acts. How easily it is read, and how easily it is remembered!

And lastly, I would say about the New Testament, although in it God Himself is revealed, — a more glorious revelation of God than the Incarnation, even eternity will not bring. A more stupendous sacrifice of Divine love than the death of Jesus on the cross, eternity will not unfold. A more wonderful mystery than the indwelling of the Spirit of God in the Church of Christ, we can never witness.

Although the majesty of the New Testament is exceedingly great, the manner of its inspiration is exceedingly human and exceedingly homely; for not, as in the Old Testament, was the Spirit of God, as it were, outside the prophets, so that they had to search diligently what the Spirit that was in them did signify. The Spirit now abiding within the hearts of the apostles, their testimony came, so to speak, in the most personal and subjective way. As Christ says, "The Spirit shall testify, and ye also shall testify." Their own individuality is allowed the freest and fullest scope, which is manifest from this simple circumstance that nearly all the books of the New Testament are letters. The gospel of Luke is a letter. The gospel of John is a letter. The book of Acts is a letter. And then comes a great number of epistles, and even in the book of Revelation we see the form of a letter.

Heart to heart, mouth to mouth, man to man, speaks in this book. Think for a few moments of what we have in the New Testament. The Jews possessed in the Old Testament all that they required as a nation — the history and origin of Israel — all God's dealings with them, all God's teaching for them, and all the plans of God for their future: all are contained in the Old Testament, so that Israel as a nation requires no more; and therefore the Old Testament to a certain extent is more difficult to understand, and is larger in its outlines, because it has not yet served its full purpose, for, in the later ages, the Jews will have occasion to go to the Old Testament as they have never gone to it before, in order to see what is the will of God concerning them in those latter days, when God begins again to deal with the remnant of Jacob.

In the New Testament we have the four gospels, the history of Christ on earth, — His sufferings, death, and resurrection.

First there is the gospel of Matthew, connecting the New with the Old Testament, showing how the promises were fulfilled in Jesus; and as Matthew himself had been a publican, what was more natural than that he should treasure up all those sayings and acts of Christ, in which Christ showed that His righteousness was different from that of the Scribes and Pharisees, and that his idea of the Messiah was different from that entertained in those days by the Jews. It is the humility of Jesus that strikes us in the gospel of Matthew.

Then comes Mark, evidently written under the influence of the apostle Peter, an eye-witness, and therefore there are so many graphic details, as if he were a painter; an ear-witness, and therefore we have the words, "Talitha cumi," "ephphatha," "eloi, eloi, lama sabacthani," — as if he was still hearing and seeing the things, showing to us the energy of Christ, declaring the gospel by word and by deed.

Then we have the gospel of Luke, written under the influence of the apostle Paul, — Luke the historian, showing what Christ is, not merely to the Jews, but to the whole world; not merely the Son of David, but the Son of Man, Saviour of sinners. Physician of the sick, — free grace abounding to the poor and the needy. This connects the gospel with the whole history of the Church in the future as Matthew connected it with Israel in the past.

Then there is the gospel of John, which is neither of the past, nor the present, nor the future, but of all eternity, and shows us Christ as the Son of God in the bosom of the Father, and the whole life, sufferings, death, and resurrection of Christ illumined by the light of eternity — both the counsel of God and also the consummation when there will be the everlasting separation between Christ's people and the world.

This foundation is like the five books of Moses, describing the fundamental dealings of God — the former with Israel, the latter with both Israel and the Gentiles.

Then comes the book of Acts, connecting, as it were, the gospels with the rest of the New Testament, like the head with the rest of the body, and showing how the gospel began in Israel, how it afterwards went to Samaria, and how then it went to the Gentiles, and ending not merely with the fact but with the condition of things namely, the gospel among the Gentiles, Paul yet testifying to the Jews in Rome.

Then come the wonderful epistles. What was more natural than that the apostles should write to their congregations, when they were separated from them, teaching them, warning them, explaining to them the manifold errors and heresies which were creeping in. We have the apostle Paul with his fourteen epistles, all, as it were, originating in the most natural way. We may say that these are occasional epistles. Thus the human and historical elements appear in the most natural manner. Historically they give us a picture of the Church of Christ in the beginning; and every kind of heresy, both Jewish and pagan, both theoretical and practical, are in these epistles shown and refuted, so that the Church of Christ requires nothing more, either for exposition or for polemics.

If we look again at these epistles in reference to the doctrine — the epistle to the Romans shows us how Christ is righteousness and life; the epistle to the Galatians shows us the same thing, — how Christ is righteousness and life, but shows further how law and gospel, flesh and spirit, cannot be combined. Higher still we rise in the epistles to the Ephesians and to the Colossians, where the centre is Christ They may be called Christological epistles. In the Ephesians we see the Church in Christ from all eternity elect in Christ, redeemed in Christ, adopted in Christ, called in Christ, and raised to be with Christ in heavenly places, whereas in Colossians we stand upon earth, and the apostle tells us of the glory of Christ, and draws from it this inference: If Christ is this glorious Being in whom dwelleth the fulness of the Godhead bodily, and who is the substance of all types, then you who belong to Christ must never think of righteousness or sanctification produced by any earthly thing, — "Touch not, taste not, handle not"; but must seek the things that are above, — the righteousness, the merit, the fulness, the power of Christ, who is at the right hand of God. Or if we look again at Thessalonians, there we have prophetic truth; or at the epistles to Timothy and Titus, there we have practical questions regarding the Church, simplicity of the Gospel against all artificial antinomian corruption and caricature of the truth as it is in Jesus; or at Corinthians — there we have the simplicity which is in Christ Jesus, the love which alone edifieth, while wisdom and knowledge puff up, and the representation that Christ is everything in the Church, and that in Him is our life and our strength.

The epistles of the apostle Paul are, as it were, confirmed by the epistles of John; they are confirmed also by the epistles of Peter. Peter looks upon the Church of Christ, as between the first advent and the second advent — strangers and pilgrims here below — exhorting them to hold fast to the hope. He sees Christ coming for the consolation of His people. He sees Christ coming also for judgment upon them that are ungodly and that reject the Gospel. The relation of these two aspects of the coming he now explains; and because at the time that he wrote the 2nd epistle, the Church had become lukewarm, and many false teachers had crept in, the tone of that epistle is different. In the I St epistle he knew that the Christians were holding fast the hope. In the 2nd epistle he had to urge them strongly to hold fast the hope, and therefore he shows them the importance of the sure word of prophecy. The epistle of James gives us a picture of the earliest condition of the Jewish Church. The epistle of Jude warns us against the latest and yet future inroad of grievous blasphemy and error; and, lastly, we have in the book of the Apocalypse the revelation which God gave to Jesus Christ — a manifestation of Christ's glory itself, a description of the Church of Christ in this dispensation, of the great events of the latter days, of the advent of our Saviour, of the establishment of His kingdom, and of the victory over Satan, and, finally, of the beginning of that period which shall have no end.

Everything that the Church can require is contained in this wonderful collection of books which we are in the habit of calling the New Testament.

Let me briefly point out to you a very important element, namely, that all these books are one book. There is no discordance between the gospels and the epistles. There is a most shallow view, constantly propounded nowadays, when people say that they would rather listen to what Christ says in the gospels than to what is written in the epistles of the apostles. The Holy Ghost alone could bring to the remembrance of the apostles the things that Christ had spoken; and the reason why Christ did not tell the apostles all that is in the epistles was not because He was not able to do so, but because they were not able to bear it; but besides, Christ told them everything in germ, although, in Jerusalem, and afterwards, all was more fully revealed. Everything that the apostles taught was contained in the teaching of our blessed Saviour, nor did the apostle Peter in any way contradict the apostle Paul, nor was there any difference of view of the truth, only different aspects of the tnith brought out, in accordance with the different graces and gifts bestowed upon the apostles; but all their writings are harmonious, and he who does no, receive the words of the apostles rejects Jesus Himself, even as he who rejects Jesus rejects the Father. "He that heareth you heareth Me," not "heareth as it were Me," but Christ Himself speaks in the apostolic word; and so we find that the apostles knew when they wrote that their writings had a distinct authority. "I beseech you that this epistle be read of all saints," says the apostle. "These things are written that your joy may be full." The Apocalypse itself, we may say, is the very word of the Father given to Jesus Christ, and the apostle Peter speaks of the epistles of Paul as collected already, and as on an equality with the other Scriptures, liable to be misunderstood by those who do not seek in humility and earnestness of heart. But at first, although these individual Churches greatly valued the epistles that were sent to them, and although the greatest part of the New Testament — namely the four Gospels and the Acts, all the epistles of the apostle Paul (with the exception of the epistle to the Hebrews), the 1st epistle of Peter, and the 1st epistle of John, and the book of the Apocalypse — was acknowledged from the beginning, by all the Churches, there were other epistles which were known and acknowledged in the congregations to which they were originally sent. It took some time before the other Churches were fully convinced of their apostolic authority, and added them to the canon.

Yet this question has been most satisfactorily cleared up. The western Churches, looking upon the apostle Paul as their apostle, divided all the books in the New Testament which they possessed into what they called gospel and epistle; that means the four gospels and the Acts, and the writings of the apostle Paul and the Apocalypse and the 1st epistle of John. In the east there was no doubt as to the epistle to the Hebrews being apostolic, and also written by the apostle Paul. The 2nd and the 3rd epistles of John being addressed to individuals, took some time, as was natural, before they were recognised as of general Church authority. Still, nearly all the books in the New Testament are referred to in the year 150 by authorised and well-known teachers of the Church; and during all the previous period the reading of the Old Testament was constantly maintained in the meetings of the Christians.

And now I come to a point where it is necessary to speak plainly — namely, that antiquity has no authority to us as regards matters of faith, because immediately after the death of the apostles there was a most marked deterioration in all the Churches; so that when we compare the writings which were produced immediately after the death of the apostles with the writings of the New Testament, there is not the slightest difficulty in perceiving that we are breathing a very different atmosphere. There is no longer the fulness of apostolic testimony and the light of God, but human error and weakness, and I might say even childishness, mixed up with the leading truths of salvation; so that those who are called the apostolic fathers are of no authority to us; and although they were diligent in reading the Old Testament, and fully believed in its Divine authority, they did not fully understand it, for the simple reason that from this very early period there began that deterioration which afterwards developed in the papacy. They did not know Christ as our only righteousness, but looked upon Him rather as a new law-giver, so that the Old Testament was viewed by them as a preparatory law and the New Testament as the real law. Even the sacrifices they did not understand in their typical meaning. The great importance of the Old Testament to them was that it furnished proof of the divinity of Jesus because it foretold His coming, and also because — the whole ancient Church was clear upon this point — it foretold the return of Jesus. That was the point most deeply impressed upon their minds and upon their hearts, and therefore we find more quotations from the book of the Apocalypse in the first four centuries than from any other book. Most melancholy is it to note how, from the fourth century to the time of the Reformation, the glimpses of light, of truth, and of evangelical liberty are exceedingly rare. It happened to the Church as it happened to the Jews. The Jews had the Word of God, but they made it void by the traditions of the elders. The Jews had revealed in the Old Testament righteousness by faith, but they sought a righteousness by their own works. The Jews not merely thought that they could keep the law, but they thought they could do more than keep the law, and therefore invented works of supererogation. Exactly what happened to the Jews happened to the Church, it having again tradition — it having righteousness by works — and therefore, instead of the clearness and sweetness of the Gospel, the spirit of bondage again to fear.

Not only so, but in exact opposition to the Word of God, Christ was obscured. Instead of Christ bearing the love of God to the chief of sinners, there were now mediators required between the sinner and that awful and terrible judge Jesus Christ. Christ was no longer seen as the prophet, because the Scripture was made of none effect, and the authority of the Church was set up instead. Christ was no longer seen as the priest, for if Christ is the priest, He is the only priest, with the exception of all believers who are a priesthood in Him. His sacrifice as complete requires no renewal or supplementation. Christ was no longer seen as the king. He alone has authority, being the head of the body from whom all life flows directly into the members, and who shall come again in glory. The Church of Rome said, "Lo, I sit as a queen, and am rich and powerful," and it sought to establish a Church kingdom, which is a contradiction in terms. Of course, blessed be God, there were many who believed in Jesus during these periods. There were many glorious teachers in the Church. There were many who, although they taught error, were also firmly based upon the foundation which is Christ. There were many who protested against the errors of Rome, and who had to suffer martyrdom on account of their faithfulness. But as a whole it was the period of darkness. Why are people so astonished about the history of the Old Testament, with its long centuries of darkness and of apostasy, when so many centuries of the Church of Christ form an exact parallel?

But now, let us look to the great change. What is that movement of the Reformation which, I am sorry to say, even among those who keep themselves separate from the Church of Rome, is so little understood, and so very languidly acknowledged? The Reformation was not an ecclesiastical movement, as if the chief question had been the authority of the Pope. The Reformation was not a philosophical movement, as if the question had been the emancipation of the human mind. The Reformation was not a political movement, as if its chief importance had been the introduction of liberty into the kingdoms of Europe, tyrannised over, as they had been, by the papacy. The Reformation was the power of the Holy Ghost, and nothing less. That selfsame Spirit who had been in the Church, who had watched over the Church all these centuries, notwithstanding her darkness and her apostasy, was now working mightily in the hearts, consciences, and minds of many men, and this was the great question that was engrossing their thoughts — "How can we have certainty of salvation and of communion with God?" That had been the question for centuries in the Church, and no clear answer had been given to it. Nothing will teach a man but the Holy Ghost — no experience, no reading, no knowledge, no tradition. The Holy Ghost alone glorifies Jesus. We can do nothing. When the Holy Ghost comes, it is then the time for us to yield ourselves to Him. Augustine, from his own experience, and by the teaching of the Holy Ghost, knew the power of sin and the utter impotence of nature to enable a man to save himself He also knew the power of grace. Bernard of Clairvaux entered still further into the truth as it is in Jesus, At first sight it might appear that he was rather departing from the doctrine of justification. He started with this point: "We can do nothing pleasing to God unless we are branches grafted in the vine"; that was the fundamental idea of "the good" of mediaeval mysticism — that there is nothing good in thought, word, or work, unless it be wrought out by the influence of Jesus Christ Himself But then he entered into this question: "How can I be a branch of the vine, if I have not the assurance of the forgiveness of sins? The feeling of dread and fear is a barrier between me and Jesus." And therefore much more clearly than any of the Church teachers did Bernard of Clairvaux say this. These are his words — "It is by God's righteousness that in Christ Jesus he forgives our sins." And when the Reformers, through reading the Scriptures, following the guidance of the Holy Ghost in their hearts and consciences, saw that Jesus was the full salvation of God to every one that belicveth, it was then that the authority and true character both of the Old and New Testaments were fully manifested to their minds, so that the two doctrines— the Bible alone, and Christ Jesus alone — went hand in hand, and nobody could say which came first and which came second. They really came simultaneously. It was by finding God in Christ that they found that the Scripture and the Scripture alone was the Word of God.

The authority of Scripture was acknowledged as a theory in all the Churches. It was only that horrible Council of Trent that made it a doctrine that tradition was of equal importance with the Word of God, and that introduced again the Apocrypha which all the ancient Church had condemned as no part of the Word of God. During all the centuries preceding the Reformation there was not the slightest dispute as to the fact that the Scripture was the Word of God and the only authority. There is a very wonderful illustration of this in one of the splendid manuscripts on parchment, preserved in the library in Paris — a manuscript of the orations of Gregory of Nazianzen. There is frequently an illustration at the beginning of a chapter. One represents the Council at Constantinople in the year 381. It met to judge the doctrine of Macedonius about the procession of the Holy Ghost, and of Apollonius about the will of Christ. The bishops are seated in a semicircle; the emperor Theodosius is also there; but in the middle of this semicircle there is a throne. Neither emperor nor bishop is sitting on that throne. On that throne there lies the roll of the Holy Scripture. The idea of this picture must have originated at the end of the fourth century. What could be a more striking proof that the Council held, that nothing was to decide doctrine or faith but the Scripture? But to hold the truth in theory and to hold it in heart — conviction and experience — are two different things.

Now what did the Reformation do? First, it said the Scripture is the only authority, because it alone is the Word of God. Tradition gives us only the opinions and views of men.

And besides tradition there was also a great element of rationalism in the Church of Rome; in fact, several popes and many cardinals were downright infidels who did not believe in the historical facts about Christ, or even in the resurrection. Martin Luther said — and I do not think he ever said anything better or more important — "The Church of Rome is founded not upon the rock of Scripture, but upon human reasoning. It is a rationalistic Church." And this is another saying of Luther, and exceedingly pregnant: "Up to this time we have been taught in our schools and colleges that nobody can be a theologian unless he begins with Aristotle" (that is, with metaphysics), "and I say that nobody can be a theologian unless he first gets rid of Aristotle"; that is to say, that Scripture has its own teaching and its own philosophy, and that we must not take human philosophy and apply it to the judgment and exposition of the Word of God.

The Scripture is the Word of God. The Scripture is the only revelation in which God makes known to us the things concerning our salvation. Therefore we must listen to nothing else.

The second point was this: The Scripture has a centre, and that is Christ. Once we understand this centre, we understand everything. Now we understand the law that it is a schoolmaster to bring us unto Christ. Now we understand the prophets that they predicted Christ. Now we understand the apostles, that they explained the person and work of Christ. Now we understand the patriarchs and David and all the saints, that their experience was that, where sin abounded unto death, only grace could abound unto eternal life. Therefore now the whole Scripture is but one. Your traditions, your philosophies, your explanations, can never be harmonised and reconciled. They have no unity, they have no centre, because Christ is the centre of all unity, and Christ is the centre of the Scripture.

Third point: We are sure that we are saved when we believe in Christ according to the Scriptures. You, Church of Rome, have never given us any certainty. You are like a kind of insurance society telling us that we ought to credit you and that you promise us, and you cannot promise us with any certainty. Not even after death. There is the vague, illimitable stretch of purgatory. This kind of feeling of safety, or of thinking we have done the best thing that can be done, is not what the Scripture gives us. God gives us assurance. Faith is *fiducia*, trust, a placid conviction of the heart that Jesus is our Saviour. That was the very nerve of the Reformation. What is the reason that the old Catholic movement in our present day can never come to anything, unless it pleases God to give more of His Holy Spirit to the men that are engaged in it? It does not speak to the conscience; it does not speak to the heart; it does not show the fulness of salvation in Jesus; and after all, all other blessings are secondary. That for which the Church of Christ exists is to stand aside and let the full light and love of Christ flow into the heart of every poor and trembling sinner.

The next point the Reformation proclaimed was this: The Scripture is its own authority. We do not believe in the Scripture because you guarantee it. A Romanising clergyman once said to me, "And who has given you the Scripture?" Who has given me the Scripture? I know who has given me the Scripture. The synagogue has given me the Old Testament, and am I therefore to deny that Jesus is the Messiah? Because the synagogue has given me the Old Testament, am I bound to interpret the Old Testament with their blindness? I am thankful that it has given me the Old Testament, but it has no authority to interpret to me the Old Testament. And as for the Church that has given me the New Testament, I am thankful to the Church that has given me the New Testament. But the authority of the Church in interpreting the New Testament, specially when it says exactly the opposite to what is written in the New Testament, certainly no Christian can acknowledge, for the Scripture is very simple and plain.

The next point proclaimed by the Reformation was the perspicacity of Scripture. There are many difficulties in the Bible, but they are as great difficulties to the learned as they are to the unlearned. In the Church of Christ there is no distinction. These things are written for all the children of God, and if we do not understand everything, we must wait till it pleases God to make it plain to us, and perhaps it will never be made plain to us; but all that is profitable and necessary and salutary and enjoyable is plain to the Christian. I admit that the Bible is very obscure to two classes of people. The Bible is very obscure to those who wish to find in the Bible what is not there. If you wish to find that there are many mediators and intercessors between God and man, it will be very difficult to find it in the Bible. If you wish to find the Virgin Mary seated upon a heavenly throne, you may read the whole New Testament carefully; you will find the Virgin Mary mentioned in the 1st chapter of the book of Acts with the other disciples and women, praying for the Holy Ghost's advent; and in the book of the Apocalypse there are the four living beings, and there are the twenty-four elders, and there are the multitude of those that have washed their robes and made them white in the blood of the Lamb; but any special mention of the Virgin Mary you will not find there. Therefore the Bible is very obscure on that ground. The Bible is also very obscure if you want to find in it all those doctrines of righteousness by works, and of penances and saints and the worship of angels and such things. If you wish to find in the Bible what is not there, the Bible is very obscure. And if we are determined not to find in the Bible what is in the Bible, the Bible is also very obscure. Oh, what difficulties have those rationalists had! They did not wish to find in the Bible the divinity of Jesus. They did not wish to find in the Bible the substitution in the death of Christ. They did not wish to find in the Bible the necessity of regeneration. They afterwards did not wish to find in the Bible anything miraculous. Oh, it was exceedingly difficult to explain the Bible, until at last a man like Strauss came and said, "Now, what is the use of deceiving yourselves and deceiving the world and being simply jugglers? You do not believe it, and it is much better to say that you do not believe it, and there is no explaining it. It is simply a mythical representation of ideas." But if we are willing to find in the Bible what is in the

Bible, the Bible is simple. And the Reformers said, "The Bible is abundant. We do not want anything more. What are all your silly stories and legends of saints who did not know what the real point was between God and the sinner? We do not want them when we have the life of Abraham, when we have the Psalms of David, when we have the experience of the apostle Paul. As for your little commandments about eating meat on Friday, and all the things that you have invented, we do not want them when we have the beautiful ten commandments of God, and all the law of Moses, and the precepts of the apostles, and the Sermon on the Mount. As for your sifting people, — trying to find out all the sins they have committed, — we do not want it, for the Bible is a sharp and two-edged sword, and there is no other father confessor but the Scripture that will search and probe the conscience. We want nothing. The Bible is God's Word, and 'profitable for doctrine, for correction, for instruction, for reproof, that the man of God may be perfect, thoroughly furnished unto every good work.'" That is what they said.

But they also said that there were to be in the Church teachers and pastors, for the explanation of the Bible. The Reformers acknowledged that people require guidance, and this is the great object of the ministry — not to perform ceremonies, and not to call themselves "priests," but to be expositors of Scripture; and not merely expositors of Scripture, but also men who are able to apply the Scriptures. The man who said, "How can I understand unless some one guide me?" was quite right. This is a favourite text with the Romanists, who tell us, "Do not circulate the Scriptures. How can people understand them? They do not know what they say." "How can I understand unless some one guide me?" Yes, quite true. When the evangelist Philip had explained to the Ethiopian that Jesus died for our sins and rose again for our justification, he guided him. He had given him the key. "Now you can understand the Scripture." And then Philip was taken away from him, and yet the Ethiopian went on rejoicing, with the prophet Isaiah in his hand, and with the key that opens the prophet Isaiah. The Church in the person of Philip had fulfilled her mission and laid the foundation. When the Church of Rome will preach Jesus, it will find out that this is the way in which people are guided to understand the Scriptures themselves.

But the great point which we must put, and which the Reformers were foremost in bringing before people, was the necessity of the Holy Ghost. The Holy Ghost uses the Scripture. We do not rely upon the Scripture in itself We rely upon the Holy Ghost, who, by the Scripture, enlightens the mind and persuades the heart to accept Christ as offered to us in God's Word. And therefore it was the unanimous teaching of all the Reformers that the basis, upon which our certainty of Scripture being the Word of God rests, is the testimony of the Holy Ghost.

And now, dear friends, I must conclude with this one word. The apostle was anxious that all the churches should enter fully into the knowledge of God's counsel. That was his constant prayer to God. He therefore expected, that not merely by teaching, but by prayer, he would indoctrinate the people whom he loved. Oh, what a lesson is given both to ministers and people to seek continually the light of the guidance of the Holy Spirit; and the object of the Holy Spirit is given in the words, "He shall glorify Me." To bring us to Jesus, to give us peace and joy through faith in Jesus, and to keep us in Jesus faithful to our Saviour and obedient to our heavenly Father — this is the object of the Spirit, acting through the Scriptures. May God grant these gifts unto each one of us.

VIII - Present Aspects of Doubt and Unbelief As Regards the Scripture

I wish this morning to lay before you my views on the present aspects of doubt and unbelief as regards the Scripture. The words which Jesus Christ addressed to the Sadducees when He said, "God is not the God of the dead, but of the living," apply also to Scripture. It is impossible for us to have a true understanding of Scripture unless the Word of God is living within us. They who stand on the shore may take an objective view of a ship, but they only who are in the ship are carried along by the current of the mighty river. And thus the Scripture, while in one respect it has to be viewed as the revelation which God sent from above, may likewise be viewed as the diary of the congregation, the record which the congregation keeps of the dealings of God, and of His words, and promises to her. There is a river the source of which is in eternity, as revealed to us in the New Testament, the visible and timely source of which is in the Garden of Eden, where God gave the first promise of redemption; and this river must flow on until it enter the ocean of blessedness and glory, at the appearing of our Lord and Saviour Jesus Christ. In this river of the history of redeeming love, prophets and apostles sent by God from time to time, and entrusted with His message, are above us, being the representatives of the Divine mind; but in another respect we are on a level with them. Our fellowship is with the fellowship of prophets and apostles, and the same life which animates them animates our spirits also.

The continuity of Scripture as of a river is a point of the greatest importance, for revelation does not consist in oracles and prophecies given from time to time without any connection, but it is one connected and united chain, in which link gives strength to link. And thus it is that unless Moses had believed in the God of Abraham, of Isaac, and of Jacob, he could not have received the new revelation of Jehovah and of the covenant which He was about to make with His people. Every prophet refers back to the past until, at last, in John the Baptist the whole law and prophets are raised up again and appear to us concentrated in his voice, for he reproduced the Old Testament Scriptures, knowing that the 1st Psalm and the 40th chapter of Isaiah, and the 3rd chapter of the prophet Malachi, were incarnate in Jesus; and all those of Israel who accepted the testimony of John the Baptist were thereby directly in the current both of the Scripture history and of the Scripture books. And thus was it also with the disciples of Jesus when He told them that the Scriptures referred to Himself, and when, after His resurrection, He opened their understanding, so that they understood the Scriptures, and remembered the words which He had spoken to them. They were immediately in possession of the whole Scripture, whilst the scribes and the Pharisees, with all their traditional law and exegetical skill, stood outside the Scripture, on the shore. They were not carried along by the river; they did not know the name "Jehovah" in its power and in its blessedness.

The Scriptures are finished, but the Spirit by whose guidance the Scriptures were written is still watching over them; and the history of the Bible, during the last eighteen centuries, throws the most wonderful light upon the history which is recorded in Scripture itself. God, the Creator, after He had finished the heavens and the earth, did not leave creation to itself He is still upholding all things by the word of His power. "My Father worketh hitherto, and I work." Jesus the Saviour, after He had laid the foundation of the Church by His incarnation, death, and resurrection, did not leave the Church to itself He is Immanuel. "I am with you alway, even unto the end of this age." And the Holy Ghost, by whom the Scriptures came into existence, did not leave them after they were finished, but still breathes in them and breathes through them the breath of life and of everlasting blessedness.

Therefore if we compare the history of the Church of Christ up to the time of the Reformation with the history of the Jewish nation from Moses until the time of Ezra and Nehemiah, we find a most striking resemblance. During the first four centuries the Church of Christ, suffering great persecution, even unto death, was kept in an attitude of faith and of living hope; but no sooner had Christianity overcome heathenism outwardly, than heathenism began to corrupt and to modify Christian doctrine and Christian life, just as it had been with the Jews, who, when they had received the fulness of divine revelation, when Jehovah had made known His name to them, and given to them the fiery law upon Mount Sinai, immediately fell into the idolatry of the golden calf; and the whole subsequent period was only a series of apostasy and idolatry and world-conformity, lit up occasionally by gleams of revival, — the people being remembered in great mercy by God, when He sent to them judges and prophets to testify for Him. But what had the judges and the prophets to do but to refer back again to that perfect revelation which God had given to them, in Moses? And if it had not been for that revelation through Moses, and for a written record of that revelation which was acknowledged to be authentic, Samuel and all the prophets would have been utterly helpless and without strength, in the face of an idolatrous and sinful nation. The prophets were not men of genius who anticipated the future, and who therefore could only be understood by a few chosen members of their nation; the prophets, instead of being leaders in advance of their age, pointed back to the ages that were behind. Their watchword was not "Excelsior."

Their watchword was "Repentance." "Seek ye out the old paths." "Remember the law which my servant Moses gave unto you on Mount Horeb." And so it was with the Reformation. Just as Ezra and Nehemiah stood between Moses and the first advent, the Reformers stood between Christ and the second advent. What they did was this. Leaving tradition and philosophy, they went back again to the New Testament revelation. Nothing can be added to that; nothing must be taken away from that; and the greatest fallacy of all is to say, as is often said, that the doctrine of the apostles had to be developed in the Church, Nothing had to be developed in the Church. It was all perfect there; it was all complete there. God's thoughts, God's ultimate message, philosophy must not modify, philosophy must not attempt to defend or to make palatable to the wisdom of men. Just as the naturalist can do nothing to modify nature, but must stand in the simple attitude of a child and an observer, to see and to worship, and just as a man who goes into mines, where gold and silver and precious jewels are hid, takes no money with him, but only the capacity of receiving and treasuring up what he may discover, so, for all ages, the New Testament doctrine stands high as heaven above us, and we have only to wait for the Holy Ghost to take, out of that fulness, what it seems good to Him to reveal to us.

They reproduced the Word of God. This is what I want to impress upon you. The Word of God is written in Scripture, but it is a living word which is also written by the Holy Ghost in the hearts of His elect, and which they utter again. Take, for instance, the Reformation testimony as it was delivered by Luther. The whole epistle to the Galatians is a perfect description of all that the Reformation taught, and of all that the Reformation did. What is that epistle? There is only one gospel. This gospel is not of man. It came down from heaven. It is absolute truth. If even an apostle Paul or an angel from heaven were to preach another gospel, he would be excluded from the kingdom of God. And this is the Gospel — that in the fulness of time God sent His Son, born of a woman, made under the law, to redeem them that were under the law, by being made a curse for them; and this substitution of Christ must be received by faith, quite apart from the law, and without any works. And the proof that it must be received by faith, and by faith alone, is this — that no good works can ever be produced by the law, for the Holy Ghost never comes by the preaching of the law, but by the preaching of the Gospel. Is this then Luther's epistle? A man might as plausibly say that the epistle to the Galatians was written by Luther, as many say nowadays that the book of Deuteronomy was written, centuries and centuries, after the death of Moses. When the Reformers, having found Christ, and having found that the only way of taking hold of Christ was by faith, and that the one way of pleasing God, and bringing forth fruit unto eternal life was by the Holy Ghost given by faith, and by faith only, — believing in the truth of Scripture, they could not fail also to believe the Scripture of truth. And this was their great testimony — that in producing the message of Scripture they were able to speak from their own experience, and with a divine certainty and assurance. There were many philosophers, lovers of literature, lovers of national liberty, who at first joined the Reformation, but they were not of the same spirit, nor had their testimony any beneficial effect upon the progress of the Reformation. In reference to Erasmus, Luther writes: "The Holy Ghost is not sceptical. He does not write upon our hearts objections and doubts, but convictions more clear than that of our own existence and the outer world that surrounds us." But while the Reformers had thus tasted the old wine, and while they thus had themselves imbibed the Scriptures so that they reproduced them, — the current of the divine word flowing again, — they taught all the people, high and low, rich and poor, old and young, learned and ignorant, that the Holy Ghost would be given to every one that truly searched the Scriptures, and that Scripture explained itself, so that it made the whole Christian people independent of human tradition and erudition. No longer did they depend upon the fathers, and upon the consent of the fathers, and upon all those things which keep the Bible at a distance from the people.

It was natural that the Reformation should dwell chiefly upon the Gospel, but the Reformation had a wonderful insight into the whole Scripture, and specially must we notice the great light which was shed by it on the Old Testament, and this according to the nature of things. It would have been impossible for the Reformers to bring before the Church the truths of the New Testament without going back to that which is the foundation — Moses and the prophets. The first reason of this is that the idea of God — the fundamental idea of God — was the constant thought and the constant soul-exercise of Luther; for in the papacy the idea of God that he had received was, in the first place, the metaphysical idea — God infinite, God incomprehensible, God dwelling in light that is unapproachable; and this divine majesty filled him with such misery and terror that he was not able to approach with confidence, for, as he says, not merely did his reason not take hold of anything infinite, but his conscience also was terrified by the idea of perfect and absolute purity and justice. But when he read the Old Testament, and especially the book of Psalms, he found that the God that was revealed there is not God as He is in Himself in His absolute and impenetrable darkness and perfection, but God who condescends, who clothes Himself, as it were, in a human form, who is full of mercy and compassion, who reveals His name unto mankind that they may be able to call upon Him, and who gives to them the promise of absolute and ever-blessed redemption. And therefore he says in his commentary on the 51st Psalm, "When David says 'Have mercy upon me, O God,' he does not say 'O God' in the way in which the Turks (that is the Unitarians) and the hypocrites and the monks say 'O God,' knowing only the absolute God as He is in Himself; but he means the God who has promised to send Christ, the God of all grace, of consolation, and of salvation." Thus they had to go back to the Old Testament.

Secondly, they had to go back to the Old Testament because the people no longer knew what was the true nature of sin and what was the true nature of godliness; for since the papacy had invented its own commandments, stigmatising things as sinful which God had never called sinful, and giving forth, all round, precepts and commandments which were not spiritual in their character, it was impossible for the Reformers to know what was the will of God, both for themselves and for the people, unless they looked into the bright mirror of the law as revealed to us in Moses and the prophets. That was the great consolation that Luther had when he read the Psalms of David. Here were none of those imaginary saints who in will-worship and castigation of the flesh, and in doing a number of useless and unprofitable things, fancied that they were better than other people, and that they were really bringing themselves nearer to God; but here he saw a man who, like himself, wished to be spiritually-minded, and wished to have his affections set upon the things that pleased God, but who felt the burden of sin and the snares of temptation, and who therefore continually appealed to God that He, by His grace and by His Spirit, might draw him into fellowship with Himself.

But thirdly, as I have already hinted by this last sentence, the Reformers being deeply exercised, and feeling continually the attacks of the world, the temptations of Satan and the evil that was within them, and striving against it, found in the Old Testament what they did not find in the New Testament except only in germ and in principle — the whole analysis and anatomy of the human heart, and such a minute description of the road which we have to travel, which is not always in a straight line, but crooked and winding, — with all the different exercises of the soul and of the mind, as described in the life of Abraham, of Jacob, and of David, and in the lives of all the prophets.

And lastly, you must notice that since the New Testament appeals to the Church, whose calling is a heavenly one, and which is hastening through the world unto the coming of the Lord Jesus, it cannot dwell upon those principles of God's government in the world, of his dealings with nations and with families, that we find in the Old Testament; and therefore, whenever there is any great turning-point in the history of the nation, when there is any great national calamity or national victory, — in all such junctures we turn instinctively to the Old Testament, for there in the history of Israel we see the divine philosophy of all history, and the principles which lie at the foundation of God's dealings, in judgment and in mercy, with the nations of the earth. Never, it may be said, since the days of the apostles, had the scriptures of the Old and New Testaments been expounded with so much light, with so much spirituality, with so much truth, and with so much experience, as by Luther and Calvin. It was very natural for them to dwell on the divine aspect of Scripture — that Scripture was the Word of God, and that nothing was of authority in the Church but the Scripture; for on the one side there was the Church of Rome with its theory of tradition, and on the other side there were the philosophers, the intuitionalists of their day, who said that it was not the written word that was of the highest authority and importance, but that it was the inner consciousness, not the shell but the kernel, not the letter but the spirit, making the light which is within us judge and rejector of the things that are written. Against this heresy the Reformers contended with all their might. As Martin Luther said, "Christ did not say, 'My Spirit is spirit,' but 'My words are spirit and life.'" And as for the separation of letter and spirit, of kernel and shell, it is perfectly impossible for us to make such a separation; for the written Word, as we have it, is written by the action and under the guidance of the Holy Ghost.

Another way in which they showed that they dwelt chiefly on the divine aspect of Scripture was that, instead of pointing out the diversities of Scripture, they dwelt rather upon its unity, showing that Christ, the gospel of redemption, grace, faith, ran through the whole Scripture from Genesis to the book of Revelation. Quite true; yet they did not sufficiently bring into prominence that the Scripture was given at sundry times and in divers manners, and that, although the ultimate meaning of the Holy Ghost was always the same, yet the understanding of men from the time of Abel and from the time of David, and from the time of Isaiah and from the time of John the Baptist, expanded and grew under the guidance of the divine dealings with them, so that they understood that, although the Bible was God's Word, it was a divine treasure in earthen vessels. They were fully aware of the human character of Scripture. Luther, in a preface which he wrote to the Old Testament, and which might have been written to-day, speaks of those who say that they do not require the Old Testament any longer, as they have got a much clearer and fuller light in the New Testament, and says to them, "Do not be offended when in this Old Testament you meet with lowly and homely narratives, but be fully assured that notwithstanding this outward lowly and homely appearance, you meet there nothing but the word and majesty and judgment and mercy of the Most High, for thus it was with the dear child Jesus, who was found in the manger wrapped up in very mean and homely clothes."

According to a very sad law, which we must observe in all the history of God's people, revivals like gleams of sunshine, like sudden showers, fertilising and refreshing, are short-lived and transient in their duration. Such were the revivals under Hezekiah and under Josiah, and such was the revival under the Reformers, It is not orthodoxy that overcometh the world. It is our faith that overcometh the world. After a time of dead orthodoxy there began rationalism, and this is the second movement which has influenced our present state, as regards our attitude to the Bible.

Only a few words in regard to this movement. The former rationalistic interpretation of Scripture could only be understood by the view which it took of man and of man's salvation. It confirms what I have been endeavouring to impress upon you in this address — that in proportion as we believe the things that are in Scripture, shall we have a clear understanding of the authority and position of the Scripture. The man on the shore' cannot understand the authority of Scripture. You must be in the ship, one with the apostles and the prophets, and carried along by the self-same living river, in order to understand it. A rationalist argued in this way. Not believing in the fall and in the sinfulness of man as the Bible explains them, he said, "Man does not require a salvation, coming from God in a supernatural way. He has within himself all the resources which are necessary for his enlightenment, for his elevation, and for his temporal and everlasting blessedness. By the light of reason he can discover God, and by an effort of will he can do the things which are right and pleasing before God. He does not require a divine Saviour; he does not require an expiatory sacrifice; he does not require a regenerating Holy Ghost He has in himself everything that he requires, but he must use and develop his powers." As he does not require anything supernatural for himself, it is clear that the Bible cannot be the record of anything supernatural, because it is not wanted. They still adhered to the Bible, partly from reverence for it and the position which it had held in Christendom, but now their great object was to explain the Bible, in accordance with their inward experience. Therefore Christ was only the best of men. Christ's death was only the death of martyrdom. The Holy Ghost did not mean anything special, but the development of the human mind and of the human conscience. It was only by the greatest straining and by the most artificial methods that such views. could frame an interpretation of Scripture; and this soon became so manifest that the whole world was disgusted with it, for they said, "It is not true, it is not honest. A revelation which reveals nothing is an absurdity." And therefore, as the human mind progressed in this direction, and as theism developed into pantheism and into materialism, the whole artificial and rotten fabric of old rationalism fell to the ground, not without having left deep traces which remain on the minds of the nations up to this day.

When men gave up faith in God and faith in the supernatural, when they started with the axiom in short that miracle was impossible — this pantheistic supposition was applied to the explanation of the New Testament, for the Old Testament had been already consigned to a very inferior and unimportant place. It was by very ingenious theorising that the New Testament was brought into harmony with the pantheistic supposition. The historic reality of Christ in the gospels was, of course, an impossibility. The doctrine of the apostles did not flow from Christ; and in the same method as it is now maintained that we ought not to say "Moses and the prophets," but that we ought to say "The prophets and Moses," it was shown that the narratives of the gospels were myths, poetical garments woven in order to make plain a spiritual story, and that what we call "Christianity" was not the teaching of Christ, but was gradually developed, especially by the apostle Paul, and that after that development the New Testament was formed in accordance with it; and this pantheistic theory has also left its deep impress on the human mind. Men who have no liking for metaphysics, but who are attracted by the world — I mean by the outward — sink into materialism, that is to say, they dwell only upon the things that are seen and upon those second causes only which we can observe and trace. The result of all this has been to leave three impressions upon men's minds, and it is upon these radical impressions that we must base the difficulty which many have in believing in the Scripture. There are a great many difficulties connected with Scripture, but if there was strength within, it would be able to overcome them all. It is owing to the fundamental corruption of man that the numerous difficulties appear to be insuperable.

I would direct your attention to these three impressions. The first is this: men have lost faith in God. There was a time when men had faith in God, and at that time they tried to find out arguments to prove the existence of God. Then there came a time when men's faith in God was not vital, but still they adhered to the arguments for the existence of God. There then came a time when they said that the arguments for the existence of God were not cogent; and afterwards there came a time when they said that the arguments were false, and theism fell away into pantheism and into materialism. Let me speak freely upon this point. There is only one God, and that is Jehovah, and there is no other God beside Him; and all the knowledge that the ancient nations had of God was a reminiscence of that which had been revealed to them. The living God, God who is from everlasting to everlasting, God who takes an interest in us, God who condescends to man, and shows to him his salvation, is a God whom human reason cannot discover. We dwell upon second causes. We do not rise to the only source and origin. Scientific men acknowledge that both the beginning and end of things are utterly beyond the reach of science; and what else is this but a corroboration of what God says, "I am the first and I am the last."

The antipathy of men against the God who is revealed to us in Scripture shows itself in their antipathy to miracle and prophecy, for a living God, who interferes by action, is a God that doeth wonders, and the living God who interferes by revelation is a God that maketh known His mysteries to the prophets whom He hath chosen.

The second impression is connected with the relation between reason and revelation. It is often said that revelation is contrary to reason, but before that position is discussed the question ought to be asked, "Do we require a revelation? Is there any necessity for a revelation?" The view of reason which God gives us in His Word is this. He appeals to reason, God often appeals to reason, for reason is His work, and it is the light which He has kindled. But the reason which God has given to man is not sovereign and independent. It is not able to create truth; it is only able to receive truth. Adam was created in the image of God unto knowledge, and the knowledge which he possessed was not a knowledge which had its fountain in himself; but he had the capacity of receiving the knowledge as it was delivered to him by God. Through the fall of man, reason and the understanding have been blinded and darkened. God addresses Himself to reason, but not to reason alone, for reason does not exist in man, isolated. God addresses Himself to all that is within man, and the reason and the will meet in that centre of humanity which is the heart. Therefore God speaks to the heart, and the Bible says, "The fool hath said in his heart that there is no God."

But, when God speaks to the reason, He brings light with the word which He speaks. God does not speak to the reason in the Socratic method, under the idea that there is already in the reason of man all that He wishes to bring out, and that it needs only to be developed, but the entrance of His Word itself giveth light, and the things which God reveals by the Spirit enlarge the understanding and raise it to a higher level. So that by faith we understand that God has created the world. By faith we receive the things which eye hath not seen nor ear heard, neither have entered into the heart of man. Faith docs not kill reason, nor is faith in conflict with reason, nor is reason passive when it receives the message of God. It is receptive. Still there are many things of which we can take hold, but cannot grasp round and round; and therefore did Lord Bacon say that the authority of God extends over the whole man— over his reason as well as his will; and just as it is our duty to obey the commandments of God when the will is reluctant, so it is also our duty to believe the revelation of God when the reason is reluctant. Abraham is the emblem of faith which receives the promises, while Sarah is the emblem of the reason which mocks and does not receive the promises. But if the revelation of God has taken possession of us, our faith will always remain faith until we come to that region where we shall see these things, and know even as we are known.

But there is another thing to be remembered in connection with this, and it is that reason cannot deal with that which is life. It cannot understand birth. It cannot understand the origination of anything. It cannot understand the individual. Every individual that you obtain knowledge of, reason has nothing to do with such knowledge, either one way or the other. It is a new life that is made known to you. It is a new individuality that comes into contact with you. God is the only true "I Am," the only person; and, when He reveals Himself to us, all that is within us must keep silence, for the Lord God is in His holy temple, and all that is within us — reason, will, feeling — will be stirred up to magnify and praise the name of the Lord.

There is a third impression, and it is also of great importance, namely, the view that the generality of people take of this world as well as of themselves. They think that it is a good world, and that it will become better. What is the view which the Bible takes of this world and of us? That it is an evil world and will become worse until the regeneration of all things, and that we are bad because what is born of the flesh is flesh, and therefore we must be born again. Now, as a pantheist truly said, all human beings are either Hebrews or Christians or Greeks. The Hebrew is ascetic, spiritual, striving to get rid of the outward, of the shadow, of the mere picture. The Greek is joyous, loves the world, feels his strength, boasts of his development, loves the things that are in it, in all their serenity and in all their colouring. For a long time people imagined that because Christianity said that there was no difference between the Jew and the Greek, and that all were one, Christianity did away with the stern and the puritanical spirit of the Old Testament; but Christianity is yet more puritanical than the Old Testament. As the Old Testament said, "Thou shalt have no other God beside Me," and "You are a chosen nation of God, and you must not conform to the other nations"; and as the prophet Isaiah said that in the latter days the name of the Lord alone should be exalted, and every mountain and every cedar, and everything that is lofty in spirit, should be swept away, and the idols be utterly abolished, so says the New Testament, "Ye are not of the world, even as I am not of the world"; "Love not the world"; "All that is in the world is not of the Father"; "The whole world lieth in wickedness"; "We are strangers and pilgrims here upon earth, and we are waiting for the coming of the Lord Jesus Christ from heaven." Now think of this nineteenth century with its proud consciousness of its strength, of its wealth, of its science, of its culture, with its worship of civilisation, and of art, and of the beautiful. Is it not diametrically opposed to the very spirit of the whole Scripture? It is on account of these things — the result of all those movements which I have endeavoured to describe, the impressions which are made upon men deep-seated in the heart, and ramified in all our literature and our daily life — that there is such a conflict between Scripture and the modern mind. There are many difficulties; but difficulty after difficulty may be answered, objection after objection may be removed, and the same conflict still continues. Remember what the apostle of love has said to us, speaking of Jesus Christ, "This is the true God and eternal life. Little children, keep yourselves from idols."

IX - Alleged Discordance between the Old and New Testaments

We have this morning to consider the prevalent and popular difficulties and objections raised against the Old Testament Scriptures by people who profess that they believe the New Testament. I do not consider now difficulties which are raised by those who reject the whole testimony of God; but I consider the fact, which must be obvious to all of you, that there are a number of people who, while they profess to believe in the New Testament, have a feeling of perplexity and doubt and unbelief with regard to the Old Testament, and have well-nigh rejected it. And the reason why I state these difficulties, is because this will prepare the way for the analysis of the structure, and for the explanation of the peculiarities of the Old Testament Scriptures, which I purpose to give.

I shall notice six difficulties. The first difficulty may be expressed in this way. We find that the God of the Old Testament is different from the God of the New Testament. The God of the New Testament is love, — full of mercy and tenderness. The God of the Old Testament seems to be a God of wrath and of anger. If this difficulty is correct, it is fatal, because the whole object of the Old Testament is to reveal Jehovah; and if the Old Testament does not give us a true view of Jehovah, the Old Testament has been written in vain. I wish to show how this objection is rooted in a deep misunderstanding of the teaching of the New Testament.

According to Scripture there is no knowledge of God inherent in man. Man was created in the image of God unto knowledge, with soul and spirit capable of receiving the revelation of God; and after the strivings of God with mankind in general came to an end, at the dispersion of nations at the tower of Babel, God left the Gentile nations to themselves; and all that they thought of God, and all the longings that they had after God, must be viewed as remnants and reminiscences of that primeval revelation which God had vouchsafed to mankind, — and the witness of the Spirit of God in the consciences and minds of men.

When the apostle Paul says to the Ephesians, "Ye who were once afar off hath he brought nigh," he does not merely refer to the atonement of Christ by which sinners are reconciled to God, but he expresses a great general and important fact, that all the Gentile nations up to the time of Christ were at a distance from God, — outside the circle in which God manifested His light and His presence. Therefore the apostle Paul, when he spoke to the Athenians, although the Athenians were the wisest and most cultured of all the nations of the world, said to them that all their previous history, with all the great thinkers and philosophers which they had produced, was the time of ignorance, in which they were in darkness, without the knowledge of the true God. Therefore the Gentiles were brought nigh in Jesus when they were brought into the commonwealth of Israel, and when the light which shone upon the chosen nation of God reached also their minds and hearts; for there were only two circles in which God became known as God, — as a living one, — as a person, — as a loving one. The first was Israel, for God revealed Himself to Abraham, Isaac, and Jacob. He dealt with them as their friend, and the whole nation afterwards knew that God was not a distant God, but that He was very near to them, because He was the friend of their forefathers, to whom He spake, and who had experience of His presence and of His power. Likewise, the subsequent generation stood at the foot of Mount Horeb, and they heard the voice of God, — and Moses afterwards says, "Was there ever a nation like you to whom God manifests Himself so that you can have no doubt that there is a God and that this God is dealing with you?" Likewise when God became manifest in the person of Jesus the apostles testified, "We have beheld the glory of the Only Begotten of the Father. We have seen and we have heard and we have handled the Word of life; and this Jesus, who is the true God and eternal life, behold, Him declare we unto you." So that Israel and the Church alone have the knowledge of God as He is God, — the person, — the living One, — the only true and blessed One.

When people, without receiving this fact, still imagine that they are able to construct God out of their own intuition and reason, and when they select from the Bible the passages which are according to their mind, leaving out all others, they fall into the error of supposing that they themselves have discovered those beautiful and attractive features of the divine character which they have selected. But in this respect they are mistaken. Man never could have found them out of himself. And in another respect they are mistaken. By separating what they like from those declarations which they do not like, they lose entirely the right understanding of their favourite passages. Now the whole world says that what it likes in the New Testament is the declaration that God is love, and indeed this is the sum and substance of all that God has taught us; but if we ask the question, "How is it that no one else ever said that God was love? — that none of the Gentiles, however great their learning, and however deep and acute their powers of mind, ever rose to this conception, and that the Romans and Greeks thought rather that the gods did not love us, that they were envious of our prosperity, and that all that we could do was to appease them, — and how is it that this declaration that God is love was uttered by him who leaned on the bosom of *Jesus?*" what is the answer? Again, what is meant in the New Testament when it says that God is love? It is easy for me to believe that God loves me as long as I think that I am lovable; but just in proportion as I find that I am unlovable, full of sin and guilt and pollution in the sight of God, is it difficult for me to believe that God is love. Now the New Testament emphasises this difficulty to the very highest point. Surely God Himself must know wherein consists the excellency and wonderfulness of His love, and God commendeth His love to mankind — not in that He is nothing but love, but in this, that while we were ungodly, sinners and enemies, Christ died for us. "Herein is love, not that we loved God, but that God loved us, and gave his Son to be the propitiation for our sins."

But if there is nothing else in Sod but mercifulness and what the world calls "love," why was it necessary that there should be a propitiation for our sins? Therefore you find that all the New Testament declarations which speak of the love of God also show the dark background of the wrath of God against all ungodliness, and of our utterly lost condition in the sight of God, on account of the justice and holiness of God. Take any passage that you like — "The gift of God is eternal life." "Oh," everybody would say, "yes, that sounds beautiful." But what precedes it? "The wages of sin is death." Why are the wages of sin death if there is nothing else in God but love? "God so loved the world that he gave his only begotten Son" (oh, that is beautiful) "that whosoever believeth in him should not *perish*." But why should anybody perish with Christ, or without Christ, unless it be that God in His holiness turns away from sin, and that the very love of God reacts against sin, and that God is a consuming fire against it? Therefore the very point which is the excellence of the New Testament, namely, the atonement, the sacrifice of Christ on the cross, cannot be understood at all, except on the basis of the Old Testament teaching as to the character of God — namely, that God must punish sin, and that the wrath of God is the great obstacle which stands between fallen sinners and blessedness and communion with Him. And thus it is that the expression, "The wrath of God," which is so obnoxious to this nineteenth century, and on account of which they feel so estranged from the Old Testament, is a leading idea in the New Testament from the beginning. What did John the Baptist preach? Wrath against evil. What is declared to us in the 3rd chapter of the gospel of John? He that believeth on the Son of God hath eternal life; but he that believeth not the Son shall not see life, but the wrath of God abideth on him." What does the apostle Paul write to the Thessalonians? "You are waiting for the coming of the Lord Jesus from heaven, even Jesus, who delivered us from the wrath to come." And what is the whole meaning of the book of Revelation but this— that the Lord Jesus Christ at last is revealed in order to take to Himself those who trust in Him, while the judgment of God must be executed on those who have despised the Gospel. Therefore the Old Testament conception of God is the very basis and foundation, on which the wonderful love of God in the sacrifice of Jesus shines forth in the New Testament. If Christ crucified is the centre of the New Testament, if, there, the love of God shines forth most brightly, then the cross of Christ is misunderstood and misinterpreted (and so it is in fact) by all those who reject the Old Testament idea of God, and the atonement is made to be nothing else but a manifestation of God's love (wherein it consists I do not see), and a death of witness and of martyrdom unto the truth of God.

The only difference between the Old Testament and the New Testament is this — that the arrangement of subjects is different. The Old Testament puts it in this way, "God is holy; you are sinful; therefore the wrath of God is upon you. Oh that the Redeemer would come to deliver you." The New Testament puts it in this way. "He has come; He has redeemed you. Now understand how holy God is who could not save you except through the blood of Jesus Christ, and now understand how great and evil a thing sin is, that it required the stupendous sacrifice of God's own Son to remove it." But the character of God is the same throughout.

There is another point which strikes people, and it is this. In the Old Testament we read of judgment upon judgment, of God. Adam and Eve are banished out of Paradise, and the earth cursed on account of their transgression; then comes the judgment of the Flood; then comes the judgment on the Tower of Isabel; then come the repeated judgments on the Egyptians and on the enemies of Israel, and a great many on Israel itself, — and people think that the Old Testament God is the God of judgments, and so He is; but the reason of this is exactly the opposite of what they imagine. The reason of it is the mercy of God. God, who had Christ always before Him from the beginning of the world, did not wish that the history of the apostate race should come to an end. He desired to postpone the last judgment as long as possible, and therefore He sent these preliminary judgments, in order to make it possible for Him to carry on the history of mankind. Adam and Eve could not have remained in Paradise. It would have been an end of all history. The human race could not have continued in the days of Noah, but God wished to continue it, and therefore there came a judgment, and out of that judgment the nucleus of a new development in Noah and his household. All the judgments are sent, in order, as it were, to make it possible for God to continue the dealings of His mercy.

In the New Testament we have the same principle, only the order of things is different. There what God says is this. There is now before you a clear space, a long period in which there is an amnesty. There will not be judgments, but the declaration that God is reconciling the world unto Himself in Christ Jesus — nothing but pardon, nothing but grace. It is the acceptable year of the Lord. But the judgment is to come at the end! — the judgment is at the end! Of how much sorer punishment shall they be thought worthy who reject this great salvation of God. They who do not accept the Gospel invitation are treasuring up to themselves, as the apostle Paul says in the New Testament, not in the Old, wrath against the day of wrath. Therefore just as in the Old Testament God is a God of judgment, because He wishes to postpone the final judgment, in the New Testament we have revealed to us the amnesty and the time of the gospel dispensation — not because God is not a God of judgment, but because He hath appointed a day in the which He shall judge all nations through that one Man whom He raised from the dead. So you see that the same elements are in the New as in the Old Testament

Now I must go still further. Believe me, I do not want to utter a paradox, but I declare the simple truth. As there are in the Old Testament most wonderful expressions of the loving-kindness, the tenderness, of Jehovah God, such as shine forth, with most extraordinary brilliancy and sweetness, even after the New Testament revelation — "I will abundantly pardon," "With the Lord there is plenteous redemption," "Can a woman forget her child?" "The mountains shall be parted, the hills be removed, but my thoughts of peace towards you cannot be removed," "How shall I give thee up, O Ephraim? Why will ye die?" "With the Lord our God there is forgiveness that He may be feared," "Ho, every one that thirsteth, come ye to the waters," — so there are in the New Testament all the fearful declarations of the Old Testament, as I have already proved; but the New Testament severity is far greater than that of the Old Testament.

And why is that? For the simple reason that now the fulness of truth has come in Christ Jesus, God in the Old Testament did declare to Israel what a great evil sin was, but He never could tell them what He has told us — by Christ. God could not say to Israel, "Sin is this — that you would like me not to exist: you would like to kill me." Such a severe arrangement of the sinner was never made in the Old Testament; but when men crucified Jesus, then sin in its true character came to light. You never find in the Old Testament such a severe saying as this— that sin is enmity against God. Why, then, do people not say that the New Testament is too severe for them to endure it? Why do they single out, in their ignorance, the Old Testament? Why do they not tremble at the New Testament? Not merely is the infinite evil of sin described in the New Testament as it never could have been in the Old Testament, but it is not from the Old Testament pages, but from the lips of Jesus and the words of the apostles, that we learn what hell is, where "their worm dieth not, and the fire is not quenched."

The Old Testament and the New Testament both combine in declaring to us God. "God is love" must be written over both, with this distinction: What is God? The Old Testament answers that question. But what is love? The New Testament answers that question. Unless you know the Old Testament when you read "God is love," and do not know what God is — the sentence has no value or meaning to you. In the New Testament, the whole depths of the eternal counsel and the light and love of God, are made manifest; and we see now what wonderful obstacles, what mountains, what huge difficulties were removed, through the stupendous sacrifice when God spared not His own Son but gave Him up unto death. What death? — the just for the unjust, bearing the wrath of God and tasting death, in its penal connection with sin.

Jesus Christ is the interpretation of God, but if you misinterpret Him, how fatal will be that misinterpretation — and all misinterpret Christ and the New Testament who do not take Christ and the New Testament according to the light which God has given through Moses and the prophets. And therefore it is that Jesus cannot say to this generation what He was able to say to His contemporaries, "Ye believe in God" as He is revealed in the Old Testament; "believe also in me." And the apostle Paul in his epistle to the Hebrews tells us most distinctly, "God, who at sundry times and in divers manners, spake unto the fathers by the prophets, hath in these last times spoken to us by his Son."

I pass now to the second point. The second point is this: In the New Testament God does not deal with nations, but with individuals. He makes no difference between one nation and the other. He addresses Himself to the individual. In the Old Testament we have the history of a nation, and therefore there are in the Old Testament a number of things which are difficult to understand. When God chose a nation, whom He formed for Himself from its very beginning, He acted with the greatest condescension, for now God had not to take cognisance merely of that which was mental and spiritual and individual, but of everything which referred to a nation's life— of their food and raiment and property, and all that concerns their social life. And as they were not an isolated nation, but a nation that had relationship with other nations, all those difficulties and problems that meet us in the history of the world are here brought under the direct cognisance and superintendence of God. We are astonished at war, at its cruelty, at the apparently innocent and purposeless sufferings which it entails; and yet we know that God permits wars, and that wars have been the turning-points in history, and have often introduced great blessings. And thus when we come to Israel, they have their wars, they have their soldiers. There are to be considered the peculiar circumstances and characteristics of that rough and cruel age. There we find the divine justification. The nations who inhabited the land of Canaan had filled up the measure of iniquity, and those who have read the history know that their lives were most pernicious, and that the abominations and cruelties of those nations were something appalling, and therefore God in His justice had to deal with them, for the good of Israel and the world. In all this there may be many things that are difficult for us to understand, that pain us, that shock us — even as in the current history of the world there are many such startling problems.

Another difficulty is that the Old Testament condescends to all the questions of a nation's life — the questions of property, and all that is associated with this earthly condition; to the government of a nation, to the well-being of a nation, and all those evils and difficulties that are connected with national life. The adaptation and accommodation of God to the weakness and sinfulness of that particular age, having to deal with the facts as they existed — His permission of polygamy, and His permission and modification of slavery — all these stagger people. But why? Because they do not see the purpose that God had in them. It was necessary that there should be a nation out of which there should arise Jesus for all nations. This nation was chosen for the benefit of all mankind and all families of the earth. Neither when God chose this nation, did He intend to deal with them as with favourites, but rather to deal with them with greater judgment and severity than with the other nations. Because He had chosen them, therefore He educated them and chastised them, and brought them under the influence of His holiness and His justice. This nation was not merely for a time. There is no new covenant nation of God. In the new covenant there are the children of God scattered abroad — all of them brought to Jesus. There is the flock of Christ, the Church, the body of Christ; but there is no nation that is God's nation in the New Testament. God has only one nation — Israel; because when He means to revive His direct dealings with the world, and to renew His direct governmental manifestation and acts in the world, He has no other medium, by which to benefit the other nations, than the nation of Israel. Therefore there can be no beginning of the millennial age except through the ingathering of the people of Israel. In the light of the future will the past be explained.

People think when they call the Jews God's "ancient" people that they are making a great concession. They are not God's ancient people. They are His present people; they are His future people; they are His everlasting people; they are His only people. What does the apostle Paul say? "Hath God cast away His people?" — not His "ancient" people. If it were "ancient" people, He had cast them away, because they were of the past. "Hath God cast away His people? God forbid!" he says, as if it were a blasphemy to suppose so. Let this be noted. Thus is this national history of Israel explained. But, in the meantime, what a benefit has it been to all the nations! While we have not got in the New Testament the principles that ought to guide kings, and rulers, and judges, the social difficulties of poor and rich, all these are considered in the Old Testament; and there we have the laws of God as to national life and all that pertains to it.

The third difficulty. There are some people who say, "It is a strange thing that in the Old Testament there seems to be only a present-day religion. The rewards promised are earthly; the punishments threatened are temporal. The future seems altogether dark and vague. In the Psalms and Prophets it seems as if they were afraid to die, and as if the future were dark to them." On this question of the gradual revelation of the future I do not enter now, but I will say this: it is a very true characteristic of the Old Testament, and full of instruction, and the instruction lies in this, that God taught the people, and God teaches us, by this: Eternal life means spiritual life. It is not a future life, and the question of how long it will last has nothing to do with the essence of God. "Walk before me in the sunshine of my favour, and then you please me, and I am your God." Whereas the Egyptians were always dreaming and speculating about immortality and about the future, and how to secure for themselves a future existence, being all the time in darkness and bondage. God said to the Israelites, "I Am. Love me and serve me." It is quite true that God promised to the Jews temporal prosperity if they would obey Him, and that He threatened them with judgments in case of disobedience. God wished thereby to help our weakness, and to incite and encourage the people to walk in His ways, as we propose rewards to children. [1] Lord Bacon has said, "The Old Testament is the religion of prosperity, and the New Testament is the religion of adversity." There is a truth in this, but a truth that requires to be very carefully guarded. There are two things to modify it. In the first place, it was only the idea that was put before Israel, not the reality. God wished to teach Israel this: "Although this is a bad fallen world, I am the Ruler, and I have connected righteousness with happiness, sin with misery. This is My principle in all realms which I have made," even as the New Testament says that godliness has the promise of this life and of that which is to come.

But was it so always among the Jews? Were not Abraham, Isaac, and Jacob, strangers and pilgrims who dwelt in tents? Was Moses a happy and prosperous man? Was David not a man acquainted with grief and with sorrow? Had not all the godly men in Israel, in proportion as they were godly, to pass through much tribulation? "Many are the afflictions of the righteous." "Whom the Lord loveth, He chasteneth." That was the problem which sometimes was a great difficulty to them, and they had to say, "Fret not thyself because of evil-doers," because of the ungodly" spreading himself like a green bay-tree." So in actual experience can you say that when individuals served God, He rewarded them always with earthly rewards? What is more striking than this? The book of Ecclesiastes presents to us a king, honoured, full of power and influence, wealthy, intellectual, artistic, tasting everything that this world could give, and he says, "It is all vanity." And the book of Job shows us a man who suddenly, in one day, was bereaved of his sons and daughters and sheep and cattle and property, and he said, "Blessed be the name of the Lord." Is that an earthly religion? Is that a carnal religion? That is the one point.

The other point is this. One reason why God in the Old Testament laid so much stress upon prosperity following obedience, upon judgment following disobedience, was, that it is His intention to bring about a state of the world when there shall be righteousness, truth, and godliness within, and when there shall be no evil without, but peace and abundance for the poor and considerateness and equity for all men, and when justice and beauty shall be established here, and the will of God shall be done upon earth even as it is in heaven. And therefore all this earthly character of the Old Testament is prophetic of the millennium, of that future condition which shall be brought about — not as the Utopian people imagine, that the world is getting gradually better and happier, and that they will be able to do away with poverty, crime, injustice, cruelty, sickness and pestilence and war, but by the coming of Jehovah in the person of Jesus Himself to establish the kingdom. As it is written in the 72nd Psalm, when the true Son of David shall come, then there shall be bread for the poor, and then there shall be the manifestation of God's bountifulness and loving-kindness over the whole earth.

There is a fourth difficulty. People say, "The saints in the Old Testament are so vindictive. They ask God to send down judgment upon His enemies. They seem to contemplate the destruction of the ungodly, nay, to wish for it, and to pray for it. That is not a spirit that we admire, nor is it the spirit of the New Testament." Now this question has been attempted to be solved in different ways. Some have said, "Yes, it was wrong in them, but it is recorded because it was so. They had these feelings, but they were wrong." This is no answer at all, because all these expressions to which I have alluded are embedded in psalms and chapters in which the highest spirituality expressed itself — faith in God, love to God, hope in His Word, devotedness to His cause; and, moreover, they are embedded in prophecies which Christ has taken to Himself The three psalms that are apparently most vindictive are psalms that are quoted by our Lord when He said, "They hated me without a cause," "He that eateth bread with me hath lifted up his heel against me," "They gave me vinegar to drink"; and by the apostle Peter, when he speaks of the judgment that has come upon Judas. Therefore these feelings are ratified in the New Testament, as feelings in harmony with all that the Spirit of God had wrought in these saints.

A second explanation is this: that it was only under the Old Testament dispensation that there could be allowance made for these feelings, but that they have disappeared, and there is nothing in the New Testament to correspond with them. This also is a false answer. If that is so, the Old Testament is not the Word of God as the New Testament is, and the God of the Old Testament is different from the God of the New Testament. Therefore we must consider the question in a more calm and candid way.

The first question is this: What is the teaching of the Old Testament as regards our relation and our duties to our enemies? because, after all, that is the point. I give a very simple answer. When the apostle Paul, in the epistle to the Romans, speaks on this subject, he does not know any better, higher, more perfect commandment than that which is given in the Old Testament: "If thine enemy hunger, feed him; if he thirst, give him drink." He quotes from the Old Testament what, those people say, is not in the Old Testament, and is peculiar to the New Testament. From the very beginning God taught Israel that they were not to be vindictive, that vengeance was His. "If thou meet thine enemy's ox or his ass going astray, thou shalt surely bring it back to him again. If thou see the ass of him that hateth thee lying under his burden and wouldest forbear to help him, thou shalt surely help him." And there are many passages in the book of Proverbs where we are warned not to be pleased when they that hate us stumble. Therefore, the idea that we are to forgive, and that we are even to help our enemies, was commanded in the Word of God by Moses, and was well understood by all the Old Testament saints.

Again, you remember those passages in the book of Job and in the Psalms of David, where these saints of God, arguing with God and pleading with Him, are able to bear this witness to themselves: "We have never done harm to those that did no harm to us. On the contrary, even when our enemies were in distress, we went to their help and their succour." Only remember the way in which David treated Saul, who was his most bitter enemy without any cause, when he was in his power in the cave; and remember that triumph of the forgiveness of injuries, when, after the death of Saul, David poured forth that magnificent elegy. The wonder is, how he collected together so many bright and beautiful features in the character of one in whom there was so much to blame. Here there was an illustration, such as the world had never before had, of the maxim, "Do not speak of the dead, except what is good and favourable." Now when we find this spirit, the question is. How are we to account for those passages in which David implores the judgment of God upon his enemies? What was the motive? It was not a personal motive, but this was the motive — the glory of God, the establishment of God's kingdom, the manifestation to the whole world that there is a righteous God, and that He judgeth, the preservation of God's chosen people for His honour, and the preservation of those things which God had entrusted to His nation — His Word, and the knowledge of His name. It was for this reason that they implored the judgments of God to come upon those who.se enmity was implacable, and whose resistance and violence against God and God's people there was no hope of conciliating, for there are other passages in which David calls upon the nations to consider the judgments of God, and to turn to Him ere it be too late. Many of those passages are prophetical, for God promises that He will judge and establish His kingdom; and being given in the spirit of prophecy, there is nothing else but an assent of the believer to the purposes of God. So in the book of Isaiah, it is said that on Babylon, which was the cruel enemy of God's people, and which in the future should appear again as the great anti-Christian power, seeking to destroy God's people and to root out the truth from the earth, there; would be judgments from God, and that the little children should be dashed against the stones; that is to say, that the whole race, root and branch, should be exterminated because of the evil which they did on the face of the earth. In poetical language this is reiterated, as Deborah sang before, "So let all thine enemies perish, O Lord; but let them that love Him be as the sun when he goeth forth in his might." When the prophets and psalmists uttered these sayings, was there no mixture of earthly passion with them? No. David, we know, was of like passions with us — that he was indignant, that he was vehement, that he was carried away. So you remember in that beautiful passage, when he had gone against Nabal to punish Nabal on account of his behaviour to his followers, and Abigail came and pleaded with him, and David burst forth with such humility, saying, "Blessed be the Lord God of Israel, who sent thee this day to meet me; and blessed be thy advice, and blessed be thou, which hast kept me this day from coming to shed blood, and from avenging myself with my own hand." He knew very well what was of the earth earthy, and what was the inspiration of God.

Is there nothing corresponding to this in the New Testament? That is the question. There certainly is, only in the New Testament the judgment is placed at a distance. Thus Jesus says, "Woe unto thee, Capernaum, which art exalted unto heaven, thou shalt be brought down to hell" and to the Scribes and Pharisees He says, "Woe" again and again; "Ye serpents, ye generation of vipers, how can ye escape the damnation of hell?" and the apostle Paul says, "Alexander, the coppersmith, hath done me much harm. The Lord reward him according to his doings." In the book of Revelation, the Lord Jesus praises the Church, "This good thing thou hast, that thou hatest the Nicolaitanes" — not the heresy, but the men — "whom I also hate"! And when the judgments are described in the book of Revelation — those fearful judgments which it is difficult for us to read without awe and trembling — what is the feeling which those judgments call forth, not in Jews as they are called, carnal Jews, but in the holy and loving angels? "Fear God, and give glory to him, for the hour of his judgment is come," "Thou art righteous, O Lord, which art, and wast, and shalt be, because thou hast judged thus. For they have shed the blood of saints and prophets, and thou hast given them blood to drink; for they are worthy. Even so. Lord God Almighty, true and righteous are thy judgments"; and in another chapter, "For her sins have reached unto heaven, and God hath remembered her iniquities. Reward her even as she rewarded you, and double unto her double according to her works: in the cup which she hath filled, fill to her double."

The dispensations were different. God is the same; and the lesson to us who are living in this present age, is to remember the glory of God, and the one great aim of all His dealings, namely to show forth His praise, and to establish upon the earth His kingdom, in righteousness and peace and love, which will bring happiness to all the nations of the world. There is a very striking confirmation of this in the 104th Psalm, The 104th Psalm is an echo of the 1st chapter of Genesis, The 1st chapter of Genesis gives us the creation of the world, beginning with the creation of light, and ending with the creation of men, and it sums up everything and says, "It is all very good." David in the 104th Psalm responds to this, and he describes all the universe, so to speak, beginning with God, who clothes Himself with light as with a garment, and ending with man, who goeth forth to his work and to his labour till the evening. This fills him with great joy, so he concludes in the 33rd verse, "I will sing unto the Lord as long as I live; I will sing praise to my God while I have my being. My meditation of him shall be sweet: I will be glad in the Lord." Now there comes an abrupt transition: "Let the sinners be consumed out of the earth, and let the wicked be no more." I remember when this first struck me, I was staggered. Up to this verse he shows how beautiful the world is, and how good God is, and he is full of gratitude and joy, and he sings, and his meditation is sweet, and now there comes this thunder and lightning. The explanation is this. In the 1st chapter of Genesis, before sin has entered, all is very good. "The Lord beheld, and it was all very good." And now this beautiful universe has been poisoned, has been defiled, and the thoughts of God frustrated by sin. It is as if a great artist had produced a wonderful picture, and then some one comes and spoils it all, and mars it. Then David wishes for the restitution, or the establishment of those things which God has promised from the beginning by the prophets, namely, the kingdom of Jesus Christ and His saints, and Israel, and all the nations upon the earth. "Let the sinners be consumed out of the earth, and let the wicked be no more. Bless thou the Lord, O my soul. Praise ye the Lord." These are very solemn truths. We should never think of them without awe, without feeling personally humbled to the very dust, without feelings of the greatest compassion and tenderness towards those that are without, and without being stirred up to pray and to work for the ingathering of those who are still without the knowledge of Christ. Not with a cold heart, or a dry eye, ought these great and awful things to be viewed, and it is for us to cleave unto the Lord our God, and to seek His glory and His only.

[1] This is universally God's method with nations, because they have as nations no future existence, and all rewards and punishments must be visited on earth.

X - The Perfect Harmony of the Old and New Testaments

I brought before you in the last lecture a few of those popular objections which are brought against the Old Testament, by people who profess to have faith in the New Testament. It is a very strange thing that there are not a few who, professing to believe in the scriptures of the New Testament, regard the Old Testament with a feeling of perplexity and doubt, not to say of antipathy; and the objections which are brought forward by them against the Old Testament, I endeavoured to show, were rooted in their insufficient understanding of the teaching of the New Testament. I have only two more to bring before you this morning, and I must pass over them rapidly, because there are so many other points to which it is necessary to allude, in connection with the subject of this address.

A fifth objection which is brought against the Old Testament is on account of the miracles which it contains. This objection is brought forward not by people who doubt the miracles of the New Testament — in that case it would be necessary to consider the question of miracle in general; but these people believe the miracles that Jesus and the apostles wrought, and still they think that the miracles of the Old Testament are of a character that makes it very difficult to believe in their actual occurrence — a strange objection in which there is no reason, in which there is only a kind of obscure feeling and antipathy; for if we compare the miracles of the Old and of the New Testament, we shall find that their character is the same. At whatever period of the world's history they occurred, they could never be interpreted or accounted for by the natural law of things. To convert water into wine, to raise the dead, to open the eyes of one that was born blind — all these things are evidently what we call "miracles."

In the second place, so great is the similarity between the Old and the New Testament miracles that it has been one of the arguments of the defenders of the mythical theory of the gospels, that it was evident that the authors of these books were anxious to show, that Christ and the apostles were able to do the same wonderful things which Moses and the prophets had done, and that therefore as there was the feeding of the children of Israel in the wilderness with manna, so there was the miraculous feeding of the multitude in the desert; and as there was the raising up of the dead through Elisha, and the healing of the leper, so there were similar miracles recorded of Christ and of the apostles.

A third point is this. People are under the impression that on every page of the Old Testament there is some wonderful prodigy which entirely stops the course of nature, and which disorders the natural development of things. They say, "Are we to believe those wonderful stories about the wife of Lot being turned into a pillar of salt, about the Red Sea, about the sun standing still, about the whale and Jonah, and so on?" giving you the impression that, according to their view, the Old Testament was a series of prodigies. Against this it must be said very simply, that, during a period of about three and twenty years, there occurred a far larger number of miracles in the New Testament time than during all the centuries of Israel's history. During the three years of Christ's earthly ministry, and during the twenty years of which the Acts of the Apostles give us a record, there is a far greater number of miracles narrated than in the whole history of the Old covenant people through many centuries. So this objection at once falls to the ground.

And all those miracles that are recorded in the old history are recorded as having happened in periods of great importance, and of transition, when a new thing had to be ushered in — when Israel had to be brought" out of Egypt, when they had to be supported in the wilderness, when they had to conquer the land which the Lord had promised to them, and again, in the time of general apostasy, when they had adopted the worship of Baal in the times of Elijah and Elisha; so that it is not for the love of prodigies that these miracles are introduced, but as acts and manifestations of a living God who transacts supernatural events, the object of which is His glory and the salvation of mankind.

Another point to be noticed is this, that all these miracles, which form the stumbling-block of people in the Old Testament, are ratified by Jesus Christ and by the apostles; so that if you do not believe the miracle of Jonah, it is not with the book of Jonah that you have to do, but with our Saviour Jesus Christ Himself; or if you do not believe in the Flood, or in the turning of Lot's wife into a pillar of salt, you have to do with Jesus, who said, "As it was in the days of Noah," and "Remember Lot's wife"; or if you do not choose to believe that Balaam's ass spoke, you have to do with the apostle Peter, who mentions that through the voice of an irrational creature God reproved the false prophet. There is no miracle spoken of in the Old Testament that is a stumbling-block to the present generation, that has not, directly or indirectly, been ratified by the authority of our divine Lord and of His inspired apostles. But to do perfect justice, as it is our bounden duty to do, there is a difference between the Old Testament miracles and the New Testament miracles, and this difference I wish to point out very briefly.

I think that the miracles of our blessed Saviour Jesus Christ stand quite by themselves, because He is both God and man; and when Jesus performed miracles, He was able to say truly, as recorded in the gospel of John, "If I had not done such works as none other man did," — not Moses, nor Elijah, nor any other man, — for out of that which was in Him, He, the Lord, manifested His power. In the miracles which are recorded in the Old Testament it is always said that they are wrought, that Jehovah's glory, not the glory of Moses, might be made manifest. But when Jesus performs miracles, it is that the glory of Jesus may be made manifest. The miracles of our blessed Saviour range themselves under these several aspects. He is the Mediator, the Saviour, the Restorer. All things are under His sway. Nature — he can intensify and multiply nature in a miraculous way. Thus the five loaves and two fishes are sufficient for thousands. The water is changed into wine. And He can conquer the adverse powers of nature, so that He rebukes the winds, and the waves of the sea, and there is a great calm. As He is the Lord of nature, so He is the Saviour and Restorer; therefore He changes disease into health. He has the power over death; therefore He is able to raise the dead, because He is the resurrection and the life. And He is the Lord whom all angels and devils must obey. Therefore He is able to drive out and to banish the servants of Satan. So He is Lord over all, — Son of God and yet Son of Man.

But the miracles of Jesus Christ and of His apostles have all reference to the individual, to salvation, to the idea of redemption and restoration. The Old Testament, as I explained to you on the last occasion, has not so much to do with individuals as with a nation. What the Old Testament history sought to prove was, that Jehovah the God of Israel is the true God, and stronger than all the powers in which the nations trust. It did not seek to prove that Jehovah pardons the sins of very contrite one, and is able to renew the heart, and to restore peace unto the troubled. It sought to show that the God of the nation is above all other gods, that Israel, in contrast with the, nations, has pre-eminence and power over all the worldly powers. Therefore the miracles in the land of Egypt had, so to speak, a cosmic character. They were to show to Pharaoh and to the Egyptians that all those natural powers in which they trusted were under the control of Jehovah. Likewise was this the case with the miracles wrought, when, under Joshua, Israel entered into the land of Canaan. They were meant to show the Canaanites that God was greater than the sun and the moon, and greater than all powers in which they had confidence. So the miracles of the Old Testament have, in one respect, a very striking, if I may so speak, stupendous, anti-natural character, because they relate to the national history and to the manifestation of God, as the God of the nation, *versus* all the other nations who trust in gods and powers which are only subordinate or altogether non-existent.

I pass on now to the last point. Many people object to the Old Testament because the sins of God's people — Jacob, and David, and Jonah, etc. — are there told with such great plainness, that it is difficult for us to believe that men, who were guilty of such sins, should continue to be regarded as the favourites and saints of God. Now this is an objection which is of great importance. Let me quote the remarkable utterance of one of the greatest speculative theologians of the present century, — the great authority on questions of theological ethics, — Professor Rothe says, "The opinion which has been so often asserted in modern times, that the ethics of the Bible do not reach clearness and purity until we come to the New Testament, is altogether false. The ethics of the old Testament and of the New Testament are perfectly identical. The Spirit of God must always announce the same principles. The Old Testament," he says, "never would have been written except it had been for the intended New Testament, and although the individual saints, who are brought before us in the Old Testament, did not attain to the idea which is revealed, the revelation of God in the Old Testament concerning ethics is a perfect revelation."

The object of the Bible is not to glorify and eulogise man, but to glorify God. It is not to give us ideal pictures of human characters. We are very much inclined to suppose this, and people are very ready to talk of a "holy man," "a very holy man." There is no degree in holiness. A holy man is a sinner saved, who, by the electing love and power of God, is brought nigh to Him. And, therefore, with perfect truthfulness, the Scripture records the great sins and falls of God's chosen ones. It wishes to impress upon us that all is by grace, that it was not on account of some natural superiority of character that God's servants were chosen, and that after they had been brought to the knowledge and the fear of God, it was only grace that sustained them, while there was still within them, even to the last, that other law striving against the holy will of God. But when Scripture lays bare to us the sins of God's saints, with perfect truthfulness, does it approve of the sins of God's people? Does it represent them in a fascinating and seducing light? Does it palliate their guilt and culpability? Does it not show to us that God condemned the sin, and that God severely chastised each one of His saints who fell into sin? And more than that The world knows about the sin of David, but does the world know about the repentance of David, — how deep it was, how spiritual it was, how sincere it was, how self-humiliating it was — so that, in the face of the whole nation, the king confessed his guilt and wrote those Psalms, the 51st and the 32nd, in which he showed, before the whole world, how deeply he had fallen, and that it was only the mercy of God that had restored him? You know well regarding Jonah, who was disobedient to God, and ran away from God, and afterwards murmured because God pardoned the Ninevites, and because the gourd was dried up. Do you ever think that it is Jonah himself who tells you of these things that he did? It is the power of divine grace, which restores God's people after they have fallen into sin, when they truly repent. God delights in His people, but He punishes them and rebukes them for all their trespasses.

But the root of the objection, which, after all, I have not touched, lies in what I have already explained — the importance attached in this age to what people call "ethics" and "morality." The world does not know the difference between morality and godliness. Morality is a very good and excellent thing, but it is not Godliness. Godliness includes morality. Morality can never be a substitute for godliness. The Bible does not divide the human race into men who are more or less moral, or who are moral and immoral; but the Bible divides men into two classes — the godly and the ungodly, the regenerate and the unregenerate — those who belong to Christ's flock, and those who do not belong to Christ's flock. And therefore it is that you will find so many people say, — what they ought to be ashamed to say, — that they like Esau better than Jacob, when God says, "Jacob have I loved, and Esau have I hated." And why do they like Esau better than Jacob? Because they do not understand Jacob. They see a few blemishes in Jacob's character (who is there that has none?), but they do not see that the whole bent of the man was Godward, that during all his life he was walking in communion with God, and that the prayer which he uttered on his death-bed, interrupting the prophetic prediction concerning the twelve tribes, "I have waited, Jehovah, for Thy salvation," was the pulsation of the man's whole heart. And the Pharisees did not understand why the publicans and sinners came to Jesus, just as the elder brother did not understand why there was so much rejoicing over the younger son who had returned. Thus it is, that men who do not know the principle of grace, and who do not know the corruption of their own hearts, are so staggered at these narratives of the fall and sins of God's people.

But now I must hasten to the subject that is further and chiefly to occupy us to-day.

In my first lecture I showed you the effect which had been produced by the interpretation of the Bible through rationalism; by the mythical theory which was produced by pantheism; by that atheism which most illogically and unnecessarily has, through alleged results of science, fortified itself in want of faith in the living God, in an undue exaltation of reason, as if it were the judge of revelation or needed no revelation, and in the Pelagian view of man that he was not so sinful as to require an expiation, or so corrupt as to require regeneration, and in the idea also that the world will improve naturally, — not, as the Bible tells us, through the judgments and direct interference of Jehovah.

I must notice some defects in the Reformation interpretation of Scripture, and what is generally called the evangelical interpretation of Scripture, under which we still labour to our great disadvantage. The Reformation had two defects. I have spoken at great length, and out of the fulness of my heart, of the glory of the Reformation. Let me point out now these two points in which the Reformers were deficient. In the first place, they did not distinguish the dispensations, although Augustine had already said, "Distinguish the times, and all difficulties vanish." If they had distinguished the dispensations of the kingdom and of the Church, they never could have approved of Servetus being put to death because he was heretical on the doctrine of the Trinity, for in the Church, in the family of God, there is no sword. The sword is only in the kingdom. If any man deny the truth as it is in Jesus, he certainly ought not to be a minister of the Church or a member of the Church; but in this world we Christians, as Christians, have no rights: we have only duties. In the second place, they did not understand clearly the important position of the Jews in the economy of God, nor did they see clearly the second advent of our Lord. Not that either Luther or Calvin held those shallow Pelagian views, so common, of a gradual amelioration and Christianising of the world. Calvin says, "It is a superstition to think that the world is improving in religion and morality. It is not improving, but it is always going back." Luther says, "I know that the world is becoming epicurean; that is to say, they will lose faith in God and immortality, and give themselves up to the pleasures of the things of this world, and then suddenly shall be heard the voice, 'Behold the Bridegroom cometh.'" But still they did not see clearly the second advent of our Lord, or the difference between the Church dispensation and the position of Israel, both in the past and in the future kingdom. The error which was made subsequently by those who preached the saving truths of the Gospel was this — that they thought that it was sufficient to preach personal salvation, man's sinfulness, the atonement, the renewal by the Spirit, the fruits of the Spirit — everything that referred to the individual. That is the centre, but all the circumference they left out, — the whole counsel of God as it is revealed in Scripture, the plan of God, the kingdom of God, the creation of the world, the creation of man, the unity of the human race, the judgment of the Tower of Babel, the elective dispensation under Israel, in its contrast to what came afterwards. The consequence was that, while it was all very good for those who spiritually and experimentally knew about sin and salvation, the world in its philosophy and in its science was constantly undermining the circumference; so that on all the other points on which the Bible touches, false and anti-Biblical ideas became current, and each of these points afforded a position from which to attack and to assail the whole Scripture.

Now this is one important thing in the controversy which is going on at present, that it obliges Christians to read the whole Scripture, that we cannot limit ourselves to a few points, which bear upon personal revelation, but that we must now acknowledge that God has taught us nothing but what is profitable, nay, what is necessary. What people generally call "edifying," — by which they mean something that touches upon their feelings or upon their present course of action, — is not the biblical idea of "edifying." The biblical idea of "edifying" is that we should see the character of God and the will of God, and that thus we should be built up in our most holy faith. It is as if I were to begin the Lord's Prayer by saying, "Give us this day our daily bread," and to pray for bread and for pardon and for guidance and for deliverance, and to forget "Hallowed be Thy name, Thy kingdom come, Thy will be done on earth as it is in heaven." These are the things in which is our life, and from which emanate all the strength and the guidance that we need for our daily conduct and our daily difficulties. The Old Testament, at present, is the great battlefield, and it is a very good thing that it is so. The reasons I must reserve for my next address.

I wish now to speak about the Old Testament in its distinction from the New Testament, and to ask this question, "What is the leading idea which will enable us to see the whole, both in its unity and also in its characteristic peculiarities?" That the Bible consists of two parts is evident — historically evident. This is not a theory; it is a fact. The one part was written before the advent of Christ, the other was written after the advent of Christ; the one in Hebrew, the other in Greek; the one believed in by the Jews, who reject the other; the other as well as the Old Testament believed in by the Church of

103

Christ Now this last fact is the clue to the whole question. During the times of the Gentiles, while Israel is under the displeasure of God, and estranged from Him, there is the Church as a witness for God, and the name which was formerly "Jehovah" lives among them as "I Jesus." Therefore the one set of books belongs to Israel, and has reference to the past history of Israel, and to the future glory of Israel; and the other set belongs to the Church, in which there are both Jews and Gentiles, having reference to the peculiar position which shall be assigned to them at the second coming of our blessed Lord and Saviour. A simple Christian who has been instructed in the saving truths looks upon the whole as one. He sees the continuity. The books of the Old and of the New Testament appear to him like a ring, or like a circle; for as in the first three chapters of Genesis we are told of the creation of heaven and earth, and of Adam and Eve, and afterwards of the serpent by whom our first parents were led into disobedience, so in the three last chapters of the book of Revelation these points are taken up exactly in the same method. First, Satan is cast into prison and made harmless; then there is the marriage of the Lamb and of the Bride; and then the new heaven and the new earth, in which the full glory of God is made manifest. The history is also continuous. Malachi says, "There will come the precursor." The gospel virtually begins, "There was a man sent from God, whose name was John." The 1st chapter of the book of Matthew shows to us that Abraham, David, the captivity, and Jesus, form a continuous history. So it appears to them as a ring or a circle. Or again, when they think of promise and fulfilment, it appears to them as a tree which is an organic whole. Or again, when they think of the history going on, it appears to them as a river which flows with increasing force and beauty until at last it passes into the ocean. Or again, when they think that the one thing is preparatory to the other, it appears to them as a house, — the Old Testament the foundation and the New Testament the superstructure. Or it appears to them as a riddle: the Old Testament states the problem in all its complex difficulty; the New Testament gives the solution in its majestic simplicity. Or it appears as a lock and key: the lock is very complicated with many wards, some of them very delicate; the key exactly fits in, and, without straining or altering any of the wards, opens it. Or again, it appears to them like that glorious scene when there were multitudes before Him and multitudes behind Him, and in the middle there was Jesus, and both they that were before and they that followed after, said, "Hosanna to the Son of David." Or it appears like those two men who brought the grapes from the promised land to show to Israel what a blessed, fertile country it was. Both carried the same bunch of grapes, but the man who went before it had only a passing glance of it when he took it up. The man who went behind saw the grapes, and he saw the man that went before. Thus were the prophets, Christ in the middle, and the apostles who saw both Christ and the prophets. But my favourite comparison is this. It is like a day, and you know that in Scripture the evening comes first, and then the morning. It was evening and it w-as morning — one day. So there comes first the night, so to speak, of the Old Testament, in which the moon of promise and the stars of prophets were shining and gladdening and comforting the hearts of God's people, and then there came the brightness of the morning — yet one day. Still more is it like that child of whom King Solomon said "Divide it," and the mother cried out, "By no means slay the child"; for to divide Old Testament and New Testament is to take away the life of both, for they are not merely connected, nor are they merely harmonious, but they interpenetrate one another. The same breath of life and the same covenant blood of Him that died for us pervades them all.

But if we see the unity of Old and New Testament and the contrast, also, between the Old and the New Testament, the question now is this: What holds the Old and the New Testament together in such a way that the Old Testament never is superseded, — that what is peculiar in the Old Testament is secured, that what is peculiar in the New Testament is secured, and yet both live together? To answer this question, I must begin by saying that the usual designation "Old" and "New" Testament appears to me not merely imperfect, but liable to great misunderstanding. Why should the books of Moses and the prophets be called Old Testament? Certainly "Old" conveys the idea of antiquity, as if it had passed away, and the idea of old covenant conveys the idea of the law. But I say Moses and the prophets are not Old Testament at all. The Gospel is everywhere. One of the objections that modern criticism has brought against the later books, the later historical books and the prophets and the Psalms, is this — that they seem to think little of the Levitical institutions; that they ignore, as it were, the law; that they lay great stress upon other things — the attitude of the heart towards God and the coming salvation of our Lord. Now, the object for which this argument is pressed is altogether erroneous, but the idea is not erroneous, for let us look away now from the five books of Moses which are generally considered the law. All the other books are full of the gospel, are full of Jesus, are full of atonement, are full of the promise of the Spirit, are full of that spiritual relationship which we have to God, so that the Christian Church can sing the Psalms. There is nothing Levitical in the Psalms. Come we, then, to the five books of Mosea Show me the law in the book of Genesis. It is not there. There is no law there." Abraham believed God, and it was counted to him for righteousness." "I am the Lord. Walk thou before me." And in the book of Deuteronomy there is given what the apostle states: — "The law is spiritual"; Deuteronomy sums up the whole in this: "Thou shalt love the Lord with all thy heart, and thou shalt love thy neighbour as thyself" The whole of that book is what you might call an evangelical exhortation to serve the God who has redeemed us. There remain Exodus, Leviticus, and Numbers. Well, what about Exodus? It is gospel throughout. Why did God bring Israel out of Egypt? First reason: election. He had chosen Abraham, Isaac, and Jacob; and the nation that was to descend from them went back to the election. And the second reason is the blood of the paschal lamb, and the institution of the tabernacle. Is that law or is that gospel? Is not that mediation? Is not that the sacrifice of Christ, under every possible aspect? Is not that the down-coming of God — the descent of God to meet His people because He is the God who redeems them, and because He is the God who sanctifies them by the Holy Ghost? As to the book of Leviticus — read the epistle to the Hebrews, and say whether it is law or gospel. In the book of Genesis we see Abraham offering up Isaac, his only son. In the book of Exodus we see the blood of the paschal lamb. In the book of Leviticus we see the high priest entering, once a year, into the Holy of Holies, with blood. In the book of Numbers we see the brazen serpent lifted up, that whosoever looks may be saved. And in the book of Deuteronomy we see the "prophet like unto me whom the Lord thy God will raise up from among thy brethren. Him shalt thou hear." It is all gospel. Gospel is not the distinguishing characteristic of the New Testament. Law is not the distinguishing characteristic of the Old Testament. That I firmly maintain. This is the characteristic: the one is the book of the kingdom and the book of Israel; the other is the book of the Church. In the one God manifests His promise, and it is the promise that has reference to this earth. Israel is the nation. Palestine is the country. All the nations of the world are the circumference. Jehovah is the King, and He Himself will come, and, after judgments on the nations and chastisements on His own people. He will save and glorify Israel. That is the promise of the Old Testament from beginning to end. As Habakkuk says, "The prophecy is for the appointed time. It hasteth to the end." Literally "it pointeth to the end." "Though it tarry, wait for it. It will not disappoint, but it will surely come." This is the kingdom of which the angel spoke to the Virgin Mary. This is the kingdom of which Mary spoke, and of which Zechariah spoke, and of which the disciples spoke, when they asked the ascending Lord, "Wilt thou at this time restore the kingdom unto Israel?" It is the book of the kingdom; it is the book of Israel; and during the present dispensation the book, as it were, still belongs to Israel, and also belongs to the Church that is waiting for its fulfilment. We now come to the New Testament. The New Testament has also a point to which it looks; and what is that point? Oh, I will speak freely on this subject. It is the second advent of our Lord, when He will return with His saints, and when He will make Himself manifest to Israel and to the whole world, not in order that the last judgment may be held, but that another historical period may be ushered in, when God's will shall be done upon this earth as it is in heaven, and when Jesus Christ and the transfigured saints shall come to be seen and to be acknowledged; and then there shall be fulfilled the promises which God has given from the beginning of the world. When He comes, Israel will say, "It is Jehovah, and it is His first advent." The Church will say, "It is Jesus, and it is His second advent." Israel will say, "He has come to take possession of the throne of His father David, and Jerusalem will be glorified and will be His nation." And the Church will say, "He is glorified in the saints, and admired in all them that believe, and we, whom He has redeemed with His blood, shall reign with Him on the earth." This is what all the apostles taught, and taught constantly. Scarcely are the Thessalonians converted from idolatry, before the apostles teach them to wait for the coming of God's Son from heaven. There is no summary given in the apostolic epistles, of what we believe, that does not bring in "the blessed hope, the glorious appearing (notice the expression) of the great God and our Saviour Jesus Christ." Purposely the expression is the Jehovah, who will appear unto Israel. It is Jesus who appears with the Church — the same thing — "the great God and our Saviour Jesus Christ." And the angel explained it to the disciples: "This same Jesus shall so come." It is the next thing which is to happen. He has left you, and the next thing that is to happen is that He will return. Now I will confirm it; and if there are any here who are in doubt on the subject, do, I beg of you, consider it. Take, now, the position of the apostles. They were told to go into all the world and to evangelise. Israel was without the knowledge of the Messiah. The nations were sunk in ignorance and idolatry. The whole field was before them. Why do they trouble about the end? Have they not plenty to do? Many people tell us, "Do not speak to us of the second advent. It is for us to missionize and to convert the world." Nobody objects to your converting the world, if you can do it. Why is it that these apostles, who are just beginning their work, do not say to the congregations, "Only wait. It is quite true that now the majority is against us; but, century after century, that will change. Christianity will leaven the world" — leaven never used in a good sense, but always in a bad sense — "Christianity will leaven the whole world, and bring all civilisation and knowledge and art into its sphere." No; but what they say to their congregations is this: "The mystery of iniquity has already begun to manifest itself. Little children, it is the last time. Hasten to the coming of the Lord Jesus, knowing that the last times shall be perilous times,— and we wait for our Lord Himself to come and establish His kingdom."

Second objection. People tell us, when we speak about the second advent, "Have we not enough to say about the first advent, the incarnation, the crucifixion, the resurrection, the ascension, the teaching of our blessed Saviour, the example of our blessed Saviour?" Oh, yes; but the apostles who, as it were, had yet the transcendent glory of the first advent, irradiating their countenances and solemnising their hearts, who had heard the words which flowed from His blessed lips, who had seen Him die on the cross, to whom He had appeared after His resurrection, and who had beheld how He was taken up in a cloud, — although, all these stupendous, magnificent, and most blessed facts of the first advent were so close to them, they could never dissociate it from the appearing of our great God and Saviour, from the return of our blessed Lord Jesus Christ. And why should the gospel of the apostle John, which he wrote in order that faith might have its right foundation, and the epistles of the apostle, which he wrote in order that we might know the true character of love both to God and man — why should they only be read and appreciated by the Church, while the other book, the Revelation, of which he himself says, "Blessed is he that readeth and they that hear the words of this prophecy," is ignored — why should that book not be brought continually before our gaze? The attitude of the Christian, whether he lives in the first century or in the nineteenth century, or in the twenty-ninth century, if there will be such a century in the present dispensation, remains entirely the same. Some people may say, "But, you see, the apostles were mistaken — Jesus Christ did not come"; or they may say that Bengel was mistaken because Jesus Christ did not come when he prophesied He would. That has nothing to do with it, nothing whatever to do with it This is the point — that, during this whole dispensation of the Church, the world will not get better, and that the only object both for the Church and for the world is the coming of the Lord Jesus Christ. Having this expectation of the heart, we will keep ourselves from the spirit of the world, and know that in this dispensation it is for the Church to witness, to suffer, to hold fast, and to be faithful. The illustrious Bengel made this remark: "The Christian Churches have forgotten the hope of the Church, but they still exhort people to be faithful, and to be unworldly, and to be patient; but in the New Testament, all exhortations to be unworldly, and to be faithful, and to be diligent, are based upon this fact, that the Lord is coming. 'What God has joined together, let not man put asunder.'"

And now we must consider the connecting links which show in the Old Testament that the coming of Jehovah is identical with the coming of Jesus, and show in the New Testament that the coming of Jesus is identical with the coming of Jehovah. There is far more said in the book of the kingdom, as I shall now call it, or in the book of Israel, of the second advent than of the first advent; far more, and for this simple reason: If everything concerning the first advent and the rejection of Jesus by His people Israel had been plainly and clearly foretold, the coming of Jesus to Israel would have been a foregone conclusion; it would not have been possible that the nation should have been tested, as God wished to test them. "At last He sent His Son. Peradventure they will listen to Him." He had to come, as it were, incognito, and it was necessary for them to have the first advent, and the rejection of Jesus, clouded and veiled, and so mixed up with the second advent that the difficulty could only be overcome by the mysterious thing which we call faith, and which is called forth by the power of God. Yet there were many things in the Old Testament that showed to them the great problem, which we can solve now from the New Testament point of view. Our Lord Jesus referred to it. "How does David call Him Lord, when He is his Son. Why does He say unto Him, 'Sit Thou at my right hand'? That is not in Jerusalem. You expect Messiah. You expect rightly the Messiah to be your King. But this servant of the Lord, this Son of David, the Holy Ghost by David calls Lord, and His position is at the right hand above. How is that?" He refers also to the prophecy of Daniel. "From henceforth you shall see the Son of Man in power, and coming with the clouds of heaven. Daniel predicts the four monarchies; there comes direct from above, from heaven, the fifth monarchy, which is the everlasting kingdom. That is the stone cut out without hands, and it is the Son of Man coming in the clouds from heaven. But how should He get there? Whoever heard of the Son of Man from heaven? Is this the root out of a dry ground? Is this He who was born in Bethlehem Ephratah? The Son of Man from heaven, the rejection of Jesus and the exaltation of Jesus.

Now He comes down. Therefore the apostle says to the Thessalonians, "You wait for the coming of Jesus from heaven." The first time He came from heaven; the second time He will come from heaven. This shows you how, in the Old Testament, we have already indication that the Jehovah who comes to establish the kingdom on earth is none other than He who is described in the book of Zechariah: "They shall look unto him whom they have pierced; and his feet shall stand upon the Mount of Olives, which is before Jerusalem on the east." In the New Testament the apostle Peter says to the Jews, "Repent, that your sins may be blotted out, in order that times of refreshment may come from the presence of the Lord, when he shall send Jesus who is your Messiah." And the apostle Paul says to the Romans, "All Israel shall be saved." Why? Because it is written in the prophet Isaiah, that out of Zion shall come the deliverer. Therefore, in the New Testament, both in the gospels and in the epistles, the coming of the Lord Jesus is connected with the national restoration and blessing of Israel; or, in other words, the coming of Jehovah; and so until we coma to the blessed book of the Revelation. There we have all summed up in this book of the kingdom and this book of the Church. There we see the unity of the whole record which God has given to us. He will come again. Jehovah means the coming one; and now He is called Jesus, who was, and is, and is to come, and of whom the Church says, "Come, Lord Jesus, come quickly."

And now, in conclusion, let me just say one word about the attitude of the Church. In the sixth chapter of the gospel of John, we have two miracles intimately connected: the feeding of the multitude in the wilderness, and Christ appearing to the disciples in the midst of the sea, when they are in the storm. The wilderness represents the world in its poverty, in its hunger, and in its absolute destitution. It can provide nothing for the real wants of mankind. Jesus is there with His disciples! and, through the disciples, He, with five loaves and two fishes, feeds the multitude abundantly, so that there are basketfuls left; that is the word that grows and is multiplied. Simple, mean, insignificant, powerless, altogether insignificant, it appears to men. Weak are the disciples whom Jesus Christ makes His agents; but the miracle is done, and for eighteen centuries thousands and thousands of hungry ones have been fed, and have found life and strength everlasting. The sea is the emblem of the world, not in its poverty and hunger, but in its unrest, and in its opposition to, and enmity against, God; and the wind and the storms that blow are the emblems of Satan, and of all the agents of Satan, who do everything to destroy the Church. And Christ is no longer in the midst of the disciples, but on a mountain, high, apart, praying to the Father. And the disciples are left alone in the ship; and it is for them to row and to toil; but they make no progress, for the world always remains the same. No apologetics will bring it one inch nearer to the end, till at last, in the fourth watch, Jesus Himself comes; and immediately — immediately — the ship is safe, close to shore. Amen.

XI - The Books of Israel and of the Church Shown to Be Organically Connected

I wish to-day, first, to offer you a few remarks on the present state of opposition to Christianity, and to the Old Testament especially; then to confirm and illustrate, in a few words, the two positions which I maintained in my last lecture, namely, that the one central and leading idea which throws light, both upon the identity of Old and New Testaments, and also upon their contrast, is the second advent of our blessed Lord, and that, therefore, the scriptures of Moses and the prophets would be more properly termed "book of the kingdom and of Israel," and the scriptures of evangelists and apostles "book of the Church"; and, after having done this, I wish to show to you the reasons why it is both rational and according to the will of God that we should always read Moses and the prophets in the light of the apostolic writings. And lastly, I wish to say a few words on the structure of both the earlier and the later books.

It may seem strange at first sight that when Christianity has been in the world for so many centuries, and when, almost from the beginning, earnest and thoughtful defenders of the faith have refuted the manifold objections which are brought against the truth, and have pressed with great clearness, skill, and earnestness, the multiform and cumulative evidence for the Gospel, the conflict between faith and unbelief is going on at present, as much as in any age of the past. And this is still more strange when we remember that the points at issue which are debated at the present are not secondary points, but are points of the most elementary and fundamental character. If there had been ten points at issue between Christians and the world, and six of these points had been established, and now there was still controversy about four remaining secondary points, it would not be so wonderful; but what a wonderful thing it is that within the last ten or twenty years the points of debate are of the most elementary character, such as whether there is a personal God, whether revelation and miracle are possible, whether Jesus is more than man! The young especially are perplexed, because they are labouring under a mistake: they fancy that while Christianity may have been able to hold its ground during past centuries, such is the development of human knowledge, and of the powers of the human mind, that we have now arrived at a height where Christianity is no longer tenable. They forget, as the apostle explains to us, that the opposition of human wisdom and reason to Christianity is not an accidental thing, but that it is essential, and that it is based upon the inherent character and nature both of Christianity and of the world. When the Apostle Paul writes to the Corinthians, "Not many wise after the flesh are called," I should like to ask a number of people what that "wise after the flesh" means; and when he says that the Gospel is foolishness to the Greeks, he does not imagine that that is peculiar to his own period. He does not appeal from his own time to future generations, who may be more enlightened, and more wise, and more inclined to receive the Gospel; but he makes a general statement, that in every age of this dispensation, unregenerate man is not able to understand the things of God, and that they must be revealed to him by the Spirit So far, then, from being any discouragement to us, — much as we regret and lament that at the present day the opposition against Christianity is as vehement and fierce as ever it was, and that the attacks are made on the most central and vital points of the truth, — we see in this only a corroboration of the testimony of the apostle, and only a proof of what we all have experienced — that no man can call Jesus Lord, save by the Holy Ghost.

The attacks of unbelief against Christianity and against the Scripture (for to attack the Scripture is to attack Christianity) vary according to different modes of thought, and according to different historical and social circumstances, as the world advances. The assailants are always shifting their ground. According to the metaphysics of the day their objections are framed. They are modern, but they are never new. To corroborate this I bring before you a very striking fact. The first attack against Christianity in a systematic form of which history has record is the book of Celsus, written in the year 150 of our era, and in this book Celsus attacks Christianity in this way. In the first place he says: "You tell a great many wonderful things about Jesus. Why do you suppose that those wonderful things are truer than the many fables and myths which ether nations and other people tell about their gods and demigods? And what a strange thing it is that this Jesus was not able to attach to him so much even his own disciples, as to render them firm in the hour of trial. And what evidence is there of his resurrection, but the heated imagination of a woman, who was a devoted follower of his, and who said that she had seen a vision of the risen one?" Again he says, "If God" (he did not believe in God in our sense) "is omniscient and omnipotent, why docs he require a messenger to benefit mankind? And what a religion is this, that addresses itself to the ignorant, to fishermen, artisans, and poor people that have no learning, and that addresses itself also to people of bad character; for we know that no bad character ever can become a good character." And again he says, "You think far too much of man. Why is man of so much importance, that such great things should be done for him? Why do you place man so high above the animals? for we see among the animals skill, and reason, and forethought, and gratitude, and sagacity; nay, some of them are greatly in advance of us. And what do you imagine that this whole world is? Do you think that it is better at one time than at another? — that there is in its purpose and progress? The world is always the same. The combination of things remains always the same. It neither alters, nor improves, nor deteriorates." These things were written after 150 years of our era. Are they not exactly like the things said by Strauss against the truth of Christianity? Is it not the voice of the Darwinian which we hear in every sentence? The same ideas are presented, the same objections made, the same fundamental position is held. The apostles were the teachers of all nations. The apostles never descended into the territory of their opponents. They did take notice of their objections, and refuted them, but always from the standpoint of faith. The apostles never said, "Now we shall look at the thing metaphysically. We shall leave out of view the authority of the Bible. We shall argue with you as a metaphysician with a metaphysician, as a logician with a logician, as a historian with a historian," — never for a single moment. The apostle said to the Athenians, that all the time of their former magnificent history, full of metaphysical speculation and of wonderful culture, was the time of ignorance, and that God had sent him, out of the fulness of the revealed truth, to show to them the things of God. This, then, is, and will be, as long as this present dispensation lasts. Truth and unbelief will contend, and there will be no victory acknowledged. True! there are many arguments brought forward in the present day which could never have been brought forward before. The very stones are crying out. Within the last twenty or thirty years, the evidences for the historical truth and accuracy of the Old Testament Scriptures, especially as to the books of Moses, have been confirmed in the most striking way by the discovery of the Assyrian and Egyptian monuments. That is perfectly true; but the prejudice is too deep, and too much rooted in the very centre of the human heart, for any of these arguments, precious and valuable as they are, to do more than rouse attention. After that has been aroused, there remains the decision, as Christ said to the messengers of John the Baptist. Miracles are done. But these miracles will never force you to believe. Miracles arrest your attention, and then comes the decision. "Blessed is he that is not offended in Me." The Old Testament has been made specially the object of attack in the present day, and it is well that it is so. Nothing better could have happened. I will tell you why. I believe in Jesus, and I believe the revelation, which, through Jesus, was given to us by the apostles, to have been not merely the word of God, but the highest reason, — absolute wisdom and truth. Now when I find that Jesus always founded His claims and based His teaching, and explained all the facts of His life, death and resurrection, by reference to Moses and the prophets, and when I find that the apostles, even when they went to the heathen, who did not know Moses and the prophets, preached to them that Christ died and rose again *according to the Scriptures*, and did not try to prove the authenticity or divinity of the Scriptures, except by their inherent power, then I say there is no other way of proving the truth, or even of stating the truth, but by reference to Moses and the prophets. But in the latter days Christian apologists have pursued quite a different method. What they have said is this: "There are so many objections against the Old

Testament, but, after all it is not of great importance. Let us pitch that overboard, or, at all events, leave it out of consideration. Let us narrow the issue. When we speak to infidels and sceptics, let us leave out the Old Testament. We shall say simply, "Here is Christ. Look at the character of Christ — how noble, how perfect, how beautiful! Is He not different from all other men? is He not greater than all other men? is He not unique?'" Verily He is. What follows? They have imagined that by presenting Christ apart from the soil in which God made Him grow and spring up, apart from the preparation for Him by the whole history of Israel, apart from the teaching which God gave to His people by Moses and the prophets, by putting Christ before men simply as a human picture, appealing to human reason, as if He had dropped down from the heavens, they would gain the assent of people. What assent is gained? Assent is gained, but of what nature? To do justice to the Unitarians, and to the old rationalists in Germany, they had a most sincere admiration of the beauty of Christ's character, and they were exceedingly skilful in showing the wonderful features of His moral excellence, harmony, and perfection. They were quite sincere and enthusiastic about it. But between Christ being the best man, and Christ being the Son of God, — between these positions there is no bridge. Faith must bridge it over, and faith can only bridge it over, when we see that Christ is the One who is alone the fulfilment of that constant series of condescending, redemptive manifestations, of which the Old Testament is the record. But now God compels these half-and-half Christian apologists, by the unbelieving world attacking the Old Testament, to do what they ought to have done from the beginning, because Christ and the apostles plainly impressed it, and not to imagine that their philosophical method is superior to that which God Himself has laid down. This is a very important point, and those of you who know what is going on in the churches, and have watched things for the last twenty or thirty years, will see that it does not merely involve apologetics, but it refers to the whole mode of preaching and teaching the blessed Gospel of our Lord Jesus Christ. The ark sometimes fell into the hands of the Philistines, but the Philistines could not do anything with the ark of God. It was of no use to them. Sooner or later they must hand it back to Israel. The interpretation of Scripture will receive no benefit or light worth speaking of, but from the Church of Jesus Christ herself It is quite true, for I wish to do justice to all, that the rationalists, looking upon the Bible as a human book, and studying the Bible diligently and laboriously, with a vast amount of philological and historical erudition and skill, have brought out many valuable facts, and have established many very valuable interpretations. It is also true that another school of interpretation, looking at the Bible from the aesthetic and poetical point of view, like that great man Heine, have contributed much to the understanding of Scripture. It is further true that the best exponent of the modern critical treatment of the Old Testament, Ewald, a man of profound earnestness and moral elevation, finding in the Old Testament the expression of the highest intuitions and religious aspirations of the human mind, but not a supernatural inspiration from above, has brought out much, both of the spirit and of the letter of the old history and of the old teaching. But the real light on the Scripture can only proceed from those who, by the selfsame Holy Ghost which breathed the Scriptures, have been taught to believe the things that are contained in the Scriptures.

Why did the Reformers, as it were, introduce a new era in the understanding and interpretation of Scripture? Because they had hold of the central idea, — justification by faith in Jesus Christ. If you have anything that Scripture teaches firmly established in your mind, it will throw light upon the whole Scripture. For instance, the doctrine of the Holy Ghost. Well, from Genesis to the book of Revelation, if you have that doctrine of the Holy Ghost clearly established in your mind, you will see a unity, a comprehensiveness, an organic illustration of that doctrine which will confirm your faith in the whole Scripture. Now, what I asserted in my last lecture, and what I have asserted ever since I have been in the ministry, and hope to assert as long as God may spare me, is this — that the one central point, and the highest point from which the whole of Moses and the prophets, and the whole of the gospels, epistles, and Apocalypse can be comprehended, both in their unity and in their diversity, is the glorious appearing of the great God and Saviour — Jehovah coming to Israel, to Jerusalem, to restore the kingdom to the nation — Jesus, that Jehovah, coming to the Church to receive the saints, that they in heavenly places may reign with Him.

As I reminded you, to call the books of Moses and the prophets "Old Testament" is liable to be misunderstood, although I do not say that it is incorrect. Jesus Christ used the expression, "Moses and the prophets," "Moses, the prophets, and the Psalms," and "the Scriptures," and so did the apostles. But there is no authority for saying "Old Testament" or "New Testament." In the ancient Church they called what we call the New Testament "Gospel and Epistle," because, first, they laid almost exclusive importance on the writings of Paul, who was the apostle of the Gentiles. But as "Testament" is generally understood by people in the sense of covenant, and they fancy that Old Testament means that these books refer to law, I must remind you of what you all know. Law, in Scripture, in the New Testament especially, has two significations — a narrow and a large one. In its narrow meaning, it is that which is opposed to gospel — the works of the law, the covenant of works. "Do this, and thou shalt live: if you do not do this, you are under the curse." Therefore the apostle says, "They that are under the law are under a curse. The law worketh wrath. The law is the strength of sin." Only think of the Pharisee, Saul, saying this of the law! It sounds almost blasphemous. "The law worketh wrath: the law is the strength of sin. They that are under the law are under the curse." Was Abraham, then, under the law, or Moses, or David, or Isaiah, and were they under a curse? Was the law to them the strength of sin? Of course not, as little as to the apostle Paul and the apostle John; for we believe that the saints of God, from beginning to end, are saved by grace, through faith in the Redeemer. But there is another sense in which we use the word "law." When David says that he delights himself in the law of the Lord, he means the whole teaching and all the institutions of God, — God as the Redeemer, the propitiatory sacrifice, — all the teaching of God that He has given to us. And, more than that, the apostle Paul says, "We have a righteousness apart from the law," and this righteousness, apart from the law, is witnessed not merely by the prophets, but by the law and the prophets. Therefore, that very law declares, not merely that if a man transgresses the law he is under a curse, but also that there is a divine righteousness, apart from any works, given to every one that believeth. It is in this sense that John says, "The law was given by Moses, but grace and truth came by Jesus Christ." There are thus» you see, two things corresponding to law. The law consists of two things. As a covenant of works, it is condemnation. Grace came by Jesus Christ. As a type of the Gospel it contains promises, figures, types, and shadows By Jesus Christ came the substance or the fulfilment. Therefore, in this respect, although there is a contrast between the two, and although the one is only the germ and the other is the fruit, the one the promise and the other the fulfilment, yet the two go together. But the distinguishing feature, and that which will remain as long as the world stands, is this: Moses and the prophets have written the books of Israel, and the evangelists and apostles have written the books of the Church: in the one Jehovah, in the other Jesus; in the one Israel and the nations, in the other an election from among all nations — not a nation, but the body of Christ; the one pertaining to the earthly, the other pertaining to heaven. When you take this view, you will see that Moses and the prophets are not merely a ladder by which we get up to a higher platform, and then can do without the ladder; but that, after they have served the purpo.se of explaining to you the New Testament of Jesus Christ, they have a substantive importance and position in themselves, which will always continue. What I aim at in these lectures is to show to you that the Bible is not an aggregate of literary productions, but that it is the testimony and voice of the living One who is to come again — a book of history which is not yet completed. And when we call the one the book of Israel, you see the Jews scattered among all the nations of the earth, the problem of their future not yet solved. And when we call the other the book of the Church, I trust that you feel that you are members of that vast community which says, "Come, Lord Jesus; come quickly."

Now I must pass on to the next point. I have used many comparisons to show the relation of the one book to the other, but I will now add a tenth to the nine that I have already mentioned, and it is this. A stereoscope contains two different aspects of the same object, but it is of no use looking at the stereoscopic picture with one eye. You must look at it with both eyes, and then the figure will stand out as a solid plastic reality. And that is exactly the way in which Jesus Christ stands out. When we see the view taken of Him by Moses and the prophets, as the coming Jehovah; and when we see the view taken of Him by the apostles, as the returning Jesus, then we see the historic re-ality, for we must always study the ancient Scriptures in the light of the new. And as this is a very important point in the present day, I am going to ask your attention to the reasons which I have for this; for all our learned friends tell us that we must read Moses and the prophets, as we read any other book of antiquity, and quite apart from the impressions made upon us by the words of Jesus and of the apostles. Now, in the first place, what I say to this is, that it is very irrational and unphilosophical from our point of view. A few years ago I was reading the works of Schopenhauer, the great German Bud-dhist philosopher. His system of the universe of knowledge and will he has embodied in two very large volumes, and in the preface he says, "There is only one idea in these two volumes." He tried to express it as lucidly and as briefly as possible, and this was the result. I would ask your special attention to what he says. I have translated it from the German, so you must excuse the style. "A system of thoughts must have an architectonic structure, in which one part supports the other, but is not supported by it. The foundation sup-ports the whole, but is itself not supported. The top stone is supported, but it supports nothing." That is one style of book. We are first to lay down a few axioms or admitted positions that have to bear the structure of the whole. Then you go on: "What you put upon it is supported by the foundation, but does not support the foundation. But there is another kind of book which is this. A work consisting of one idea, however comprehensive, must possess perfect unity. It may consist of parts, but they must be organically connected, so that each part supports the whole and is supported by the whole. No part is, so to say, first, and no part is last. The whole is illustrated by every minute part, and even the smallest part cannot be rightly understood unless the whole has been comprehended." What he means is this: "If a work consists of one idea, although that one idea is very comprehensive and has many ramifi-cations, then the only way in which it can be set forth is as an organism. The whole idea will be in every part. The beginning cannot be properly under-stood unless you know also the end. The smaller and less important parts cannot be properly understood unless you know the whole. They throw light upon the whole, as the whole throws light upon them. In this case nothing can be done" (now listen to this) "but to read the book twice, and the first time with much patience, which can only be obtained by a freely granted confidence that the beginning presupposes the end, as much as the end pre-supposes the beginning, and the earlier part the later. Although each part may be as clearly expressed as is possible, yet its relation to the whole can-not be seen at first. When you read it the second time, all will appear in clear light." When I read this preface some years ago, I said, "That man has exactly explained the philosophy of the Bible." The Holy Ghost inspired the Book. God is the Author of the Book. You must read it the first time with a full con-viction that you can understand it only partially, for it is organically united. He, by whom the first three chapters of Genesis were inspired, saw in His mind the three last chapters of the book of Revelation. "God, who at sundry times and in divers manners spake unto the fathers by the prophets hath, in these last days, spoken unto us by his Son." And therefore when we have read the whole, and when we have got the solution and the key in the New Testament, then we must return again to the book of Genesis and read Moses and the prophets, in the light that God has given us throughout. The same Author; every minute part illustrated by the whole; the whole shedding light upon every minute part. Were, then, the apostles right in their method? Let us go back to the Lord. He opened their understanding, that they might understand the Scriptures. He explained unto them His own person and His own history, beginning at Moses, that through sufferings He must enter into glory. These dear apostles, even while they were seeing Jesus and beholding the things of Scripture fulfilled, did not understand the Scripture. Why did they not understand the Scripture? They knew Hebrew, as well as any Hebrew scholar of the present day. What made them not understand the Scripture? Because the Holy Ghost was not given, and Christ had not yet risen.

I will give you a second reason, and that second reason quite as strong and as cogent as the first. I must say again that the Bible is not a literary production. The Bible is part of God's dealings with Israel and with the Church. Therefore every portion of Scripture, as it first appeared, had already an audience prepared for it, a circle of readers who were under the divine training, and the circumstances in which they lived gave them the key to understand the books which were sent to them. Now, the readers of the five books of Moses were still in circumstances which made it suitable that they should have nothing else but the five books of Moses. The readers, on the other hand, of the Gospel, knew already that Jesus was the Son of God, and the Saviour. It was to those who, through the apostles, had obtained the knowledge of Christ that the Gospel record was sent. Before Christ came, of course, the Jews could do nothing else but read Moses and the prophets. They had no more. But now remember that Christ has come; Jerusalem is destroyed; the temple has vanished. There is no more the high-priest going into the Holy of Holies on the day of atonement. Paschal lambs are no. longer offered. The whole Levitical dispensation has disappeared. Israel is no longer in their own land. The circumstances in which the Jews now read the Old Testament prevent their understanding the Old Testament, without their acceptance of the New. It is impossible that they should understand the Old Testament. Why? Because of its not being a mere literary production, but the address of the living God to His people, in accordance with the circumstances and stage of history in which they are; and that stage of history, when the old Scriptures were given, having passed away, it is impossible that they should understand Moses and the prophets, and the fact has corroborated this. They do not understand them. I have shown you before that the very idea of God has been changed in the Jewish synagogue; that, instead of His being a living, condescending, self-communicating, friendly, redeeming God, He is regarded as an abstract conception of unity. The whole idea of the law has been changed. As the apostle says, the law is spiritual, but with the Jews the law has become a conglomeration of ceremonies, a number of precepts and injunctions. The feeling of the necessity of propitiation, of atonement, has vanished altogether, because for eighteen centuries nothing has reminded them of sacrifice; and, to accommodate themselves to their circumstances, they have changed the idea of sacrifice into the mere offering of thankfulness. The expectation of the Messiah also has disappeared, for, seeing that He came at the time when, according to the prophets, He must have come, and seeing that the Christians have always applied and urged these predictions, they have been obliged to invent other interpretations, in which the idea of the personal Messiah altogether departs into the background. A burnt child dreads the fire, and if the whole Jewish nation, with all their Hebrew learning, and with all the instinctive understanding which, after all, is still in their blood, have, for eighteen centuries, misinterpreted the Old Testament because they will not consider it in the light of the New Testament, I have no hope of the Gentiles understanding the Old Testament without the New Testament; for if we do not go to the Old Testament with the light and the ideas of the historical facts furnished to us in the New, let no man imagine, for that reason, that we go to it as little children, without any conceptions, prejudices, oppositions, and theories of our own. The practice of the Church of Christ from the beginning, based upon the example of Christ and the prophets, is binding upon us as Christians, commends itself to us as thinkers, and is ratified and corroborated by the experience of the Jews.

The last topic I can only briefly allude to, and it is this. The ancient books and the new books, the book of Israel and the book of the Church, have exactly the same structure. No twins could be more alike in figure and in feature. It is God who is the beginning, who redeems, who teaches, who guides, who commands; first come the manifestations of God in creation, in the promise of redemption, in the election of Abraham, in the bringing of Israel out of Egypt, in the planting of the tabernacle and of the whole Levitical dispensation — the mighty acts, words, institutions, gifts, and promises vouchsafed by God through Moses. That is the foundation. After that there comes the history, how these promises were carried out into actual reality and appropriated by the nation, with all their backslidings. This is in the so-called historical books, or, as the Jews call them, the earlier prophets. Then there is in the book of Psalms the response of the believer to what God has said, then the promise of the fulfilment and consummation of all God's purposes in the prophets. The order is the same in the New Testament. First comes, not what men think about God, but the incarnation, the history of Christ on earth. His death, resurrection, and ascension, the four gospels, just like the five books of Moses. Then there comes the history of how this was appropriated and actually carried out, the book of Acts, the planting of the Church in Israel, the planting of the Church among the Gentiles, and the response of believers to what is revealed, given in the various epistles, so that the epistles, to a certain extent, take the position of the Psalms, as the response of faith unto the great things of God. And then at last there comes the Apocalypse, showing how all the promises will be fulfilled. This is the first point.

The second point is this. In both Testaments, the beginning contains in germ everything that follows. Here we come to Schopenhauer's idea. All that is in the later historical books and in the prophets, is in the five books of Moses; and all that is in the Acts and in the epistles and in the Apocalypse is also in the four gospels. And the position of Moses as an individual, as the person, as the man that wrote the books, is most important, for he is not like any other prophet. It is perfectly indifferent who wrote the second book of Samuel or the Chronicles, but it is not indifferent who wrote the five books of Moses. Moses wrote them; for this Moses is not merely a law-giver; he is not merely a prophet; he is everything in one person. He is the human mediator upon whom the whole structure of the Jewish history and of the teaching of God in Israel rests. And in the books of Moses you find everything. There is no prophecy given by the later prophets which is not already contained in the books of Moses; as, for instance, that Israel shall be called back from all the ends of the earth, and by the grace and Spirit of God become again His people, and that all families of the earth shall be blessed in the seed of Abraham, and that God shall finally bruise Satan under our feet when the Lord comes. All are in the books of Moses. And in the same way the gospels contain all the teaching, afterwards more fully developed, and all the predictions which are in the subsequent parts, namely, the epistles, etc.

The third thing is this. Strictly speaking, all those elements are in all the books of Scripture; that is to say, there are no books of which we can say, "These are simply historical"; or books of which we can say, "These are simply prophetical"; or books of which we can say, "These are simply lyrical"; but all the books, and everything, as I have said, united together, planted together, wrought in together, with the most exquisite harmony — not with the harmony which we see in a book of genius, although that is a kind of illustration, but with the harmony which we see in everything on which *God* has breathed the breath of life. "Consider the lilies of the field." Why? Because God has clothed them, and therefore their beauty is *much greater* than anything which architecture or art of any kind can produce. The books of Moses are history; the books of Moses are teaching; the books of Moses are prophecy. The Psalms are not merely prayers, but prophecy. In the books of the prophets we have history. Thus, in the prophet Isaiah, the history of Hezekiah; in the prophet Jeremiah, the history of his own days; in the prophet Daniel the history of God's manifestations at the court of the pagan monarchs. And so it is also in the other Book. The gospels contain history and teaching and response, like the psalms of Mary and of Zacharias and of Simeon. And as to prophecy — the epistles are full of prophecy, until, at last, all the prophecy of the later scripture culminates in the Apocalypse, as the former scriptures had done in Daniel, the man greatly beloved, in whose book not merely Israel's future is predicted, but the future of the whole world; so all the scattered prophecy in the gospels and the epistles, and in the whole preceding scripture, culminates in that book which, in the latter days, as it was in the first ages of the Church, will become the beloved book of the Church — the revelation which God gave to His Son Jesus Christ.

And now let me just say one word about our Lord's return. Oh, not as a question of exegesis, not as a topic of polemic discussion, does it behove us to speak of this great, solemn, and most blessed hope. "Surely I come quickly." Of all announcements of Scripture, it is the one that most stirs up the depths of our conscience and of our heart. Sometimes, when we feel overwhelmed with a sense of our sin, unworthiness, and unfaithfulness, the question arises, "And am I one of the wise virgins who have oil in their lamps, and shall I be numbered among those that are ready to go in when the Bridegroom comes?" And at other times when, by the grace of the Lord Jesus Christ, the Holy Spirit bears witness with our spirits that we are the Sons of God, the solemnity is even more overwhelming in its sweetness and blessedness. And is it possible that He, whom having not seen we love, shall be at last seen by us face to face — that we shall see Him as He is, not as at present, by laboriously combining all the different aspects of His wonderful person and work, but by a glance, by an immediate vision, by the complete and comprehensive understanding of our enlarged and glorified faculties, behold Him as He is, and be like Him? Meanwhile, to us who have this hope, and who by this hope are entirely separated from the present age — not merely in its wickedness, but also in its pretended goodness; not merely in its frivolity, but also in its wisdom and in its culture — unto us poor, isolated, unknown, and enigmatic people there is the Word of God, the holy and beloved Scriptures of the prophets and of the apostles; and ye do well to take heed to them as unto a light shining in a dark place, until you see the bright morning star; and when that morning star comes, soon shall the Sun of Righteousness rise with healing in His wings, to bring us gladness, strength, and power to glorify God, and to reign with the Lord Jesus on the earth. Amen.

XII - Our Faith Based on Facts, and the Bible A Book of Facts

There are two points which I wish to bring before you this morning: that the Scripture history supplies us with the facts and principles upon which all true philosophical and universal history is based. And the second point is this: that the history, recorded in the books of Moses, and of the other writers, of the ancient dispensation, contains actual and real history.

In my last lecture I endeavoured to show why it is that we cannot understand Moses and the prophets, without the apostolic light of the gospels and the epistles, and to this I wish only to add one remark. Nothing can be said in stronger terms, concerning the evangelical history of the ancient Scriptures, than the simple remark which the apostle Paul made to Timothy, that the Scriptures "arc able to make thee wise unto salvation, through faith which is in Christ Jesus." And although there are many things, both in the ancient history and in the ancient prophecy, which will be fully explained and manifested only at the second coming of our blessed Saviour, still, as we are told both by the apostle Paul and by the apostle Peter, the whole Old Testament was written, in order that it may be understood by the Church of Jesus Christ, who live in the latter days, and unto whom there has been granted the privilege of seeing the fulfilment of God's promise; for so the apostle Peter says with regard to prophecy — that through suffering the Messiah should enter into that glory, — that it was revealed to the prophets that not to themselves, but to us, they did testify of these things. And of the ancient history, the apostle Paul declares in his epistle to the Romans that all these things happened for our example, and were written for our admonition, upon whom the ends of the world have come. Seeing, therefore, that we have the fulness of the Gospel light, and that there have been manifested to us these histories, it is for us to enter into the consideration of Moses and the prophets, in the full assurance and expectation that the Holy Ghost has there treasured up for us all that is profitable and needful for our instruction and guidance, in connection with that fuller development of history and teaching which we now possess.

A combination of history, teaching, prophecy, with the subjective response of the congregation, both in works of reflection and in the lyrical outpourings of their feelings, is something altogether unique; and it is a combination which corresponds to all the different wants and necessities of mankind, as they arise in the course of centuries; and, while it corresponds with our need, it is the only kind of book of revelation worthy of Him from whom it emanates. Ideas without facts make up a philosophy. Facts without ideas may make up a history. But that which we need is something which appeals not merely to our intellect, but also to our conscience and to our heart, and that which so appeals must be the revelation of God. And, if it is the revelation of God, it can only be the revelation of God, coming down out of His infinite eternity, into our time and into our space. It must record the initiative, creative, and redemptive acts of the Most High; and, in recording these acts, it must contain a revelation of His character and of His purpose, of His commandments concerning us, and of the promises by which He sustains us. And only in Scripture have we such a combination. All Scripture facts are full of ideas. So to speak, they are full of eyes, and light shines to us in them. And all Scripture ideas, the things which we believe and the things which we hope for, are based upon actual facts — manifestations of the Most High. If a Christian is asked, "What is your belief? what is your faith?" he does not answer by enumerating dogmas, in the sense of abstract philosophical truths; but he answers by saying that he believes in God who created, in God who became incarnate, and died, and rose again, and in God who sent the Holy Ghost to renew his heart. So what is our creed but facts; but such facts as are full of light, and in which God manifests Himself to us?

Again, the name of God, and that name, which we should not know without the Bible, is "Jehovah"; and "Jehovah" has this meaning: first, that He is sovereign, self-subsisting, and eternal; but, secondly, that He has become the God of history, and is in history; and, thirdly, that He is the God who is coming, who is fulfilling His promises, and who will consummate all the counsel which was in Him in eternity. And as this simple name, Jehovah, contains all Scripture history, all Scripture teaching, and all Scripture prophecy, so the people who accept this name "Jehovah" live in the past, and in the present, and in the future. To live merely in the past by memory is a kind of death, in which there is no activity, but simply regret. To live merely in the present, without remembering the past and looking forward to the future, is unworthy of man who was created in the image of God. To think merely of the future is simply a work of imagination and reverie. But past, present, and future — Jehovah who was, Jehovah who is, and Jehovah who is to come — this is what fills up the whole of man. He lives by memory; he lives by present communion; he lives by hope; and all the saints of God from Enoch, the seventh from Adam, until those who shall be alive at Christ's coming, remember the merciful deeds of God in the past, live in communion with the present-living God, and look forward to the glorious consummation of God's purposes. So all Scripture must be viewed in the light of history; and in this history, teaching, prophecy, and the response of the congregation are comprehended.

The Bible is a book separate from all other books, and high above all other books. That is quite true. On the other hand, the Bible is connected with all other books in the world; and, as all things must work together for good to them that love God, so all books that are written, even those that are written against the Bible, contribute to the corroboration and to the illustration of the Scriptures. Joseph was considered a dreamer and very ambitious, and yet, after all, his dream was fulfilled that all the sheaves of his brethren did obeisance before his sheaf. And thus is it that all books that ever were written, on whatever subject, must contribute to show forth that Scripture is the book of books. As a French socialist who had no faith in Scripture has said, "It is a strange thing that we cannot think on any subject but in a few minutes we come to theology."

So far, then, from granting that Scripture does not encourage the cultivation of our faculties, and the zealous investigation of truth in all its different departments, we see that Scripture is the very basis upon which all activity of mind is founded, and that all books are written in order that this one book may be understood; for there is no book in the world which so encourages the use of our reason and the active employment of all the mental faculties that God has bestowed upon us. It sets a high value on knowledge, and it continually counsels us to get wisdom. As a revelation addressing itself to man, an intellectual and responsible being, it at once quickens all his powers, and wherever the Bible has been, human knowledge has made progress.

Although the Bible does not interfere in any way with all those different branches of knowledge with which man is occupied, it connects itself with them all. No book in the world exhibits such a love of nature, such a diligent and careful observation of nature, as Scripture, — such is the testimony of Alexander von Humboldt, — and yet Scripture does not come into conflict or collision with any investigation or with any intellectual activity, defining exactly the limits which must be assigned to them, and reserving for itself that special place which, as a revelation from God, belongs to it.

In my next lecture, when I have to speak on the miraculous character of Scripture, I shall endeavour to show that this applies especially to science, and that not merely is there no collision between Scripture and science, but that without the scriptural idea of God and this world, and of this world forming one whole or cosmos, there would be no legitimate and thorough foundation, upon which science could build its superstructure. To-day my subject is rather with regard to history.

The Bible history is peculiar. It is a theological history. The selection of evidence, and the way in which the evidences are narrated, show that all the historical books were written by men of the prophetic spirit. It aims at illustrating God's dealings with men. It desires to show how the salvation which is in Jesus Christ was prepared. It wishes to lay down all the threads which are to be taken up, when the whole counsel of God shall be fulfilled.

But although the Scripture pursues its method thus, it throws light upon history in general. What is history? There is a very natural tendency of man to write down events which strike him as remarkable. It is a natural thing for a family to keep a chronicle or a diary of things that happen, and to preserve genealogies. The Egyptians could not allow anything remarkable to pass, without writing down an accurate description of it. There is a chronicle style of history which we trace in most ancient nations — exceedingly tiresome, because there is constant repetition, which, in the course of centuries, becomes endless — dynasty succeeding dynasty, war following upon war, and the different vicissitudes and the different developments of various branches barely recorded. The Romans and the Greeks had a higher style of history, yet, after all, the Romans and the Greeks did not reach the true method of history, for in the true method of history it is necessary that the whole human race should be regarded as forming one family, and the ancient nations had not this idea at all. They thought that, in the various countries of which they had any knowledge, the inhabitants, as it were, had sprung out of the earth, and that they were not connected with the nations of other countries, so that the Greeks looked down upon all the rest of the world as barbarians, and the Romans looked down upon all the rest of the world as people to be subjugated to their empire. The true idea of history as it lives now among us, even among people who do not know whence they have obtained that idea, is this — that humanity is a unity, and that events not merely succeed each other with constant iteration, but that there is a purpose in them; in fact, that history leads to some goal and to some end. And also we have got this idea, that it would be altogether impossible and unprofitable simply to chronicle all the events which happen to all the different nations and tribes of the earth, and that our great object is to select those nations, and to select those events, which stand in direct and vital connection with the whole stream of history, and which contribute something to the development of the whole race. During the last years there has appeared a history which has astonished and delighted the civilized world. The veteran historian, Ranke, has attempted to write a world-history, a history of history, selecting only those nations, and, in those nations, only those events and movements which have contributed to the general history; but whence did Ranke and all other modern historians get that idea, but from the Bible? Mark this: from the Bible — nowhere else. I had occasion to quote to you the words of a great man of science, that the beginning and the end of things are both absolutely hidden to science. Science has to do with phenomena, but the beginning of things and the end of things are both absolutely untouchable by science. The same may be said of history; and yet, unless we know the beginning of our race, the unity of our race, and that all the different nations of the world are related to one another, how is it possible for us to conceive the idea of a world-history? Again, unless we have the idea of providence, — of God, who sees the end from the beginning, who guides and overrules things for His own glory and for the good of humanity — it is a hopeless thing to read history. It leads to nothing. It is like a vessel that is drifting, tossed to and fro by the waves of the sea, without having some one to guide it, and bring it to its appointed goal.

But, thirdly, what is that end, and what is that goal? What a curious thing it is that before geography had made any great progress, the Bible anticipated that the whole earth would be inhabited, that the uttermost ends of the earth would be peopled, and that the whole earth would be united in the knowledge and worship of one God, and in righteousness, and in prosperity. You remember that Moses said, that when the Most High divided to the sons of Adam their inheritance. He did it according to the number of the children of Israel. And this is the very thing that the apostle Paul preached to the Athenians — the philosophy of history. He says, "God has made of one blood all the nations of the earth" — not, as you imagine, that you Athenians are of a different blood from the barbarians. Not merely has He done this, but He fixed the bounds of their habitations, as well as regulated the different periods and epochs of their history. Here you have a chronology, and here you have a geography, and here you have a teleology which is of that purpose or aim that alone gives eyes to history. Without it, history would be like a body without eyes. Is it not a wonderful thing?

And as for the beginning of the human race, no inquiring mind, no lover of humanity, no enthusiastic pursuer of history can rest satisfied without asking himself the question: What was the beginning of the human race? All things in both physiology and ethnology, as well as in all the sciences which bear upon the subject, confirm the idea of the unity of the human race, and also that all human language was originally one. Max Müller has often asserted that the more languages are examined, notwithstanding all their diversity, the more it is seen that they consist of a very few elementary roots, and that they must all have originated in one common source; and as another philologer says, it is just as when an earthquake has come, and has broken up what formerly was one continuous mass: you see the parts are diverse, but you see that they formerly were a unity.

The 10th chapter of the book of Genesis is a very remarkable chapter. Before God leaves, as it were, the nations to themselves, and begins to deal with Israel, His chosen people from Abraham downwards. He takes a loving farewell of all the nations of the earth, as much as to say, "I am going to leave you for a while, but I love you: I have created you: I have ordered all your future"; and their different genealogies are traced. Ranke says of this chapter, "It is impossible to read this chapter without seeing that there is something here different from all other history, and that the national pride and separation which we see everywhere else has here been entirely subjugated by the religious idea that all the different tribes of the earth are related to one another by their common descent from Shem, Ham, and Japheth."

More than that. The end of history is given to us in Scripture, and here it is. Whereas, as I have said before, the common view of history that is taken in the world, and taken also by many Christians, is the real reason why the Bible is not believed, and why many who profess to believe the Bible, if they knew what was in the Bible, would also reject it. But the history of the world is given to us in Scripture, without entering into the history of the different nations. That was not necessary. For that we do not require a revelation — as to write a history of the Greeks, and of the French, and of the Russians. That we can do ourselves. But to show us what is the programme, what is the divine idea, what is the real way and purpose of this history — for that we do require the teaching of the Most High.

Now, this is the history. From the fall of Adam there goes down a line in which judgment succeeds judgment. There is also a line in which deliverance and grace succeed deliverance and grace. The fall of Adam, the banishment from Paradise, the wickedness of the world in the days of Noah; the Flood; the judgment on the Tower of Babel; the judgment upon Israel at the destruction of Jerusalem; the judgment upon an apostate Christendom and the anti-Christ, when our Lord comes. This is the downward line. But there is an upward line of grace. There are the Sethites, who called upon the name of Jehovah. In the Flood, Noah and his household are saved to form the beginning of a new period. After the destruction of Babel, Abraham is selected to form again the beginning of a new period. After the destruction of Jerusalem, we have already a church both of Jews and Gentiles to form the beginning of history till after the coming of Christ, to destroy the anti-Christ with his might and power, and to judge the anti-Christian nations. There is the godly remnant of Israel, there are the nations of the earth, and there is the Church of Christ, which is transformed and with Christ.

The Babylonish captivity is an event of great importance in God's plan of history. Babel at first was the human race combining their own resources of strength and wisdom and culture, for the Cainites were the beginning of culture, music, and art. It is the combination of humanity, relying upon their own power, wisdom, and culture, to form an independent and united organism, without God; and from that day, Babel became a type of the world-power as opposing God, until at last we read in the book of Revelation, "Babylon is fallen, is fallen."

Now, when Babel was judged, Abraham rose. Again, when Israel was judged, Babylon rose. From the time that Israel was led into captivity, until Christ comes again and restores Israel to His own land, is one period. It is "the times of the Gentiles," during which there is no outward and visible theocracy or Christocracy. This was revealed in a dream to Nebuchadnezzar, which was interpreted by the Most High to. Daniel, the "man greatly beloved." And here we have an outline of the whole history of the world — gold, silver, brass, iron, clay. Outside this seen world there comes a crisis, and this passes away, and there comes a new crisis. This shows us the outward character of the world-kingdom, which, contrary to our usual idea, is not a progressive but a deteriorating one, for the metals deteriorate as we go on, by which we are taught that a nation which is extremely civilised and advanced may, in God's estimation, be much inferior to a nation which is only at the beginning of this process. Civilisation is a very good thing. That we have railways, and telegraphs, and intercourse between nation and nation, is of great importance. But though many live by those things, rely upon those things, boast of those things, and think that these are the kingdom of God, it is perfectly evident that such is not God's estimate. Such is not even the verdict of history, for the most civilised nations, as Greece and Rome, perished by their very civilisation. The things in which the life of a nation consists are righteousness and justice, reverence and obedience to the sanctity of the family life, and not culture. Let the whole race of Adam reach the highest point of civilisation and unity, and it may be, as the Colossus, ready for destruction.

But the 7th chapter of Daniel shows us the inward character of the world-kingdoms, namely, Babylonian, Persian, Graeco-Macedonian, and lastly Roman, under which we still live. They have to be compared to beasts; that is to say, they have not the character of humanity. They are strong, they are cunning, they are wise; but they have not the mind and heart of man, until the

Son of Man comes down from heaven, and unto Him is given the dominion. That is the Scripture sketch of history.

Now here I have left out the consideration of the Christian Church; and in Daniel its origin only is left out. Do not misunderstand me. The Old Testament prophecy sees the first coming of Christ clearly, but it sees it as a point and not as a line. It sees the second coming of Christ not merely as a point, but also as a line. But the Church of Christ is exactly in the same position, as regards the world, as that in which Israel was as regards the nations. As the apostle says, "He has redeemed you out of the world," and as Christ says, "Ye are not of the world, and my kingdom is not of the world"; it will come into the world, but it is not of the world.

And now let me go on to the next point. This latter point will come up again for our consideration when I view the Jewish history in its prophetic light.

I wish now to speak of the actual reality of the Jewish history. This is a very important point. I wish to say, in the first place, that the Bible professes to be history. There is no distinction made in the Bible between certain parts of this history and other parts — some which are more credible than the others, some which are more historical — none whatever. The prophets, our blessed Lord, and the apostles, treat all the parts of Bible history on a perfect level. The serpent that tempted Eve is a historical fact. The Flood and all the things that are narrated in the earlier portion of the Bible, just as much as in the later are historical facts. There is no distinction made.

Now, I wish to treat this subject with all fairness. I say it is exceedingly difficult for a man to accept the history of the Bible, not because there is not abundant evidence of its truth coming out every day, of its historical and geographical accuracy; there the difficulty does not lie. The difficulty lies in this, that the things which are spiritual — and, above all, God Himself — can only be the object of faith; and this whole Bible history is a history in which God is the great agent, and Israel only responding to His agency, and afterwards the Church only responding to His agency.

Now, people have said — and it is quite natural — "The Jews are not the only nation of antiquity. There are a great many other nations." We notice in the history of all other nations that the early portion of their history is full of wonderful things, what we must call "myths." A myth is not a lie, but it is not a historical reality. There is generally some basis of fact in every myth, some hero, some great wonderful event which actually existed. But a myth is not historically true. It is the action of imagination and of reflection, which, as it were, spin out a narrative in order to illustrate some truth, or to represent some idea. Now, we find Grecian history and Roman history in their early stages to be mythology; but when the Greeks advanced in knowledge and in their whole intellectual activity, they rejected their early mythology; and so we find that Plato and other thinkers, both among the Greeks and among the Romans, criticised their early history with great severity and irony. And for this there was a twofold reason. In the first place, the myths themselves were so grotesque and so evidently fabulous that it was impossible to believe them, except in an age of childhood, when people do not seek for truth, but rather for amusement, as children like to hear something that is imaginative, knowing themselves that it is not true, and yet not analysing whether it is reality or not. It pleases them, and it also, perhaps, instructs them in some degree. That was one reason of the criticism. But the other reason was this. These mythologies are full of immorality. The gods and heroes of which these mythologies speak are by no means illustrative of a high ideal of human character; and as the conscience was aroused in these men, and they knew what were truth and honesty and magnanimity and the different virtues which men ought to have, they said, "It is pernicious to exalt such gods and heroes, because the influence of them is immoral." So in proportion as light advanced, and in proportion as the conscience was roused by reflection, ancient history was discarded. That is perfectly true.

But now I come to the Scripture history, and upon this very fact I base an argument. The argument, in short, is this: that, because there is a good deal of base coin circulating, that is no proof that there is not genuine coin, the superscription of which is that of God the Lord Himself. As the idols of the nations were either nothings, or simply heroes or demons, so the mythology concerning them docs not belong to the realm of fact, but of fiction. But as the God of Israel, which is our postulate, is the true God, the living God who created the heavens and the earth, the history which tells of Him does not belong to the realm of fiction, but belongs to the realm of truth.

And, secondly, the Greeks and Romans, as they advanced, discarded their early history, but the people of Israel as they advanced, and (to speak with reverence, and humanly) as Israel reached its culmination in Jesus Christ and in the apostles, their regard for their ancient history did not decrease, but rather advanced, and the God of Abraham, Isaac, and Jacob is the God of Jesus Christ; and thus the apostle Peter preaches, "The God of Abraham, Isaac, and Jacob hath glorified His child Jesus." And Abraham, Isaac, and Jacob are no mythical characters. There is nothing about them that is fictitious. They are not described as being different from other men. Theirs is a most intensely human history; and so the word "patriarch" has remained up to this day to describe what is genuine, unsophisticated, real humanity. No miracles were performed by these men. There is nothing in the record, showing that there was an intention of putting a halo around them, or of regarding them as demigods.

But the second argument is this. The tone of the historical books of Scripture is sober, severe, unadorned, negligent, as regards the form. The myths of the ancients, because they were not fact, required all the embellishment which poetry and rhetoric could give them in order to make them attractive. But the history of creation and paradise, of the patriarchs and Moses, of the children of Israel in the wilderness, of David, of Christ, and of the apostles, requires no ornamentation. It is quite true that there is nothing so grand, because there is nothing so pathetic, there is nothing so beautiful, as these beautiful histories. But the authors of these books did not want to make them beautiful. It is not the result of art You know how, in poems and in books of fiction, there is great art in the grouping of things, in making the complication of the knot as exciting and interesting as possible, and in leading up everything to a grand dramatic solution at the end. We have nothing of that in Scripture. Sometimes, when the history is, so to speak, most exciting, there comes a long interruption, a chapter of names and genealogies, and a statement of stations and places, as if the man who wrote it was just noting down the facts, and entirely careless of producing any effect of art. This is the divine negligence of style which is grander than all human art.

Again. In all other histories we find an element which has to be largely discounted. Niebuhr says that the Old Testament history is the only exception to ancient history, in that it is free from what he calls all "national patriotic falsehood." What that means is evident. The other nations always wished to magnify themselves. They are never defeated in battle, or if they are defeated in battle, it is owing to some extraordinary perfidy and some very extraordinary combination of circumstances, and they always aim at glorifying themselves. You see this tendency continually breaking out, even unintentionally. But Israel's history is a history that shows what a wicked, ungrateful, bad nation they were, and how God punished them by making other nations come and subdue them; and so the defeat of Israel is not merely narrated faithfully, but a most humiliating reason is given for that defeat — "Because Israel forgot the Lord, and walked not in the way of His commandments." That is another very remarkable element in sacred history. What other nation has so recorded its iniquity, and the constant chastisement which it drew down from heaven?

There is another evidence of its veracity, and it is this. In other histories we see the great tendency to hero-worship. The historian has some favourite character. He wants to show what a grand man that was. The Bible never wants to show what a grand man anybody was. There is no hero-worship in the Bible. I have already referred to that which is made an objection against the Bible— that Abraham and Jacob and Moses and David are so full of faults and sins, and Peter denied Christ thrice, etc. There is no hero-worship in the Bible. Israel and the Church have great men; but what was their greatness? Read the nth chapter of the epistle to the Hebrews. Faith was their greatness; or, in other words, their greatness was, that they were nothing, but that they trusted in God. Now, that is another argument for the actual history.

I come to a third argument, very important. I have already alluded to the genealogies. Of course when people read these genealogies, or, rather, do not read them, they think, "Why is so much of the Bible taken up with a dry list of names?" Well, it is dry to us, but it is not dry in itself These genealogies are of the greatest importance in proving the historic character of these books. The book of Genesis is made up, as it were, of ten genealogies, into which the history is framed. The book of Exodus begins by a very cool and prosaic enumeration of the families descended from Jacob. The book of Chronicles, at its beginning, chapter after chapter, contains nothing but a list of names. What an extraordinary thing this is! Now, notice, if a man writes a fiction which he wants to have the appearance of truth, like Robinson Crusoe, he will make use of this in an artistic way, to a certain extent, to give an air of verisimilitude, as in Hg>mer we find a catalogue of the ships. But look at these statements in the Bible. Look at the book of Numbers, — a description, with the names of all the stations where they halted, and the distances. Is this fiction? Look where these interruptions and these genealogies are placed, and you will see that it is not done by an artist, but by one who states that which is true. And what wonderful disclosures in the names! I will mention only one instance, the names of Moses' parents, Amram and Jochebed. The parents of Moses, living in Egypt, lived by faith in the God of Abraham, Isaac, and Jacob, and they knew the things and the truths recorded in Genesis, although the book was not in existence. The facts were in existence. Amram means "the nation that is exalted." Jochebed means "to Jehovah belongs the glory." Are not all the five books of Moses in these two names? Whence came these names? These genealogies and statistical statements which we find throughout the Bible, down to the New Testament, where Matthew begins with a genealogy, are a very strong proof of the historic character of the Scripture.

I wish to mention another point that is very striking. The Bible history is quite different from all other history. I not merely admit this, but the point of my address is to prove that it is different from all other histories. Yet it always keeps sight of the other nations. We never, as it were, leave the coast. We are always reminded that we are on *terra firma*. The monuments and inscriptions that have been discovered within the last thirty years have brought to light the accuracy of the allusions in Scripture to surrounding nations and to the earlier world. Professor Dawson has written a very interesting book on the Lands of the Bible, in which he throws much light upon the position of Paradise. This has been a subject of research among the Assyriologists. I quote a sentence from one, who is a great German authority on Assyriology. He says, "The 14th chapter of Genesis, in which there is recorded the war of the four kings with the five kings, has been proved by lately discovered cuneiform inscriptions to be the grandest relic of ancient Scripture history." That is a wonderful fact. Take, again, the history of Egypt. It was once objected that, because it was mentioned that the king of Egypt made a present to Abraham, in which were included asses, camels, and sheep, the narrative could not be true, because, at a later period of Egyptian history, it was found that Egyptians kept no sheep, and had no camels, and had a great abhorrence of asses. But the latest discoveries have shown, that in the more ancient period there were rich men in Egypt who possessed thousands of sheep, while bones of dromedaries have been found; so that this statement has proved to be a confirmation instead of an objection. And — to mention the name of a writer whose works of fiction may be known to many of you, and who is a great authority on Egypt — Ebers declares that the whole narrative of Joseph, and the picture it gives of the history and the customs and the spirit of Egypt at that time, is most faithful and accurate. Then we have the Egypt of the time of Moses. Then we have the other nations of which we read in the earlier Scriptures, — the Assyrians, the Babylonians, the Persians, all the surrounding nations, — always kept in view. The whole ancient history is referred to, although the Scripture only touches upon it, because in the Scripture view the great and mighty conquerors were of no vast importance; and all those great kingdoms, under which men at that time trembled, the Scripture knew to be ephemeral. It says in the 40th chapter of Isaiah that they will not take root, and that they will not be found in future on the earth, while Israel should abide. Thus the incidental light the Old Testament throws upon the surrounding history is confirmed, and makes us perceive that real history is related.

In the New Testament, in the gospel of Luke and the Acts, because Luke's was eminently an historical mind, we find the birth of Jesus in Bethlehem, the miracle of miracles; He was conceived of the Holy Ghost and born of the Virgin Mary; but it happened on this earth of ours; in Judaea, and in Judaea at a certain time; when Caesar Augustus was the emperor of Rome, there went forth the edict, that all the world should be taxed; and again in the book of Acts there is constant reference to the Roman history of the time.

I sum up by saying that the evidence for the accurate veracity of the history of the Bible is accumulating day by day, and comes to us from all sources, and, if I may so speak, from independent and impartial, and oftentimes hostile, sources. I believe that it is all actual history. I believe that the evidence of its veracity is very great, and yet at the same time I must confess that it is difficult, that it is impossible, to realise it, unless there is given to us grace. The Scripture history does not demand credit merely. The Scripture history demands faith. We can prove to a person that it is impossible to account for the apostolic Church, if Jesus did not rise from the dead. Here is an effect, and there is no cause to produce it; and then all these men said publicly in Jerusalem that Jesus was risen from the dead. We can also prove to him from the different statements of the Gospel narratives that this is a fact and not an imagination, the disciples themselves not expecting it, and, after it had happened, scarcely able to believe it; and yet he will not be convinced that Jesus Christ is risen from the dead. A man may say, "I cannot disbelieve it," but not disbelieving a thing is different from believing it. He says, "I cannot contradict it." He says, "I cannot account for it in any other way," but still he does not realise it. I find that when the apostles preached to unbelievers that Jesus Christ was risen from the dead, they did not produce a mass of evidence and say, "We will prove it to you. It was only a few weeks ago that you saw Him crucified. You know what was done to the sepulchre, and that there was the stone and the seal and the Roman guard; and He has appeared to Peter, and

He has appeared to Thomas, and He has appeared to these women, and He has appeared to five hundred. We can prove it to you." Afterwards, when Paul wrote to believers, to the Christian Church at Corinth, when heresy had sprung up regarding the resurrection, he says, "I preached unto you that Christ was risen according to the Scriptures, and that He appeared on such and such different occasions." But the apostles preached the resurrection of Christ as a divine fact, as in accordance with the prophecies, as a link in a great chain which God made, and therefore the acquiescence on the part of the audience was not credence, but faith. Ah, wonder of all wonders, that on this earth of ours He by whom this earth was called into existence lived thirty-three years, that the sun which was created by Him shone upon Him, that He ate our bread and drank water out of the springs of our habitation, that He lived among men, and that with Him also there was yesterday, and to-day, and to-morrow, that He wept human tears, and that He died upon the cross, and that His blessed feet shall stand again upon the Mount of Olives, and that on this earth there shall be again a miraculous divine history. It needs faith, faith. It is a mystery of godliness, and blessed are we if we believe.

Bible history to us is not a matter of indifference, nor merely does it satisfy our intelligence, but it is our very life and consolation.

XIII - Objections to Miracle Have No Basis in Reason

The subject of this morning's lecture is the supernatural and the miraculous character of Bible history. Abundant and various as are the evidences, and the corroborative testimonies attesting the truthfulness and accuracy of Bible history, yet, as I stated at the conclusion of my last lecture, this Bible history requires not merely credence on the part of man, but also faith. And this seems at first sight a contradiction, because if there is sufficient evidence to attest the truthfulness of a history, then the human intellect, unaided, ought to be able to receive this history. But the reason why the human intellect is not able to realise this history, is not because there is any lack of evidence to attest its veracity, but because it is a history of a supernatural and miraculous character. It is the revelation of God, and of a kingdom which is spiritual and eternal; it is the manifestation and development in time, of the counsels of redemption, which God had in Himself, before the foundations of the world were laid; and it is because God, and the things that refer to the eternal and spiritual kingdom, are inwoven into this history, that without the light and power of the Holy Ghost man is unable to realise it. And therefore this history is an object of faith, and faith is the gift of God.

As God, who is unseen, reveals Himself in this history, and the plan which He has purposed in Himself develops in this history, we are brought altogether out of the region and realm of that which is seen, and that which can be apprehended by human reason, or taken cognisance of by the limited powers of human intellect. It is here that the opposition of science has always come into collision with that which has been the object of the faith of Christ's Church. But, as I endeavoured to show in my last lecture, that not merely does history not come into collision with the records of the Bible, but that the Bible alone contains the facts and the principles upon which a philo-sophical and universal history can be based, so I may also assert that there is no collision whatever between science, if science keeps to its own limits, and that revelation of God and a supernatural kingdom which is given to us in the Scripture, They who do not believe in a personal God, but are atheists or pan-theists, cannot logically accept the possibility of miracles; but all who believe that there is a living God, full of wisdom, and of power, and of love, can find no difficulty in accepting a testimony which shows us that God reveals Him-self, and that God acts here upon earth, and within the history of mankind. Therefore, all that the Scripture tells us of God and of the unseen world, in-stead of interfering with the discoveries of science, only lays the basis and firm foundation for the activity of science. To quote a man who. speaks of this subject with authority, Professor Dawson, "Any rational or successful pursuit of science implies the feeling of a community between the Author and Con-triver and Ruler of nature, and the mind which can understand it. To science nature must be a cosmos, not a fortuitous chaos, and everything in the histo-ry and arrangements of the universe must be a manifestation not only of or-der, but of design. The true man of science must believe in a divine creative will, in a God who manifests Himself, and is therefore not the hypothetical God of the agnostic; in a God who must be distinct from and above material things, and therefore not the shadowy God of the pantheist, who is every-where and yet nowhere; in a God who causes the unity and uniformity of na-ture, and therefore not one of the many gods of polytheism; in a God who acts on His rational creatures daily in a thousand ways by His fatherly regard for their welfare, and who reveals Himself to them; a God, in short, who made the world and all things therein, and who made man in His own image and likeness." And with this corresponds the fact that science has only pros-pered in Christendom, and that the nations who are polytheists, or who are pantheists, are not able to cultivate science for the simple reason that they do not believe in God, who is the creator and upholder of all things; and there-fore the phenomena, of which they take cognisance, have not to them any coherence and unity, attributing as they do the different things which they see to the powers of nature, or to personifications of these powers. But we who believe in a living God, although we see nature and trace the laws of na-ture, yet do not conceive of these laws of nature as if they put any limits to the power of God or to the liberty of God. He who has made the laws, for laws pre-suppose a law-giver, uses them as His servants and as His medium, but He asserts within them, and above them, His own power and His own wis-dom. Therefore it is the same thing whether the heathen nations deify the various powers of nature separately, and worship the sun or the moon, or the god of the ocean, or the god of trees, or whether scientific men worship nature as a whole and as an organism. This idolatry of nature and of the laws of nature is the very thing against which the miracles which are recorded in Scripture history do testify, declaring to us that Jehovah is the God who hath made the heavens and the earth, and who ruleth over all. If there is a kingdom which is visible, and which has its inexorable laws, there is likewise a kingdom which at present is unseen, the laws of which are still more inexorable and more binding. There is a kingdom of which science can take no cognisance. There is God; there are angels; there is the kingdom of evil, with Satan at its head; there is the inheritance that is incorruptible and undefiled, and that fadeth not away — even heaven; there is the abyss which is prepared for Satan and his angels. Now, of all this unseen kingdom which is ruled over by God the Lord we know nothing, except by the revelation of the Most High, both in His word and in our hearts, through the Holy Spirit. The laws of the spiritual kingdom are, if comparison be possible, far more stringent and far more unchangeable than the laws of this outer world which we can trace. But more than that. Before God ever thought and carried into execution the creation of heaven and earth, as we see them now, there was, in the depths of the Divine Mind, the idea of the new heavens and the new earth wherein dwelleth righteousness; of a new creation in Christ Jesus, in which there would be no sin and no sorrow; of a new race born again of the Spirit, to whom it would be impossible ever to fall away from communion with God. And it was only because of this purpose, which He purposed in Himself before the foundations of the world were laid, that the heavens and the earth which we behold were created, and that the whole history took place which is recorded in Scripture, and which culminates in Christ, and which shall end in the manifestation of His glory. Therefore this is the God who, out of this unseen realm, in order to carry out the purposes of His love, manifests Himself in that history which is recorded in Scripture; and this is the law which, out of the unseen world, is made manifest in the visible world: "With man it is impossible, but with God all things are possible." Salvation is of Jehovah, and of Jehovah exclusively. Only by the intervention of divine power and wisdom, actuated by love, can man be redeemed, this world transformed, and the kingdom of the Most High set up upon earth. Hence the eternal necessity, founded in the very essence of things, of the supernatural and miraculous, in the history of redemption. When we come in this light to the consideration of the Old Testament history, which can never for a moment be separated from Christ, — for without Christ it could never have taken place, without Christ it could never have been carried out, without Christ it could have had no end and no purpose — I say, when we come to the consideration of the miracles recorded in the sacred history in this light, then what we cannot comprehend appears full of wisdom and consistency.

And before I enter on the enumeration of the special points, let me remind you of a few facts in connection with the miracles. It has been said that miracle is beyond nature, and that miracle is above nature, and that miracle is against nature. It would be better to say that miracle is entirely apart from nature. In miracle, for great reasons and purposes, God acts here upon earth, apart from the laws of nature. The thing that is important in a miracle is not that something extraordinary has happened for which we can give no account as to its origination; but the important thing in a miracle is that God acts. It is nothing to say that something remarkable has happened, and that we are not able to account for the phenomenon. The essence of a miracle is this, that God interferes, that God acts, to reveal Himself and to carry out His purposes. Therefore every miracle is regarded in the Bible as full of teaching and instruction. It is the revelation, the manifestation, the exposition of God's character and purpose. Those miracles that occur in the Bible are not isolated and unconnected with one another, but are all links in a chain, and by these links the history of God's kingdom upon earth is carried on, for without them it could not have been carried on. They appear at the important junctures and times of crisis when, to speak with reverence, it is necessary, according to the divine wisdom, that God should interfere. And further, it is a mistake to say that in these miracles the laws of nature are suspended. The laws of nature are by no means suspended. When Jesus changed the water into wine at the marriage at Cana, all water was not changed into wine. All the water that was in Cana was not changed into wine. Only this water upon which the will of Christ acted was so changed. If, when the axe of iron was cast into the water, somebody else had cast an axe of iron into the water, it would have sunk. The laws of specific gravity were not suspended, but in this particular instance there was an action of the divine omnipotence, for His gracious purposes. And nothing illustrates this principle more than that most remarkable instance of the divine power — God raising the dead. When our blessed Saviour raised the little maid. He said, "Give her something to eat." The laws of nature were not suspended. He raised the little child, and, immediately after He had raised the little child, there was not the slightest disturbance upon the face of the waters of nature; she had immediately to go back again to the general course. And when He raised the young man, the son of the widow of Nain, He gave him back to his mother; and when He raised Lazarus, who had been four days in the grave. He said, "Loose him, and let him go." Nor do miracles nor prophecy interfere with the action of human liberty and of human responsibility. Miracles never forced people to believe in Jesus, or to believe in Jehovah. The decision of the will was left untouched by the miracle. We see from the 9th chapter of John that, although the most persistent minute cross-examination of the man that was blind took place, the Pharisees resisted the most circumstantial evidence that could have been brought before a judge. And the raising of Lazarus from the grave only accelerated the decision of the enemies of Christ that He must be put to death. Where is there in the miracles that are recorded in Scripture anything that interferes with science properly so-called, or that interferes with all the ideas and instincts of reason and of feeling?

Look then at the chain of supernatural and miraculous events. I call events supernatural when God speaks, when God appears, when God Himself acts. I call them miraculous when God, through the agency of His chosen servants who have faith, breaks as it were through the phenomena that we behold, and manifests His own presence and His own purpose. Supernatural in the strictest sense of the word is the history of the creation of the world, which reason could never have elaborated, and of which human testimony could not possibly have given witness — that God created the heavens and the earth, and that God created man in His image, that God formed Eve out of Adam because the whole human race was to consist in one, and not in two beginnings. Supernatural is the record of the fall of man — that the idea of evil emanated not out of the depths of his own being, but that, from a realm beyond our ken, the Prince of Darkness suggested to him disobedience to God. Supernatural is the record that Enoch, the seventh from Adam, was taken up into heaven, in order to convince a secularised race, which sought its safety and its happiness in the present, that there was another world and another life. Supernatural was the judgment of the Flood upon the human race, and the deliverance of Noah and his household. Supernatural was the origin of nations and the origin of the diversity of languages, because God in His own mind saw already that, in Christ Jesus and by the power of the Holy Ghost, He would unite all the families of the earth into perfect harmony and concord, through the One that He had chosen. With all these supernatural manifestations and acts, which are recorded in the first part of the book of Genesis, there is associated the teaching which God designs. God teaches; that is. His light descends unto man. God works marvellous things; that is. His power is made manifest to man. There was a tendency to emigrate, at the time when Abraham lived in Ur of the Chaldees, but to no natural impulse was the emigration of Abraham to be attributed; for the beginning of the race which God had chosen must be altogether in the hands of God. It was a supernatural and divine call, when the God of glory appeared unto Abraham, that made him go into the land which God showed him. Supernatural was the origin of the Jewish race in the birth of Isaac, so much so that the apostle Paul teaches us that the faith which Abraham exercised in believing the divine promise was nothing short of believing that God was able to raise the dead, and to call into existence that which is not. When now in the providence of God the children of Jacob had got into Egypt, and were there brought into conflict, 400 years afterwards, with the most civilised nation of the world, it was not because the Jewish nation had attained to a maturity of independence and of courage that they conceived the idea of emancipating themselves from the yoke; for when first the idea was presented to them they rebelled against it; nor was it because Moses, actuated by a heroic patriotism, resolved to be the rescuer of his nation, for long after the painful experience that he had had — which taught him that that which is born of the flesh is flesh, and that the unhallowed and unbridled enthusiasm and energy of human nature are not able to do anything in the kingdom of God — God appeared to him in the burning bush, and had to persuade and command the unwilling Moses to go to Pharaoh. By miracles and signs He persuaded Closes that the God of his fathers was also with him. By miracles and mighty wonders did God deliver Israel out of Egypt, when He made manifest to Pharaoh and to all the Egyptians, that the powers of nature which they worshipped were altogether under the subjection of the Most High. And on that memorable night when the first born in Egypt, and only the first born — when not *many* of the first born, but *all* of the first born of Egypt — died, God brought Israel out of Egypt with His mighty hand and outstretched arm, and by the blood of the paschal lamb redeemed them, to show them that it was not merely His power nor His faithfulness, but also His mercy (which was to be exhibited in the atonement), that made them, who were as guilty as the Egyptians, to be His witnesses and His people. By miracle they passed through the Red Sea; for all that the rationalists have suggested about the natural tide and flow cannot account for the passage of two millions of human beings just at that time, and for the destruction afterwards of their enemies. By miracle, and through the faith of Moses, they passed through the Red Sea, in order that they might witness that stupendous and magnificent manifestation of Jehovah, when, with His mighty angels, He promulgated the fiery and blessed and everlasting law of Mount Sinai. Not in any other way could it have been done; not in any other way could it have been impressed upon Israel and on other nations, that Israel was the nation of God, chosen by Him in His sovereignty, formed by Him for Himself, and that all that was to come out of Israel ("Salvation is of the Jews") was not because in Israel there was any worthiness or any material but of which there could come a deliverance and a redemption, but because God Himself in Israel, and among Israel, and through Israel, was about to carry out His gracious promises. For forty years in the wilderness there was a supernatural and miraculous history. The angel of His presence went with them. The manifestation of glory was vouchsafed to them. Manna came down from heaven and fed them. Out of the rock came water, and they drank. Against their enemies they were protected by the might of God. By looking at the brazen serpent they were healed, in order that they might learn the doctrine of sin and of salvation. God did mighty works, and revealed Himself in a marvellous way to the children of Israel in the wilderness. Here comes an episode frequently used by the opponents of revelation, who see only the surface, and who are very easily satisfied with the most feeble satire upon what appears to them to be grotesque. When the Israelites first come into contact with their enemies, the Amorites and the Moabites, just before they are going to take possession of the land promised to their fathers, there is a wonderful witness raised up for Jehovah, not from among the Israelites, but from among the heathen nations — Balaam, who was a seer and knew that Jehovah was God. Whether he had retained some of the primaeval knowledge, handed down among the heathen, or whether the report of the mighty acts of God in Egypt and in the wilderness had reached him as it had reached many others, he was a seer, one who used divination, a soothsayer, many of whom were to be found among the heathen. These were, as Scripture teaches us, not merely deceivers, but they possessed a real knowledge and a real power in connection with demons. Balaam wished to combine his heathen magic with the knowledge of Jehovah. Deeply rooted in his heart was the love of money— covetousness, which is idolatry. He was a double-hearted and a double-minded man, yet full of light and knowledge — a great psychological miracle, and several times held up for our instruction and warning in the books of the New Testament. When God permits him to go up to Balak, — but on the condition that he should speak only what God commanded him, — God, seeing the perversity of his heart, wished to rebuke him and to hinder him, and then there came the angel with the drawn sword. But he that was a seer became blind and saw not, and he that was as a prophet, above the level of humanity, sank below the level of humanity, so that, as the apostle Peter teaches us, the dumb animal rebuked his madness. God rebuked his perversity by making this irrational animal speak to him. The ass saw the angel of the Lord, and was frightened. The ass also perceived the injustice of his master and resented it; and in both these acts the animal did not transcend the limits of what we see all animals around us continually do. That the ass expressed both its fright and its indignation at being wrongfully treated is according to natural phenomena. The miracle begins here — that with the human voice he rebuked the perversity of Balaam. And that all this happened not in an ecstasy or a dream is evident from this fact, that not until after this rebuke did Balaam behold the angel of the Lord. But this miracle, striking as it is, is only one of the incidental and accidental features of this wonderful narrative. The importance of Balaam and his predictions lies in quite a different territory. Balaam himself, in wonderful words, shows to us the great distinction that there is between prophecy, and the enchantment and divination common among the heathen nations — as the consulting the flight of birds, or the foreshowing and foretelling of future events from the configuration of the intestines of sacrifices, and so on. In Israel it was the living God who, by His word, was to direct their history. Many of the sayings of Balaam have become household words among the faithful: his declaration that God was not man that He should lie, or the son of man that He should not be faithful to His promise; or his prediction of the king that was to arise in Israel and give to it the victory — the star that was to come out of Jacob and the sceptre that was to come out of Judah. Wonderful were the predictions of Balaam, and this was their significance: that here God raised up a witness out of heathenism, to show to Israel that, weak and powerless as they were in themselves, and about to enter upon a task which appeared and must appear to man impossible, that of conquering the nations, they were strong in the Lord. Here is a heathen seer, who beholds heathen power after heathen power rise up, while all of them are destroyed and

138

disappear, and Israel alone remains. There is no prophecy, until we come to the prophecy of Daniel, which passes forth to the utmost distance, like the prophecy of Balaam, for, as a heathen, he was more concerned with the relation of Israel to the world than with Israel to itself. So in this prophecy of Balaam we find, what is afterwards more fully revealed by Daniel, that from the west, the Isles of Chittim in the Mediterranean Sea, that is Greece, there should come the victory of Israel over Asshur that was to rise up against her. As Balaam says, Israel is a nation apart, separated by God for a great purpose.

When Israel was now before the land of Canaan, and Moses had been taken away, miracles continued to be wrought, and for good reason. Only think of Joshua's position. For forty years he had come into contact with Israel, and become acquainted with their unfaithfulness and their want of courage. The task that was before him was one of stupendous magnitude, for Canaan was full of fortified cities, and was inhabited by warlike nations, and he was to succeed Moses, that unique man in antiquity — the man of God. No wonder that God said to him, "Only be not afraid, and be of courage; as I was with Moses, so I will be with thee." And therefore as miracles were wrought by Moses, miracles were wrought by Joshua. Again, by miracle they crossed the Jordan, as they had crossed the Red Sea. By miracle the walls of Jericho fell down. By miracle the sun and the moon had to serve the purposes of God, the sun being deified by these nations as Baal, and the moon as Ashtaroth. The angel of the covenant appeared to Joshua, even as God appeared to Moses in the fiery bush. The Prince of the Hosts of the Lord spoke to Joshua, and assured him that he would be with them. Thus it was necessary, in order that Israel should take possession of the land, for miracles to be performed.

When we come to David, who is the type of Christ, the man after the heart of God, and whose reign was not to be like the reign of an earthly monarch, then again we find that the election and appointment of David to be king was brought about supernaturally. He was not chosen by Israel, for Israel had regard to that which is outward, and the man who appeared a hero and valiant in battle was the man that attracted their attention; but David the son of Jesse, that kept the flock of his father, was pointed out by God Himself to the prophet Samuel. And again God appeared to David, and showed to him the sure mercies of David, and that future One in whom God would lay the foundation of the kingdom. Then there was no miracle for a long period until the days of Elijah and Elisha, when the whole nation had fallen into idolatry, when the king was a worshipper of Baal, and hundreds and hundreds of priests were priests of Baal. Then God, to arrest that downward progress, and to prepare and retain the land for the future kingdom, sent Elijah. Sudden was his appearance, mysterious was his ascension. Like fire his word burned, and lit up the darkness of that idolatrous race. He by prayer shut the doors of heaven, so that it rained not for three years and a half; and he opened again the clouds of heaven, and the rain descended. Fire came down from heaven upon the altar, and it was made manifest to the nation that "Jehovah, He is the God"; and although, as was necessary for the exigencies of the time, the miracles of Elijah were chiefly of this terrible and solemn character, yet the mercy of the Lord was also made manifest by Elijah, even as God spoke to him in the still small voice. And the trust of Elijah in the mercy of God, who was able to feed the hungry and to bring to life again those that were dead, we are shown in his miracles. And as Elijah, so Elisha. As Joshua succeeded Moses, so Elisha succeeded Elijah; and in him the healing, saving, redeeming power of Jehovah was made more manifest. These were the two witnesses that God chose. They did not prophesy in word. They did not look forward so much to the Messiah as did the other prophets. Their miracles were their sermons. God, by mighty signs and wonders, roused this idolatrous nation to seek Him and return to His favour.

I refer now, further, to two miracles which it is necessary for me to mention: one, because it is often made the object of ridicule, while the importance of it is not seen. For a thousand people who will say, "Do you believe that Balaam's ass spoke?" there is scarcely one who has read the history of Balaam — so wonderful, so instructive, so sublime, and with such strong evidence — in its prophetic character and world-wide predictions — of the revelation which this man had from God. Likewise is this the case with the miracle of Jonah. What a wonderful book is that little book of Jonah with its four chapters! even in Scripture history it is conspicuous for its vivid and graphic character. As Dr. Pusey says, "There is not a single line in this book which does not advance the history. Here there is no reflection; here everything is fact and picture." What a large idea is in this book of Jonah! God is not the God of the Jews only, but also of the Gentiles. God sends him to Nineveh. There are two miracles recorded in the book. One belongs to outward nature, and the other belongs to the inward kingdom. How great was the miracle of the conversion of the Ninevites — that this great city which contained millions of inhabitants, from the king upon his throne down to the lowest of the people, repented, simply by hearing the message of a strange prophet who was landed on their shore. So deep was their repentance, that they caused even the "beasts to be covered with sackcloth." Who but the mighty Spirit of God could have wrought this?

But as to the other miracle, that God prepared a monster of the sea to swallow Jonah, and preserve the life of Jonah for three days, and afterwards bring him forth on to the dry land — "improbable," "impossible," as it appears, — there are many instances corroborative of this miracle, to be found in secular history, of great monsters of the sea which are only able to swallow their prey entire, or to break it in pieces. But when we come to remember what God purposed by this history, when we see first the sublime idea of this history — the pity of God upon the Gentiles—and how God afterwards would, through Israel and through Him who was typified by Jonah, command men everywhere to repent and to turn to His love; when we remember how our blessed Saviour repeatedly alluded to this book of Jonah in both its aspects, first, as typifying Himself, — His being buried in the earth, and afterwards raised again from the grave, — and, secondly, as referring also to the repentance of the Ninevites, who would stand up in judgment against those who did not obey the voice of Him who was greater than Jonah — then we see the magnificence of this book, and we see also that this miracle is not a grotesque prodigy of human imagination, but the manifestation of Him who is perfect wisdom and perfect love.

And so also of the miracles that are recorded in the book of Daniel. The great besetting sin of Nebuchadnezzar, and afterwards of Darius and all of these mighty men, was pride, as if they by their own wisdom had built up these great and mighty empires. And how easy it was for them to suppose that the God of Israel was a weak God, for if, as Sennacherib afterwards said, He were a strong God, how could He have allowed His nation to be subjugated by other nations? Therefore God showed to Nebuchadnezzar and to Darius that He was the God and the only God, and that although He allowed Israel, on account of Israel's sin, to be chastised by them, and to be taken into captivity by them, yet His power was an infinite power, neither was His love to Israel a love which could ever change or falter. And the effect of these miracles we can see in that wonderful edict of Cyrus. Cyrus says that he has written this edict in obedience to the God of the Jews — to Jehovah. But I want now to show how all these miracles were preparatory, and how they were intimately connected with our blessed Saviour Jesus Christ.

All that is supernatural in the Old Testament, all that is miraculous in the Old Testament, has its explanation, has its root and its purpose, in Christ Jesus. You who are Christians understand that on different occasions God spoke to Abraham, God spoke to Moses, and appeared to Abraham and appeared to Moses. The glory of the Lord was seen, between the Cherubim, in the Holy of Holies. That was supernatural, but all this happened only because in the fulness of time God appeared. He was made manifest in flesh. We beheld His glory, the glory as of the Only Begotten of the Father. The Shekinah tabernacled in Him who tabernacled and dwelt among us. And if God spoke. His ultimate and His perfect message to mankind was given by Jesus, and Jesus Himself is the Word, in which all the thoughts and purposes of God are expressed.

Look we to miracles, God acts; God heals the sick; God forgives sin; God subdues the powers of nature. God is stronger than Satan, and will vanquish him. God is able to raise the dead. Jesus says, "Thy sins are forgiven" Jesus cleanses the leper; Jesus restores to the blind their sight; Jesus rebukes the storm; Jesus conquers devils; Jesus raises the dead. And if God in the Old Testament performed the miracles by the agency of men who had faith — by faith Moses did this and this — so did Jesus also by faith do miracles, by the finger of God, trusting in God, doing the things which His father showed Him, and doing the works because the Father was in Him, and He in the Father. Wonderful double relation of Jesus! He does the miracle by His own power:

"My Father worketh hitherto, and I work." He raises the dead, because He is the Resurrection and the Life, and, at the same time, He thanks God at the grave of Lazarus, because the Father always hears Him. What a meeting of the two lines is there here! Theophany: God appears; God's glory is manifested; God does miracles. Jesus appears; Jesus' glory is manifested; Jesus works miracles — that is one line: and the other line, that the faithful Israelite, the servant of the Lord, trusting in God, doeth marvels. Jesus who is both the Son and the servant, believing in the Father and communing with the Father, showing great signs, as in the raising of Lazarus — "The sickness was not unto death, but that the Son of God should be glorified" because He is God; namely, that Jehovah, who says, "My glory will I not give to another." He has given it from all eternity to His Son, who is one with Him. And afterwards Jesus says: "Did I not tell thee I hat if thou wouldst believe thou shouldst see the glory of God," for greater contrast there could not be than between a body mouldering in the grave when corruption has already made itself manifest, and the glory of Him who is the Creator of heaven and earth, and who shall raise the dead and introduce His everlasting kingdom. So in Christ Jesus all the supernatural and all the miraculous finds its confirmation. But more than that, it is very difficult for people to believe that miracles happened in the past, if they do not believe that miracles will happen again in the future. The history of the world, according to them, is most unsymmetrical. There is no architectural order in it. There first comes a period in which there are miracles, — the appearing of God Himself, and the action of God Himself, — and then there comes a long period in which there are no miracles, and that period is to be ended suddenly, abruptly, and without any transition, by the eternal condition, at the last Judgment. Not such is the view of Scripture. When Jesus Christ rose from the dead, we were born again unto a lively hope and unto an inheritance which is incorruptible and undefiled and that fadeth not away, reserved in heaven for those who are waiting for the things that shall be revealed to them at the appearing of the Lord Jesus Christ. The resurrection of Jesus Christ was the beginning. It is the future. Looking back (because time does not come in here): — What Jesus is, He is to all believers, whether they lived before the advent or after the advent, and in Him is contained the actual beginning of that new period in the world's history when God is made manifest. So the prophet Micah says that the same kind of miracles shall happen again as happened when God brought Israel out of Egypt; and the prophet Jeremiah says that when God shall bring again Israel, whom He has scattered, all the ends of the earth and the far-off islands shall take notice of it, and shall say, "What wonderful things God has done!" If then we believe this, that the present period is only a pause, only an interval, even as there were 400 years between Joseph and the call of Moses, and as there were 400 years between the prophet Malachi and the appearing of the angel to the father of John the Baptist; if we believe that, in these pauses, God is still the same God, and that just as a great musician puts the thought of melody, not merely in the notes which we hear, but also in the pauses, — the rhythm of the silence of these being part and parcel of the great idea, — so shall He come again, and there shall begin again the mighty manifestations and acts of God. And in the intermediate time is there not miracle? Have there not been miracles since Jesus went up to heaven, and since the last of the miracles performed by the apostles? Is not every one that is convinced of sin and brought to love Jesus a miracle? Is it not the Holy Ghost Himself who has quickened him? Is it not the power put forth by Jesus Himself? I, when "I am lifted up," am a prince and a Saviour to give repentance and the remission of sins. Is not God's answering prayer a miracle? When God gives to a man, who by nature is impatient and proud, meekness and patience, is not that a miracle? When God enlightens our hearts, when God subdues our sins under us, is not this a miracle? There is a continuous current of miracle in the present dispensation. To the outward world it is not striking: "The world seeth me no more, but ye shall see me, and your hearts shall rejoice, and your joy no man can take from you." Thus, then, we believe in God in the past, God in the present, God who will come again.

And in conclusion, children of God, do not imagine that what the Bible tells us of miracle is to make us less thoughtful, or to make us less appreciative of that wonderful first creation in which He has placed us. It is not to make us think nature of no importance, because miracles are more striking, but, on the contrary, it is to rouse our dormant sense, that we may adore God in all the wonderful works which He has made; in the sun which rules by day, and in the moon and stars which shine by night; in the beautiful and striking way in which He renews, every year, the face of nature; in the lilies which grow, because God clothes them. Oh, how beautiful in the Psalms, when the psalmist speaks of God who created the heavens and the earth, and who created the sun, the moon and the stars, and afterwards goes on to say, "Who delivered our fathers out of Egypt, and led them through the Red Sea" It appears there as if he thought everything miraculous, and as if the Jews had no idea of nature apart from miracle. Oh, far from that. But this is what the psalmist wishes to show to us. It is because of these mighty miracles, that now we have an eye open and a heart open to adore God in all the wonderful works of the first creation. And how beautifully He attributes everything, not to the power of God, or to the wisdom of God, or to the sovereignty of God. Why did God create sun, moon, and stars? Why does He watch over nature, year by year, and bring forth the seasons in their order? Because His mercy endureth for ever — that salvation-mercy which brought Israel out of Egypt, and which afterwards sent to us His own blessed Son. It is because of His mercy that all things are around us to praise Him and to magnify His Holy name. And is the miraculous character of Bible history to put, as it were, providence into the background, so that we may not notice it or admire it? Oh, that be far from us. It is just because we believe in the living God, who hath done great miracles and will do them again, that we are sure that not even a sparrow can fall to the ground without His will, that the very hairs of our head are numbered, that He knows our daily steps, and that He takes cognisance of our daily difficulties and duties. Believe then in God. That is the sum of all things. As Jesus said to the disciples, "Have faith in God."

XIV - The Doctrinal, Typical, and Prophetical Aspects of the History of Israel

The subject upon which I enter this morning is the doctrinal, typical, and prophetical aspects of the history of Israel. My remarks will have as their centre the person of Abraham; and I hope in my next lecture to continue the subject, taking as the starting-point Moses, and to conclude the subject this day fortnight, if it please God, taking for the starting-point David.

The combination of history, teaching, prophecy and type which we find in Scripture is so perfect and excellent that it is extremely difficult to give a correct view of each of these component parts separately. If we look at the doctrine apart from the history, the tendency is to represent the doctrine in an abstruse and metaphysical method, lacking all the vitality, fragrance, and affectionateness which wc find intertwined in the Scripture statements, with the dealings of God and the development of the history of redemption. If the history which is recorded in Scripture is viewed apart from the prophecies which are still to be fulfilled in the future, the danger is that the history may be regarded merely in its abstract and doctrinal point of view, and that great violence may be done to it by an interpretation which chooses to call itself spiritual, but which, after all, is carnal, because it does not submit itself to the wisdom of God. Rather should it be called phantomising, in not fully seeing that the history was an actual and concrete reality, even as the Son of God, who came down from heaven, really and truly was made flesh. For that reason the continuous and diligent study of Scripture is absolutely necessary, and nothing can take the place of Scripture — not the most perfect and skilfully framed creeds, not the most thoughtful and earnest preaching. As we find that God has provided all over the earth certain springs which possess healing power — chemistry is able to analyse them, chemistry is also able to produce artificially a compound containing the same elements, but nothing that human skill can prepare is exactly the same as that which Nature herself produces — so is it with that teaching which God has given to us in His own Word. Botany may describe very accurately a plant but it is quite a different thing, which even the ignorant can enjoy, to see the plant, and to be impressed directly with its organic unity, with its beauty or with its fragrance. Every one who sees a splendid building is immediately impressed with the harmony, and the majesty, and the beauty of the building, but very few people would be able to understand the architect's plan of that building as it is sketched upon paper. Therefore God, who in great wisdom and love has framed the history of His people, and has also caused the Scripture to be

144

written by inspiration of the Holy Ghost, has provided for the poor and lowly, and has bound us to the continual and diligent study of the Scriptures, for only in this way can His great purpose be fulfilled in us, that, through the Scriptures, we may be brought into harmony and communion with Himself, and be made heirs of salvation.

The Scripture history is throughout written in the prophetic spirit, for the great object in that history is to show to us God's will concerning us. His purposes concerning the human race, what man is to think concerning God, and what life it is that God requires of man. But the acts of God are so sublime, and so full of manifold wisdom, that it would have been impossible for Israel and for us to understand them, unless they had always been accompanied by the Word.

It is quite true, as the proverb says, that facts speak, and so do those facts which are recorded in Scripture, but still it is necessary that they should be accompanied by the teaching given by God Himself; and this teaching we may call prophetic, not merely because it relates to the future, but because it reveals God and His mind. Therefore God says, through the prophet Amos, that there is nothing that the Lord God ever does without revealing His secret, that is to say, His plan and His idea to His servants the prophets. And thus it is said by David that God made known His ways to Moses and His acts to the children of Israel; that is, so to speak, the meaning and the philosophy were made known to the prophet, the outward fulfilment and embodiment were seen by all the people. And here it is very remarkable that the mysterious man of whom I spoke in my last lecture, Balaam, to whom in the New Testament there corresponds Simon Magus, saw the difference that there was between heathen prophecy and prophecy among the people of God, for he declares that among God's people there is no divination and soothsaying, as among the heathen. Out of a great desire to know the future, whether a god would prosper or not some war expedition, they consulted oracles. There were men and women who had some natural gift of seeing into the future, and who were often possessed by some demon. These persons excited themselves, by all kinds of outward and physical means, into a state of ecstasy, and, from observing physical signs, they predicted the future in a most ambiguous manner — purposely ambiguous — and often their predictions came to nothing. But not thus was it to be in Israel. There was to be no divination of that kind in Israel, because God Himself at the proper time, in every critical juncture, would show to Israel by His servants the prophets, the purpose which He purposed in Himself. And as thus the history was always accompanied by doctrine, and was always accompanied by the interpretation given by the prophets, so the history was always connected with the promise of the future, for it was all pointing towards the appointed end. Likewise the history itself was a prophecy of the future. As the proverb says, "History repeats itself," or "Coming events cast their shadows before them." The whole history of God in His relations, so to speak, with mankind and with Israel, was a continual repetition of the same idea and the same action on God's part, which were at last perfectly fulfilled in Jesus Christ. Thus the explanation of words in doctrine, the promise of the future in prophecy, and the prefiguration of that which was coming in type, continually went side by side, one illustrating and confirming the other, and all keeping pace together; that is to say, God did not predict anything of which the beginning was not already intelligible to those to whom the message was sent.

You see from this, that the exposition of the Old Testament in one respect is very complex; but to us who are living in the days of fulfilment there is given most abundant light, and we are provided with the clue which is to lead us safely to manifold and yet united preparation — for Jesus Christ is the end, the consummation of all things. He is the end of the Jewish history. This you can see from the genealogy in the book of Matthew. Abraham is chosen that he may lead to David. David is not the fulfilment, and therefore the genealogy goes on to the Babylonish captivity. From the Babylonish captivity there are fourteen generations which lead up to Jesus; and in Him the whole Jewish history reached its culminating point, but not its termination. The Jewish history is complete in Christ, and the future of the Jewish history is secured in Christ, but it has not come to an end, and therefore they do greatly err who suppose that the Jewish history ends with the first advent and the Christian Church. Rather, in the first advent of Jesus Christ is the foundation laid upon which the yet future history of Israel is to be constructed, for He was a minister of the circumcision to confirm the promises which were given to our father Abraham. The law is fulfilled in Christ. Christ is the end of the law to every one that believeth in Him, and thus, in a manifold way, the negative aspect of the law is fulfilled. Having confessed our sin, and seeing that the curse of God rests upon every one that abideth not in the law, Christ has removed the curse and delivered us from the sentence of the law, because He has delivered us from the guilt which we have incurred; but, more than that, the righteousness of the law is fulfilled in us who walk not after the flesh but after the spirit, and therefore, to them that are in Christ Jesus, the law is no longer outside of them as a foreign power, but the law by the Holy Ghost has been put within them, by Christ's dwelling in them. But although this is perfectly true, Christ has not done away with the law of Moses in its social and in its national aspect, but every jot and tittle of this law will yet be realised and fulfilled, when God will make a new covenant with Israel, and put His Spirit within them. Then shall they walk in all the statutes and ordinances and precepts which God gave to them through Moses. So also are all the prophecies fulfilled in Christ Jesus, and yet not one prophecy is fulfilled perfectly. If we separate the first from the second advent of Christ, it is impossible for us to explain the prophecies. The New Testament fulfilment is the key to open the lock, but there is a way of opening the lock and spoiling the wards of the lock, displacing them, injuring them, destroying them. Not thus must we apply the fulfilment to the promises, by explaining away in an artificial method what is most clearly taught When Christ said in the synagogue of Nazareth, "This day is this Scripture fulfilled in your ears," He said so truly, because He is the fulfilment of the Scripture, and yet that very Scripture was not completely fulfilled, for the day of vengeance had not come. That day was still in the future. When we read that the Messiah that was promised to Israel has come, this is true, but it is not yet perfectly fulfilled, because in the days of the Messiah it is said that the nations shall learn war no more, and that there shall be peace everywhere; and we know perfectly well that this is not the case now. Christ is the fulfilment of all the Old Testament prophecies. When we view Christ, both in His first advent and also in His second advent, then we have in Christ Jesus as He came, and as we expect Him to come, the explanation of the history of the law and of the promises, and also the fulfilment of the types, for the types, both in what they are, and are not, able to represent, have now found their end in Jesus Christ, in whom everything that God has provided for His people is treasured up, and the fulness of the Godhead dwelleth bodily.

But to make this subject still clearer and simpler, — my wish is to impress upon you that, notwithstanding all the complex and manifold character of the Old Testament revelation, which was unfolded very slowly "at sundry times, and in divers manners," and in which there were a great many elements combined, that appear to us at first sight not to be spiritual but rather ephemeral — notwithstanding all this, there was great simplicity and great unity. In Christ Jesus we have God and man. The whole object of the Scripture, and the whole object of God Himself is to reveal God, as we may know Him, and also to show how man may come into communion with God. And this can only be realised in Jesus Christ, who is both God and man. He is the Son of God. He is the Son of man. He came down from heaven. He was born in Bethlehem. He was sent of the Father; He came of His own accord. He was the Son of Abraham and yet Jehovah, "Before Abraham was, I Am." He is the Son of David, and yet He is David's Lord. Now these two lines which we see united in Christ are so wonderful that it is impossible for us to explain the mode in which they are united, so that the incarnation, and the history which dates from the incarnation, must remain a mystery to us— though we see the fact, and we are convinced and impressed by that wonderful gift which has been bestowed upon us, in One who is both God and man in one person — a truth revealed in the Old Testament, in its two separate aspects.

We have two lines in the Old Testament, which it must have been very difficult for the saints in those days to combine. The first line is from heaven to earth. God wishes to reveal Himself. He appears; He speaks; He reveals Himself in the form of the angel of the covenant. That angel of the covenant speaks as Jehovah; He gives promises which only divine wisdom and omnipotence can give, and they to whom He appears say, "We have seen Jehovah." It is of this angel of the covenant that we read, that He appeared to Moses in the burning bush and said to him, "I am the God of Abraham, and Isaac, and

Jacob." This angel, in whom was the presence of God and the countenance of God, was He who led them through the wilderness. It was again a theophany which was vouchsafed to the prophet Isaiah, and afterwards it is explained to us that Isaiah beheld Christ and His glory. In the similitude of the Son of man, God was again seen by Ezekiel and by Daniel, until the last prophets most distinctly describe to us that the Lord Jehovah Himself will come. And yet this Jehovah that comes distinguishes Himself from the Jehovah that sends Him. And in that last prophecy of Malachi, it is said that there should be sent a messenger to go before the face of Jehovah. In all these manifestations we sec God appearing, making Himself visible and revealing Himself as the redeeming, delivering, helping, and friendly God to the saints, until we come to God manifest in the flesh.

But there is another line in the Old Testament going from earth heavenwards, for from the beginning of the history, God's people were told that they were to be delivered through a man, the seed of the woman, one who belongs to Shem, the seed of Abraham, one of the tribe of Judah, the Son of David, the servant of God, the root of Jesse, growing up out of a dry ground. Now as they saw God coming down from heaven, and then saw man going up to heaven, how difficult must it have been for them to combine those two lines. When Jesus says "Salvation is of the Jews," when the prophet Jonah says "Salvation is of Jehovah," Jesus is the explanation and combination of the two things, for He who came out of Israel, out of this earth, was none other than the Only Begotten of the Father,

Let me for a few moments remind you of the historical books as they are given to us, and of the unity which they form. There are first the five books of Moses upon which the whole building rests, and these five books of Moses are inseparable. Exodus shows how God redeemed Israel out of Egypt and brought Israel to Himself. Leviticus shows us how this redeemed nation was sanctified to God by the institution of the priesthood, of the sacrifices, and of the festivals. Numbers shows us how this nation was disciplined in the wilderness, and the utter failure of the nation to accomplish their destiny in the person of Aaron, and even in the person of Moses himself, who, on account of his sin, and because he did not fully represent the character of God, was excluded from entrance into the land of Canaan. Now it is impossible that the history could conclude with the book of Numbers, because then it would conclude as it were with sunset, in the darkness of despondency. Therefore in the book of Deuteronomy, Moses appears as a prophet, showing the loving-kindness of the Lord, and how, notwithstanding all the unfaithfulness of Israel and his own imperfection and sin, God would carry out His plan. Immediately after the book of Deuteronomy there comes the book of Joshua, which is joined to the book of Deuteronomy by the conjunction "and." As the book of Joshua joins Deuteronomy by "and," so the book of the Judges joins the book of Joshua by saying, "And after the death of Joshua."" Judges and the two books of Samuel are connected together in the same way, for in the book of Samuel, Samuel is represented as judging Israel; he was, as it were, the last of the Judges, and the connecting link with David. The two books of Samuel and the two books of Kings are so blended and joined together that, in the Septuagint, they are called "The four books of Samuel," and they bring the history of Israel down to the captivity, — concluding with a gleam of hope and sunshine. Now to supplement this history there is another book of history given to us, the object of which is to show how, after the Babylonish captivity, God's people were restored to their own land, and the temple service and the priesthood were revived. And, in order to bring this clearly before us, it was necessary to give again the genealogies of Abraham, Isaac, and Jacob, and their children, and to connect them with the beginning. So the book of Chronicles begins with Adam — showing to us the genealogies, as they follow. But as the 2nd book of Chronicles ends by telling us how Cyrus gave permission to the Jews to return to their own land, the identical two verses open the book of Ezra, and in Ezra and Nehemiah we have an account of what formed the beginning of the new period of Israel's history; so all these books are united and compacted together, and all have one object in view, and what is important to that object is narrated, and what is not important to that object is omitted, however important it may appear to the eyes of the mere secular or worldly historian. But Exodus would have no meaning, unless it was preceded by the book of Genesis, for who were this people that Moses was called to bring out of Egypt? Who was Abraham? who was Isaac? and who was Jacob, the God of whom appears to Moses and gives to him that wonderful commission? It is therefore necessary that there should precede the book of Exodus a book to explain all this; and so we have not merely the history of the patriarchs, and the history of Joseph, by whom the transition was made from Canaan into Egypt, — but to understand Abraham aright, and the God of Abraham, it was necessary also to have the history of the creation of the world, of Adam, and of Noah, and of the promises which were given to the fathers. Therefore Genesis is the necessary prologue to the three middle books of the Pentateuch, as the book of Deuteronomy is the epilogue.

Now look at the first three chapters of the book of Genesis. They form a complete whole: God the creator of heaven and of earth: man created in the image of God, as the culminating point of God's creation: the Sabbath instituted: Paradise described: Eve formed out of Adam: sin introduced by an adverse spiritual power: the consequences of sin — death, spiritual, temporal, and everlasting: the immediate result of sin, the conscience acting in man and accusing him, so that he is ashamed and he is afraid: the intervention of God, in His great mercy and love, revealing the deliverance that would be brought through the seed of the woman, by One that was to suffer, and also describing the period which was now to commence, when the judgment was to be blended with mercy; the period of chastisement when man, through a severe discipline, was to learn the meaning of life, and was to be exercised unto godliness. Then there was the manifestation of God Himself at the entrance of Paradise. Now we find that the descendants of Adam, as Adam and Eve themselves, understood this teaching. They had faith in God the Creator omnipotent, all-wise, all-loving, merciful and compassionate to them. They knew that the wages of sin was death; they knew that finally there was to come a Deliverer who, by His own sufferings, was to gain the victory over death and over him that had the power of death. They worshipped God in the way in which He had appointed; they relied upon the promise, as we can see from the words of Eve at the birth of Cain, and from what Lamech said at the birth of Noah. So they believed, they hoped, they prayed, and they served God. There must have been a manifestation of the presence of the Lord identified with some particular place, as we read that Cain fled from before the presence of the Lord.

Now the New Testament shows to us the deep meaning of this history. How much the saints of God understood, who lived in those days, it is impossible for us to define, but what God meant us to learn by this history is made manifest in the writings of the New Testament, for the promise was all along developing itself. The human race was from the very beginning divided into the seed of the woman and the seed of the serpent. The descendants of Cain who left God, the descendants of Seth who knew God, called upon the name of Jehovah, for although the name Jehovah, in the fulness of its meaning, was only disclosed to Israel by Moses, — just as the meaning of God being the Father was not fully disclosed to Israel until Jesus Christ came, — yet they knew the name Jehovah, and they called upon this God of promise. And the future was seen by them, for Enoch prophesied of it, in which prophecy he saw approximately the judgment of the Flood, but ultimately also the final appearing of Jehovah with all His saints. When we come to Noah we find that there is a new beginning. He is the second father of the human race. There is a new beginning — a beginning which was made only possible through judgment and deliverance. And here we meet for the first time with that remarkable expression "Covenant." "God made a covenant." Among the heathen nations, such an idea, as that of the Deity or any god making a covenant, would have been incomprehensible. They only understood man's offering to the gods, as it were, bribes and sacrifices on the condition that they would give them successes in some enterprise which they undertook; but for God, in His sovereignty and in His wonderful love, Himself initiating a disposition and arrangement of things, in which, according to His own nature, He promised blessings which were to extend over centuries — nay, unto the end of history — this is a sublime idea which is only revealed to us in the Scriptures. Covenant, in the Scripture sense, is not a compact that is made between two parties, and which is nullified by either of the parties not fulfilling the conditions, but covenant, as is manifest from the covenant with Noah, is simply a promise on God's part that, as long as this dispensation lasts. He will not destroy the world again with water, and that the four seasons are to succeed one another, and, as a seal of that gracious arrangement which God made, He gave to Noah and his descendants the sign of the bow in the cloud. And Noah was a prophet, for to him was revealed the future history of the race — that Shem was to belong specially to Jehovah, and that Japheth was to dwell in the tents of Shem. And thus the first promise which was indefinite, speaking merely of the seed of the woman, received a more definite locality, and became limited to one of the three sections of the human race— to Shem.

To consider next the election of Abraham. There now comes a period in the history of the world where God, who hitherto has been dealing with the human race, as one, consisting simply of families, leaves all other nations to themselves, and separates to Him one nation, that among them He may kindle and preserve the light which was ultimately to illumine the whole world. Just as we see in the story of the prodigal that the younger son is allowed by the father to leave the father's house — not without the portion of goods that belong to him, — that is the reminiscence of the primaeval revelation, and the testimony of God in the heart and conscience — and then to go into a far country, so it was that all the nations of the world, with the exception of the nation that was elected in Abraham, were left to go their own ways. These were the times of ignorance. And the purpose was this — to bring out what was in man apart from God — "The world by wisdom knew not God" — and to show what was the character of sin, when unrestrained by the divine law. You find described in the 1st chapter of the epistle to the Romans how the nations forgot God, and because they forgot God, because they were unthankful, they were given up, to work out the evil of their own hearts and of their own souls. And yet, notwithstanding all this, during this dispensation God does not forget the Gentiles, and, when Abraham and the patriarchs and Moses are brought into contact with the Gentiles, they never treat them as if they were outside, as it were, of the goodness and the wisdom of God, but always testify to them in the name of God, and. appeal to that which they have still retained in their remembrance, of the knowledge of the Most High. But the question still is asked — and it is a great stumbling-block to many, whether they give utterance to it or not — Why did God for so many centuries restrict Himself to one nation, and why were such special promises given to it only? The reasons that are given to us in Scripture are manifold and are very satisfactory, although it is impossible for us to understand wholly the counsel of God. Even the apostle Paul, after having devoted three chapters to explaining the mystery of Israel, bursts forth into the exclamation: "Oh, the depth of the riches both of the wisdom and knowledge of God! how unsearchable are His judgments, and His ways past finding out." It was necessary to separate Israel in order that the fire should be kindled, and that it should be intense in its brightness and 'in its heat. It was necessary to hedge round Israel from all the other nations by the strictest injunctions, lest they should forget the knowledge which God had given them, and become contaminated with the idolatry and abominations of the nations that were around them. It was necessary that there should be prepared a soil out of which Christ, born of the Virgin Mary, was to appear. He required the whole of the Jewish nation, so to speak, from whom He was to arise. And also there was to be a godly people to welcome Him, who should form afterwards the nucleus of the Church of Christ.

It is necessary for us also to remember that this election of Israel has a spiritual aspect. Not all are Israel who are of Israel. Even in Israel the nation as a whole does not obtain the election, but a portion obtains it. It was not a carnal descent. It was not Ishmael but Isaac; it was not Esau but Jacob; and therefore of those who are really descended from Abraham, Isaac, and Jacob, it is only those who are godly, spiritually minded, the "little flock," to whom pertaineth the promise. So that in Israel also there were the godly and the ungodly, the righteous and the unrighteous, the wheat and the chaff. And that it was not in a carnal and mere outward way that God chose them, is manifest from this — that at all times, from the very beginning, there was the greatest facility afforded to those who were not of Abraham, Isaac, and Jacob, to be joined to the commonwealth of Israel. There were hundreds and thousands of strangers from other nations, who were allowed to be admitted into the Jewish nation, and to become heirs of the covenant.

Lastly, you must remember this. The apostle Paul considers those who believe in the Lord Jesus Christ to be the representatives of the nation. The others, although numerically they were the majority, he looks upon as the exception. He uses the expression, "And what if some have not believed?" Now in reality the "some" that have not believed are a far larger number than those that have believed, but viewed in a spiritual light, and according to the reality of God, they are only the exception. The real stem of the nation is represented by those who believe in Jesus; and when Israel is restored again to its own land, and the times are fulfilled, the wall of separation between Jew and Gentile, which has been abolished in Christ Jesus, will never be built up again. That which has passed away will not be restored. It will be an actual and real reestablishment of Israel in their kingdom. The law of Moses will be revived in a transfigured way according to the spirit of the new covenant, but the union between Israel; and the nations who believe in God and His Anointed will be a perfect union, and from among the Gentiles there will be chosen to be in Jerusalem and in the Holy Land those who hold a special position in Israel; and through all the world there will be offered to God a pure offering, because they shall know His name.

Now with regard to Abraham, we read the expression that God appeared to him. God appeared to Abraham. There was again that theophany of God, in which God made Himself know to Abraham, And to Abraham appeared also the angel of the Lord, who said, "By myself have I sworn," To Abraham also there was given the great promise, and that promise given to him not in itself, but in the form of a covenant; for with Abraham God made a covenant which he repeated several times, which He confirmed with an oath, which He ratified again to Isaac and Jacob, and upon which the whole future not merely of Israel rests, but also the salvation of all the Gentiles who believe in our Lord Jesus Christ. For this reason Abraham is not merely the father of Israel but the father of all the faithful, and all they that believe in Christ Jesus are of the seed of Abraham, and inheritors of the promises given to him.

Now that covenant that was made with Abraham was, as the covenant with Noah, an unconditional covenant, sovereign, absolute, unchangeable. The transgressions of Israel, even though they culminate in the crucifixion of Jesus, cannot put aside that covenant, for the gifts and calling of God are without repentance. The law, which came 400 years afterwards, cannot possibly interfere with this covenant. It only came in, by way of parenthesis, to make sin appear exceeding sinful, and to heighten the expectation of the grace of God. This covenant with Abraham is the sovereignty of God, into which He always retreats whenever the sin of Israel renders it impossible for Him, humanly speaking, to go on with them, for the history of Israel would otherwise often have come to a standstill. When they crucified Jesus Christ, how would it have been possible for God to continue His connection with the people of Israel, if it had not been that He retreated into Himself, into His own sovereignty, into His eternal counsel, into that abounding grace to the chief of sinners? And therefore it is that an oath is connected with the covenant, although the Word of God without an oath is perfectly sure and steadfast. When God says "As I live, saith the Lord," He thereby signifies that He is retreating, as it were, into His own depths, and that what Hg is going to promise is so connected with Himself, with His character, with His love, with His glory, with His purpose, that He Himself is the guarantee that it must come to pass. Oh, what a firm foundation for our own personal salvation and for the future of Israel — nay, for the future of the whole race.

And the covenant with Abraham embraces three points, and you cannot take any one of them away; first, that from Abraham was to come an exceedingly numerous nation; secondly, that that nation was to possess the land of Canaan; and thirdly, that the seed of Abraham was to be the centre of blessing to all the families of the earth. When we look at these three points, if it were not for the middle point of the promise of the land, it might be possible for people to say that when Christ came, and when Christ, by His death, became the Saviour of sinners, the promises to Abraham were fulfilled. He had become a numerous nation; the Messiah had come; and through that Messiah blessings had gone forth to all the nations of the earth. Take all the promises which are based upon this covenant that God made with Abraham in a literal and concrete sense, and never for a moment forget the land of Canaan, in which all these promises were to be fulfilled. You can find no promise in the Old Testament with reference to Israel — their conversion and the outpouring of the Holy Spirit upon them, — except in connection with their national restoration to the land which God gave to their fathers. In that very chapter in Jeremiah, when God says that He will make a new covenant with them, and give to them a new heart, and put a right spirit within them — in that very chapter, and in the subsequent chapters, are described to us distinctly that, in that very land which He gave to their fathers, all this would take place, and also that their national existence would endure as long as the sun and moon and the heavens; and so you find in all the prophets that these things remain steadfast and sure; and Jesus Christ Himself confirmed these promises — the oath which God sware to Abraham.

And when God made a covenant and revealed Himself to Abraham there was as yet no law. God simply said to Abraham, "I am the Lord; walk thou before me and be perfect." On the part of Abraham there was faith. He believed God, and he believed the promises of God. When Isaac was not yet born, the non-existence of Isaac was no difficulty to his faith. When Isaac was born and grown up, the death of Isaac was no obstacle to his faith. lie offered him up to the Lord, knowing that God was able to bring him back again from the dead. And we find the patriarchs Isaac and Jacob walking in the footsteps of the Lord, until in Jacob we see that the promise receives a fuller development, Jacob himself received the revelations of the angel, the redeemer, that led him all his life long. To Him he looked as the source of blessing for his posterity; and the nation that God has chosen does not take its name from Abraham or Isaac, but from Jacob. And why is it so? Because Jacob was called "Israel" just as Jesus, when He was upon earth, changed the name of Simon. Only the Searcher of Hearts has the power of changing the name. Jesus called Simon "Cephas." Jehovah changed the name of Abram into Abraham, and unto Jacob he gave the name "Israel," and that has become the name of the whole nation. And why is this the name of the whole nation? Because it is the divinely-given character of the nation, as opposed to all the nations of the world. Israel gains the victory. Israel gains the victory only from God. Israel gains the victory from God only through strong crying and tears and supplication; and Israel, after having gained the victory, docs not go forth with the firm and jubilant tread of a hero, but halting, even as the apostle Paul went forth with the thorn in his flesh, glorying even in his infirmities, because the strength of God was made perfect in his weakness.

And here is a remarkable thing — that at so early a stage the twelve tribes knew themselves to be one, and had one common name. The Athenian historian, Thucydides, states as a very extraordinary thing that the various Greek tribes lived for so many centuries without having any bond of unity between them, and that only recently had there been found out a name by which the whole of these different tribes could be designated — the name of Hellenes; whereas we see from the song of Deborah, the early date of which has never been doubted by any expositor, that all the tribes knew themselves to be Israel, and that their union was in Jehovah, from whom alone came the victory, and unto whom alone belongs the glory and the praise. And to Jacob there was revealed, when he blessed his twelve sons, that from among all those sons, Judah was the one that was chosen — that out of the tribe of Judah there was to come the Deliverer.

And now I wish to make one remark. The apostle Paul describes the character of the whole dispensation up to Moses in one sentence. He says that until Moses sin was in the world, but because there was no law, sin was not as yet imputed; nevertheless, death reigned from Adam unto Moses upon those that had not sinned after the similitude of Adam's transgression. And we find in the whole book of Genesis that the consciousness of sin was dormant in the people, Abraham humbles himself before God; he says, "I am but dust and ashes." Jacob, when he humbles him, self before God, says, "I am unworthy of the least of thy mercies"; but those deep confessions of sin and guilt, which we find afterwards among the saints of God, we do not find in the book of Genesis. Why? Because the law had not yet been given to make sin exceeding sinful. Of course they had the consciousness of sin and the knowledge of the difference between good and evil, but the consciousness of sin was not prominent. And therefore the types in Genesis do not refer so much to Christ the expiation and substitute, as to Christ the restorer from death unto life and from suffering unto glory. This is the typology of the book of Genesis. Abel the righteous one has to suffer. Enoch the godly one is taken up into heaven. Noah and his household are restored from death unto life, and make a new commencement of history. Melchisedek appears to Abraham not as a sacrificing priest, but as the type of Him who is the priest after the power of an endless life, and who is able to give blessing to the children of God, — offering to them bread and wine. Isaac is not so much a type of Christ as a substitute, as of the method in which God through death can yet fulfil the promise, and restore the seed to whom is given that promise. Joseph, lastly, is the type of Christ, through humiliation and prison and suffering, exalted to power and glory, to be the source of salvation and blessing to his own household, as well as to Egypt.

XV - The Deep Spiritual Meaning of the Decalogue and of the Whole Law

Let us for a few moments look back again on the teaching connected with the history recorded in the book of Genesis. Genesis is the Alpha of Scripture, and because Jesus Christ is the Alpha, Genesis is full of Christ. The higher teaching which is given to us in the apostolic Scriptures brings out deeper truths than those which we considered, when we dwelt chiefly upon the training which God gave to the human race, and to His chosen ones, Abraham, Isaac, and Jacob, limiting ourselves to what they were most probably able to understand at the time. But who that has read the gospels and the epistles and the book of Revelation can fail to see, hidden in the book of Genesis, still more wonderful truths and spiritual and heavenly realities? Before that "In the beginning" of the first chapter of Genesis, there is the eternal beginning which is revealed to us in the first chapter of the gospel of John; and in the light of that chapter of John and many declarations of the apostle Paul, who can fail to see in the 1st chapter of Genesis the revelation of the blessed Trinity? Ten times it is written," And God said, "for by the word of the Lord all things were made, and the Spirit of God was moving upon the face of the waters. Who can fail to see, in the light of the teaching given to us in Corinthians and in Romans, that the first Adam was a type of the last Adam, and that, as by the disobedience of the first many were constituted sinners, so by the obedience of Christ, the everlasting Son, many are constituted righteous in the sight of God? The formation of Eve out of Adam, we are told in the epistle to the Ephesians, is a type of the creation of the Church of Jesus Christ out of Him who was crucified, and who rose again from the dead. The meaning of God resting upon the seventh day is explained to us in the epistle to the Hebrews, as showing that God in His great love wishes to introduce us by faith into His rest, that thus we may find our blessedness in Him. The victory that is announced to be achieved over the serpent, what else is it but that victory which spiritually was achieved when Jesus Christ died upon the cross and the prince of this world was cast out, and which shall be achieved actually, as is written in the twentieth chapter of the book of Revelation, when Satan shall be chained for a thousand years, and finally accomplished when Satan shall be bruised under our heel? In the light of the New Testament also we can understand how Abel, Noah, and Enoch unitedly show forth that Jesus the Good Shepherd, the Righteous One, must die, that Jesus was the deliverer of the household of faith from the floods of God's judgment, and that Jesus, like Enoch, ascended up on high, having this testimony — that he went unto the Father, because of righteousness. In the light of the New Testament we understand that Babel had its antitype in Pentecost, when, by the gift of the Holy Ghost, all nations were united together in one faith and in the common understanding of the mysteries of God, and that the judgment upon Babel is typical of that last judgment which we read of in the book of Revelation, when Babylon shall fall. A different and a higher light falls also upon the life and upon the manifestations of God to the patriarchs, Abraham, Isaac, and Jacob; and in the final history with which Genesis concludes, Joseph is truly understood in the prophetic light, not as a type of Christ's relation to sinners in general, but a type of Christ's relation to Israel, after He has been a blessing to the Gentiles, when he rouses the children of Jacob — who, although nominally they have been faithful to the God of their fathers, yet in reality have blood-guiltiness upon their conscience, — when he reveals himself to them in the greatest tenderness and love, "I am Joseph your brother."

But however these deep mysteries may to a certain extent have been known unto the people of that age, one thing, as we have seen already, we must clearly understand. They did know that God revealed Himself to them; God showed Himself as a God of mercy; God gave to them the promise of a deliverer from death and the consequences of sin; and their attitude was simply the attitude of faith, which is the only attitude in which, during any dispensation, men are able to please God. They were believers. It was by faith

156

that they served God, and the very first time that the word "righteousness" is mentioned in Scripture is when we are told that Abraham believed God, and it was accounted to him for righteousness; and the very first time that the word "priest" is mentioned in Scripture is in connection with Melchisedek, who had in himself the right of priesthood, and who is a type of that Priest who is now seated upon the throne of glory, and brings blessings, under the covenant, unto His people.

Now when, in the book of Exodus, the history which had been interrupted for 400 years begins again, we see the children of Abraham, Isaac, and Jacob in sore captivity and bondage, for the great truth had to be typified that the people whom God has elected are a people who are in great misery, and who must be redeemed. In Egypt, Israel, according to the providence of God, was brought into contact with the highest civilised nation of the world, and yet at the same time was kept separate, on account of the antipathy which the Egyptians had to shepherds; and although the idolatry of Egypt, to a certain extent, contaminated Israel, yet, on the whole, Israel kept faithful to the remembrance of the God of Abraham, Isaac, and Jacob. So it was by faith that the parents of Moses watched over the infant that was entrusted to their care. In God they believed, and in the promises which were made to the fathers; and they had not forgotten that Joseph by faith had given commandment concerning his bones, that these were not always to remain in Egypt, but that surely God would bring Israel back into the land which He had given them, and that then they were to bury him in that land that was dear to the heart of faith.

As they had this faith in God the Creator, in the only God who had chosen their fathers, and whose covenant was an unconditional covenant, so it was necessary that these truths should be still more firmly impressed upon their mind before the great dealings of God with Israel commenced, and they beheld God in His supremacy, in the miracles to be wrought upon the Egyptians, which proved to them that God was above all the powers of nature. And the connection between sin and death was made manifest to them — how God redeemed them out of Egypt simply on account of His sovereign mercy, and not owing to any superior merit which they possessed — by that wonderful type of the paschal lamb and of the blood which was sprinkled against the door-post; showing that they also were under sin and under the curse and under the condemnation of death, but that God in His great mercy had provided a substitute, by the shedding of whose blood it was possible for Him to carry out His counsels with mercy and compassion.

And that night in Egypt— when, by faith, they slew the paschal lamb, and sprinkled the blood and ate of the lamb, having their loins girded, in repentance, in humility, in trustfulness towards God, in thankfulness, in entire dependence upon His power and His grace — was memorable throughout the whole history of Israel. It was the beginning of their history. Afterwards, in the book of Kings, when Solomon built the temple, we are told that it was so many hundred years after God brought Israel out of Egypt. This was the beginning of their chronology. It was the first month of the year to them — the beginning of every year. The whole national existence is rooted in that exodus from Egypt — a marvellous fact which will find its full illustration when, according to the gospel of John, Israel in the latter days shall look upon Him whom they have pierced, upon that Paschal Lamb of which not a bone was to be broken — Alpha of Israel's history, Omega of Israel's history. All the prophets allude to this, that God brought them out of Egypt. And you remember who it was that said, "With desire have I desired to eat this passover with you"? Not until the greater event shall happen, the still more wonderful manifestation of the power and grace of Jehovah, when He shall make Israel again His manifest and glorified people, shall that night be forgotten, or the remembrance of that great exodus be eclipsed. And not merely the exodus, but also the deliverance out of the Red Sea, was entirely by the power of God; for this also was to be made secure unto Israel. Not merely did God alone redeem them out of Egypt, but it was God only who was their sanctification, and who separated them from Egypt and from the power of Egypt. Oh, how clearly did they understand this, as we can see from the song of Moses and of the people of Israel. God only is holy; God only has redeemed His people. He has redeemed them to bring them near to Himself, into His sanctuary, where they may be in communion with Him, and where He shall reign for ever and for ever.

But the reason why He brought them out of Egypt, as was said to Pharaoh, was this, that upon Mount Sinai He might betroth them to Himself as His own people. Mount Sinai is generally viewed, and correctly viewed, as the mountain where God manifested His severe justice and His awful majesty. Even Moses himself was filled with fear and trembling. But there is another aspect of Mount Sinai, which we also read of in the prophets. It was, as it were, the place where God, who had brought His bride out of Egypt, betrothed Himself unto her. "I remember the time of thy first love, the day of thine espousals, when thou wentest after me in the wilderness."

Israel is God's son. Unto Israel pertaineth the adoption. Here we are not in the territory of creation and nature. Whatever is said about God being a universal Father — and there are some elements of truth in that representation — it does not come into contact with this. Not because God created Israel, and has created all human beings, is He their Father, else the term "adoption" would have no meaning. "Out of Egypt have I called my Son." He has adopted them to be His — "His own."

Now before I begin to speak about what God said and did upon Mount Sinai, let me remind you of that wonderful phenomenon which has become more and more observed by all historians and by all those who investigate the religions of different nations — that there is no trace of monotheism to be found until we come to Abraham, and therefore only by something wonderful and supernatural can we account for the fact that there was a race

who worshipped one God and who knew that God by name; for all the Shemitic tribes, without any exception except the Jews, were idolaters. They
were not merely idolaters, but the number of their gods and goddesses and
heroes was exceedingly large, and their idolatry was connected with great
abominations and degrading sins. In Israel, although there was often a falling
away into idolatry, or an attempt to combine the worship of Jehovah with
idolatrous usages and places, all idolatry is always regarded as a going after
strange gods and after new gods. There is not the slightest trace in Scripture,
or anywhere else, that Israel at one period of its existence was idolatrous, or
semi-idolatrous, and then gradually rose to the knowledge of there being one
God. Idolatry is always spoken of as adultery which Israel had committed, for
God was from the beginning the very God who had revealed Himself unto
them, and it was only from other nations that they adopted the idea of there
being gods, and of those idolatrous services which were connected with their
ideas of gods. There is the significant fact that there is no word in the Hebrew
language for goddess. Such an idea never entered into their minds. That entire degradation of the idea of God — whatever remnant there may have
been left in the minds of men from the primeval revelation — that thorough
degradation of the idea of God, according to which men knew really of no
God, but only a personification of the powers of life, had never any place
among the descendants of Abraham, Isaac, and Jacob. This point is so important that I would like to read to you two statements in regard to it of two
English writers; the first from De Quincey, "There is one sole idea of God. Of
this idea two things may be affirmed: the first thing, that it is at the root of all
absolute grandeur, of all truth, and of all moral perfection, the second is, that,
natural and easy as it seems when once unfolded, it could only have been
unfolded by Revelation; and to all eternity, he that started with the false conception of God could not, through any effort of his own, have exchanged it for
a true one. All idolatries alike, though not all in equal degrees, by intercept-
ing the idea of God through the prism of some representative creature that
partially resembles God, refract, splinter, and distort that idea, so that idolatry is not merely one of many evils, and one utterly beyond the power of social institutions to redress, but, in fact, it is the fountain of all other evil that
seriously menaces the destiny of the human race." The great importance of
this is evident. Men who do not wish to believe all that is written in the Bible,
select a few things from the Bible which they like, and then give themselves
the appearance as if they had found out these great truths by their own reason, or from the intuitions of their own mind; whereas they would never
have known that there is a God who has created the heavens and the earth,
except through the revelation which God gave to Abraham, Isaac, and Jacob.
And not merely would they not have known that there is one Godhead. Important as this is, it is not of the chief importance; some philosophers have
supposed that there could be only one supreme cause of all things; but that is
not God. To believe in a Godhead and in a supreme being is not to believe in

God. I may see the beautiful pictures and sculptures which some great artist has produced, but I do not know him. The little child that plays with him knows him as his father — knows his person, knows his countenance, knows his love. Of what use is that abstraction of Deity which the philosophers possess? Canon Mozley says: "The vulgar among the heathen believed in many gods; the philosopher believed in a universal cause; but neither believed in God. It is perfectly evident; I cannot understand how people can read the Bible and not see it, but they do not. The vulgar believed in many gods; the philosopher believed in a universal cause; but neither believed in God. The philosopher only regarded the universal cause as the spring of the universal machine, which was necessary to the working of all parts, but was not thereby raised to a separate order of being from them. Theism was discussed as a philosophical, not as a religious question. Nothing could have astonished him more than, when he had proved in the lecture-hall the existence of a God, to have been told to worship Him. 'Worship Him,' he would have answered; 'worship what?' Would you picture him indignant at the polytheistic superstition of the crowd, and manifesting some spark of the fire of St. Paul, when he saw the city wholly given to idolatry? You could not have been more mistaken. He would have said that you did not see a plain distinction. The crowd was right on the religious question; the philosopher right on the philosophical. However men may uphold in argument an infinite abstraction, they could not worship it. The hearer was much better fitted for worship than a universal cause — fitted for it not in spite of, but in consequence of, his want of true divinity. The supreme being among the Brahmins was a characterless, impersonal essence, a mere residuum of intellectual analysis. No temple was raised to him, no knee was bended to him; without action, without will, without affection, without thought, he was a substratum of everything himself — a nothing. Thus the idea of God was far from calling forth in the ancient world the idea of worship. It ever stood in antagonism with it. One simple nation alone of antiquity worshipped God, believed the universal being to be a personal being — God." And while Israel knew God and knew His name, they were opposed to all idolatry, and, as we have seen before, Nebuchadnezzar and Darius and Cyrus, and many of the Gentile nations, were taught by them the idea of God; and since Israel has forsaken God, and His own proper name of God, with which to go out into the world, but only prides itself in the idea of the unity of God, which sinks back again into the philosophical idea of an abstraction, they have done nothing to disturb the idolater and to convert the heathen nations. But we Christians who believe in Father, Son, and Holy Ghost, and who have the name of Jesus standing out as a personal name, even as Israel of old had the name of Jehovah — we have gone forth, and many have turned from idols to serve the true and living God, and to wait for the coming of the Lord Jesus from heaven.

Now this God brought Israel out of Egypt, and there they were before Him, at Mount Sinai; and this God was holy, and yet He was their covenant God.

What is holiness? Holiness can only be understood by what Scripture teaches us of it. All other ideas must give way, and we must be perfectly silent to hear the voice of God. Holiness has generally been explained as the love of that which is good, and the hatred of that which is evil. But that is not holiness; it is a consequence of holiness; it is a manifestation of holiness; but holiness does not consist in this. The holiness of God, as it is revealed to us in Scripture, seems to me to be this. It is not one of many attributes, but it is that out of which all the attributes of God flow, and in which they all are connected. God is holy; He only is holy; and the holiness of God is, so to speak, the infinite self-containedness of God, that He is Himself and nothing else, that in Himself there is all that is infinitely pleasing to Him, that He is sovereign, majestic; and as this holiness of God consists in there being nothing and none with whom God can be compared, and unto whom we can liken Him, the brightness of God, the majesty and transcendence of God above all things and above all persons, so this holiness has two aspects. In one aspect it removes God to an infinite distance from all that is creaturely, and therefore it is that which appears to be what prevents us from drawing near to Him. For, according to that holiness of God, God is of purer eyes than to behold iniquity; and as He is God of life, death, and everything that leads to death, is impure in His sight, and cannot appear before Him; so that the guilty, and those that are under the sentence of death from their birth onwards, are separated from God. But just as the life of God, in one aspect, is a consuming fire against everything that is opposed to God, in another aspect, like the light — although it cannot bear that anything should touch it that is not light — it is essentially communicated. Thus it is the holiness of God which comes into the hearts of people to bring them into closest communion with Himself.

Therefore we find this double aspect of holiness — Holy, holy, holy. Lord God of Hosts, not to abide alone: "Heaven and earth are full of Thy glory." Glory is holiness manifested; holiness is glory concealed. Isaiah trembles because he is a man of unclean lips, and dwelling among a people of unclean lips. It is the Holy One who sends him forth. He is the Holy One of Israel, not to condemn Israel: "The Holy One of Israel, and thy Redeemer," therefore the holiness of God has this double aspect — God is God. Sin and death cannot appear before God. But just because God is God, therefore He is able to sanctify a people unto Himself; and how does God make anything holy? Simply by His bringing it near to Himself It is not by any inherent quality that He infuses into a. person or into a place. Wherever God chooses to manifest Himself, that ground is holy; and whatever sinners God chooses to bring near to Himself, from that moment they are holy. So was the thief on the cross holy, the moment he said, "Remember me when thou comest into thy kingdom." By bringing them unto Himself, God constitutes them holy. But Israel was a sinful nation, as we all are sinful, but God said, "They are my nation; a kingdom of priests unto me, a holy nation. I have separated them unto myself."

But what is now that covenant that God initiated upon Mount Sinai? Is it a covenant of works? Is it a law, in its aspect of condemnation and of curse? In one respect it is. That was only a very limited, secondary, and, if I may so speak, negative attribute of the dispensation, which commenced upon Mount Sinai. Only think of it The unconditional covenant which was made with Noah, and of which the rainbow is the sign; the unconditional covenant which was made with Abraham, Isaac, and Jacob, and of which circumcision is the seal, could never be frustrated by anything which should happen subsequently, as the giving of the law on Mount Sinai, 400 years after, and the dispensation which followed from it. God, by an oath, had sworn unto Abraham that He would be his God and the God of his descendants, and that He would give them the land, and that He would give them the Messiah, This oath could not have been frustrated, could not have been modified, could not have been put aside, by that which God is now going to reveal to them. This is the first reason.

Second reason. If it was a covenant of works, on condition of Israel's disobedience God would reject them, and on that of Israel's obedience God would befriend them; then, when Israel made a golden calf and worshipped it, the history of Israel ought to have ceased. The covenant was broken. God had no longer anything to do with them. But so far from this being the case, God returns again to this promise, "I am the God of Abraham, Isaac, and Jacob." The history of redemption commenced. The covenant with Abraham, Isaac, and Jacob is dear to the heart of God, and the only hope of His people; it flows on, a river of mercy, with as great vitality and fulness as it ever possessed before.

The third reason. A covenant of works, with death, curse, condemnation? Yes, it is perfectly true, but why is it that God again reveals all His name? "The Lord God, gracious, merciful, slow to anger, plenteous in redemption." Why is it that in that law God gives them priests, gives them a tabernacle, and gives them sacrifice? God says, I will forgive your sins, and I will make you draw near to me. How is it that none of the prophets ever, for a single moment, thought that the covenant with Abraham had been set aside, or that they were living under the curse, or that they did not know the grace of God, God forgiving and God sanctifying them? It was necessary that it should be made plain to Israel that the law had this aspect: "You are all guilty in the sight of God, and if I were to deal with you according to that which is required by the corresponding part on your side to the law, I should have nothing more to do with you. You depend entirely upon sovereign mercy, upon grace." The law itself thus mocks, so to speak, at its own utter insufficiency, and points us to that covenant of grace which is rooted in the eternal love of God. It was with the Jews as it is with you. Every man that is not converted is under the law, and under the curse of the law, although this is a gospel dispensation. Else why do you need to say, "God be merciful to me, a sinner," and "What shall I do to be saved?" And what understanding have you of the new covenant unless you know that you are transgressors, and transgressors of what? Transgressors of the law of God. There were the wicked and the worldly, and the law was a testimony to them and bridled them, and was a hedge round them, lest they should go on to worse, and it warned them, that they might be led, if possible, to repentance. There were the people whom our blessed Saviour describes, "Blessed are the poor in spirit, blessed are they that mourn, blessed are the meek, blessed are they that hunger and thirst after righteousness." There were Zachariah and Elizabeth. They were righteous before God, walking in all the ordinances and commandments of the Lord — blameless. Do you think that Zachariah and Elizabeth thought that they were justified by the works of the law? They were righteous before the Lord in the way in which any sinner can be righteous, in the way in which Abraham was righteous before the Lord, and in the way in which all Christians are righteous before the Lord, because they believed the Word which He had given to them; and therefore, because they waited for the redemption, they walked in the ordinances and commandments of the Lord. And then there were the Pharisees and the self-righteous, as Saul of Tarsus, who did not understand the spirituality of the law, who went about to establish a righteousness of their own, by the works of the law; who did not see that the law was spiritual, and that neither righteousness nor life could come by the law. The aspect of Jesus on his appearing to Saul crushed him, revealed to him the whole splendour of the law, and the insufficiency of the law, and he cried out for a Redeemer.

To make this still plainer, it is the covenant of works, it is the dispensation of law, but only on the outside, and only as to the shell, not as to the kernel. God says to Jerusalem: I will make a covenant with you, not as the first covenant was when I gave you my law, and you transgressed it, when I was a husband unto Israel. God always was a husband unto Israel during the whole period. "Where is the bill of your mother's divorcement?" Israel went away from God, but God never said, "I give thee up." He was always the covenant God of Abraham, Isaac, and Jacob, or as we say, "The God and Father of our Lord Jesus Christ, according as he has chosen us in him before the foundation of the world."

So the covenant with David. Take the covenant that God made with David, 2nd book of Samuel, 7th chapter. God made a covenant with David — "The sure mercies of David," — a covenant which was ordered in all things, perfect, the covenant upon which salvation depends, and that also was conditional. He said, "If thy sons walk in my ways, I will bless them and be with them. If they transgress, I will chastise them." According to the work side of the covenant, the conditional side of the covenant, where is the house of David? Were not the last occupants of the throne of David led into the captivity? And for more than 400 years before Jesus came, was there anyone sitting upon the throne of his father David? Then did it come to nought? Yes, it came to nought, as everything was a dead failure, and must be a dead failure, under any conditional covenant and under the law. But the covenant with David could not come to nought, for Jesus is the son of David, and the title-deeds of Palestine are now at the right hand of the majesty of God. In Jesus the covenant is fulfilled, and thus it is that the glory of God in Jesus shines through the whole of that law which God gave to Israel.

Let us look now at the law, the law which God gave to His people — a theocracy in which God is the king, Israel is the nation, Palestine is the land. There must be a law. Oh, what a blessed thing it is that there is a divine law! Not the opinion of the majority. Majority? — if wisdom characterised human beings, or goodness characterised human beings, then we might have some faith in what the majority says. God gives the law. His eternal law, a blessed law, a perfect law. The whole authority of the law emanates from Himself, and it is to teach all the nations of the world, to show to them what God's idea of a nation is, and what government is. All experiments that are made in politics and in social science, containing as they do exceedingly great and exceedingly tender problems, will fail; and at last it will be seen that the true principles of national existence are contained in the five books of Moses.

This law is usually divided into moral, ceremonial, and political; but this division, although there is an element of truth in it, does a good deal of mischief in diverting the attention of people from what is really the character of the law. As James says in his epistle, "The law is one: you cannot divide it"; and for the simple reason that there is one law-giver, that is God; and therefore, whether God says, "Thou shalt love thy neighbour," or whether He says that you are not to do this thing and not to do the other thing, it is the same God that gives the law. The same life animates the whole. It is an organism, and as for calling one part of the law moral law, the expression moral is entirely inadequate, for it is not morality that is taught in the ten commandments, it is our relation to God. It is not that we are to love the true, the good, and the beautiful — a neuter thing — but we are to love God. We should not find this out by our unassisted reason and conscience. But here it is the first table of the law — what God is, what God is to us, and how we are to stand in Him, and in our love to Him. Therefore to call it moral law is to lead away from that which is the very glory of the law. Oh, how majestic it is to read the beginning of these ten commandments and the expression of the promises "unto thousands of generations of them that love me and keep my commandments." You remember the gentle voice in that little upper chamber in Jerusalem that said, "If ye love me, keep my commandments." That is the voice of Jehovah. No other being— angel or man — no other could say, "The root of all that is pleasing to God is that you have affection for me personally"; and no other has a right to give commandments but God.

Then, again, as to the ceremonial law. People imagine by "ceremonial" something to strike the senses, something to add pomp and beauty to services, something in which there is no reality. There were no ceremonies in Israel. It was all the preaching of eternal truths and of spiritual substances, and real transactions between God and the people. This ceremonial law, as it is called, contains the most sublime and touching aspect of the will of God: "Whether ye eat or drink, or whatsoever ye do, do all to the glory of God." God wishes to have communion with people in their daily business, in their seed-time and in their harvest, in all the relationships of their earthly life.

And as for the national law, it is only the expression and the application to the nation of Israel, of the ideas and truths and relationships expressed in the spiritual law and in the preparatory evangelical law, which God had given to His people. But all this does not preclude me from acknowledging that the Ten Commandments, spoken by God Himself and written by God Himself, stand as it were on a majestic height. They are, so to speak, the face of the law; and as you see the intelligence and the affection of a man in his countenance, so the whole law of God shows its face to us in those ten words which the Lord spoke. Now see the covenant of works, or rather, do not see the covenant of works, for you will not be able to see it. "I am the Lord," that is the holiness of God, Jehovah. Six thousand times the name of Jehovah is mentioned in the Old Testament, and the name Elohim, which describes God the Creator, only 2,500 times. "I am Jehovah" — that is the holiness of God. "I am the Lord thy God" — that is the covenant with Abraham, Isaac, and Jacob: and you are His children. And as God gives Himself to the people as their God, He thereby sanctifies the people, and draws them up to Himself And lest any one should imagine that this is based simply upon the relation of God as a creator to His creatures, or the universal fatherhood of God, He says, "I am Jehovah, *thy* God," according to the election of Abraham, Isaac, and Jacob, "which brought thee out of the land of Egypt" The blood of the covenant — that is the foundation upon which the whole ten commandments rest. That is the most precious part of the ten commandments. Let nobody speak of the ten commandments unless he understands this verse. To take away this verse is to take away the glory, the diadem, the head, the heart of the ten commandments. And this verse is the gospel, and nothing but the gospel. And because this is God, holy covenant God, redeemer God, they were to have no other God — thou shalt have no other gods beside me; and not merely have no other gods beside me, but this very idea of God which has been revealed to us is not to be formulated or illustrated or shaped according to the imagination of our hearts, or, as De Ouincey says, brought down to a lower level; and this law which forbids us to make any image of God is the "divine right" of Puritanism, that man has no right to invent ceremonies or methods of his own, whereby to worship God. God stands by Himself, and must be worshipped in spirit and in truth; and since God in His wonderful love has made Himself known to us — like the artist and sculptor of whom I spoke, who is known to his little child, who may not even have seen any of his pictures or any of his statues — so that we know the name of God, as we know now the blessed name of Jesus, you must keep this name of God separate from all your ideas and the desires of your hearts, and the manners and customs of the world, and walk in the name of the Lord only. And being thus with God,

God in His great mercy says, "Come unto me, all ye weary and heavy-laden ones, and I will give you rest." I will make you partakers of my rest, and I will give you as a sign of that the Sabbath day; and you shall rest in me, and know that, notwithstanding all the toils and troubles and afflictions of this earthly life, you are not a beast of burden merely; and you are not only to work for meat that perisheth, but I myself am your portion, and you will become a source of rest and blessing to your wife, and to your son, and to your daughter, and to your manservant, and to your maidservant, and even to your horses and to all your cattle. It was the idea of God to make His people happy before Him, so that under the law of Moses there were very few fast days, but a great number of feast days, in which the people were to rejoice before the Lord God in the beautiful harvest, and in all the bounties with which He had surrounded them. And as they are to be a nation upon the earth, — His representatives here upon earth, — He has put His crown upon all fathers and mothers, as being His representatives, and therefore He says, "Honour thy father and thy mother," which is the foundation of all national prosperity, and which includes also all reverence for authorities and governments, which the Lord in His providence establishes. And then He comes to the relation of man to man, and there He passes from the outward to the inward, commanding us to love our neighbour as ourself! doing him no injury by act, doing him no injury by word, doing him no injury in the most inward recesses of our hearts: "Thou shalt love him."

This is the law that God gave, and, like God, there is nothing to compare with it. Oh that it were taught in all our families! oh that it were taught in all our schools! and that it were taught everywhere where there are human beings walking upon the face of the earth; for the law is spiritual. Moses sums up the law, and Jesus sums up the law, but Jesus makes one beautiful reflection. He says the first commandment must necessarily be love to God. The other is second, but He does not like to put it even second, because, if it is second, it might be separated perhaps from the first. Jesus Christ is so anxious to show that the first table of the law and the second table of the law are inseparably connected, that He says the other is second, but "like unto it." And the whole 1st epistle of John is only an exposition of this — that love to God and love to man go hand in hand together, not as Cain was, who hated his brother Abel; and wherefore did he hate him? because he hated God; for if he had loved God, he would have loved Abel also.

But take a higher view of the ten commandments. The ten commandments, I have said, were the face of the law, the countenance of the law; but I am bold enough to say that the ten commandments are the very countenance of God Himself God is Spirit. "Thou shalt not make thyself any graven image, thou shalt hallow the name of God"; "God is light and truth;" "Thou desirest truth in the inward parts"; "Cleanse thou me from secret faults"; "Thou shalt not covet." And the hallowing of the name of God corresponds also with this — that God is light and God is truth.

And lastly, God is love. And what is the second table of the law but this, that God is the Father of the large family, and that the children are to love one another and to treat one another, according to the character of God Himself And therefore, when our blessed Saviour Jesus Christ has spoken of the righteousness, there is no other righteousness but that righteousness which is described in the ten commandments. When He dwelt upon the various commandments, — as Moses with the three elders that ascended up on high, even above the clouds and darkness of the Mount, and saw the God of Israel and the blue under his feet, and as the lark which soars up higher with her thrilling melody, so Jesus Christ says unto us, "What is this law, but that ye may be the children of your Father which is in heaven." It is the image of the Father that you ought to see in this law: "Be ye therefore merciful and generous, as your Father is merciful and generous. And be ye perfect, as your Father which is in heaven is perfect." This was the law which God gave to His people. But as the Lord was holy, just, and good, and as Israel was sinful and guilty and polluted, and under the sentence of death, how was it possible — what was the method by which it was possible — that there should be communion between God and the people? And yet God, because He is holy, wished to draw this people into close communion with Himself "I will dwell in the midst of them: I will be their God. I will dwell with them, and they shall dwell in me." He wished to marry them. He wished to become one of them — to become one with them. What a contradiction is there here! God says, "Then I will be merciful, I will forgive all your sins; I will bring you near to myself;" and God forgives sins in such a way that He is the Holy One, and that nothing of what He has said against sin is cancelled, and that the connection between sin and the wrath of God, and sin and death and the curse, is only made clearer. Therefore He gives to Israel the sacrifices: "Without shedding of blood there is no remission of sin." God is a just God, and yet the justifier of the guilty. The feeling of the sinfulness of guilt and pollution is only deepened in the hearts of Israel, who receive the forgiveness of sin. Observe the language of the 51st Psalm. David had nothing but the law of Moses to teach him the 51st Psalm; and in this 51st Psalm he says, "Have mercy upon me, according to thy loving-kindness: according to the multitude of thy tender mercies blot out all my iniquities, for my sin is ever before me. Against thee, thee only, have I sinned, that thou mightest be justified when thou judgest. And not merely have I sinned, but I am altogether a mass of sin. My whole existence is sin. I was shapen in iniquity." The law had impressed upon him the 3rd chapter of Genesis, that we are ruined in the fall of Adam, and inherit this guilt which separates us from God. "Purge me with hyssop, and I shall be clean" (the blood of Christ); "Wash me, and I shall be whiter than snow" (the divine righteousness imputed to us). So you see the law did what God meant it to do, and lest Israel should imagine that God forgives sins, but that we must do our part, and sanctify ourselves unto the Lord; lest there should be any such idea of cooperation in the mind of Israel, any such conditional salvation, oh, how was Israel continually taught: "I, even I, am He that sanctifies thee." For how can you explain in the Psalms the constant cry which rose out of Israel, 'Incline my heart to keep thy commandments"? Then the heart was not inclined to keep the commandments of God. Read the 119th Psalm, and if there is any Pelagianism or Arminianism in you, it will be rooted up by the grace of God; and although you often read in the Old Testament, "Sanctify yourselves," that has only reference to this ceremonial cleansing, and to outward bodily preparations for coming near to God. In the New Testament you never read about sanctifying yourselves; for Christ is our sanctification, who, by His blood, has transplanted us out of the region of sin and death, and brought us into the region of righteousness and life by God's electing love, by the power of the blood of Jesus, and through the application of the Holy Ghost — all which was shown in the law which God gave to Israel. Therefore God appointed holy persons, priests, and holy places where He would reveal Himself, and give to Israel His gifts, and enable Israel to bring to Him their gifts to the tabernacle. And He appointed holy times, festivals, in which all the various component parts of the divine dealings in redemption are broken up, as it were, into fragments, that they may be taught one aspect after another. Oh, it was a wonderfully merciful dispensation.

I must pass over this to say only one thing. With all its beauty, with all its glory, and with all its loving-kindness, the law was a failure. It made nothing perfect; the people of Israel felt that all these were shadows. They all knew that the blood of beasts could not take away sins. They all knew that the sacrifices had to be repeated continually. They all knew that the day of atonement was only for one year, starting them as it were again, so that the communion between God and Israel might be kept up for another year. Therefore, under the Old Testament, as the apostle teaches us in the Hebrews, the conscience was not made perfect concerning sin, and the forgiveness which they had was, so to speak, only through the patience and forbearance of God, waiting, as the apostle says in the 3rd chapter of the epistle to the Romans, until the blood, the real blood of Jesus Christ, was brought into the Holy of Holies. "The law made nothing perfect," and although the righteousness was not perfectly revealed and appropriated under the law, yet all who believed were accepted of God, and beloved. So God, in the strict sense of the word, was not yet revealed in the Holy of Holies, where there was darkness, for God dwelleth in light unapproachable, and the very excess of that light makes it unapproachable, and the very excess of that light makes it darkness to man. Into that Holy of Holies the priests could not go, the Levites could not go, the people could not go, and the high priest could go only once a year, the Holy Ghost thus signifying that the way into the Holy of Holies had not yet been made manifest. Well might Philip say to our blessed Jesus, "Show us the Father, and it sufficeth us." That was the desire of Israel during all the preceding years. And Jesus said, "He that hath seen me hath seen the Father"; and the true tabernacle, the eternal sanctuary of God, is above, and thus we read,

"If any man sin, we have an advocate with the Father, even Jesus Christ the righteous." And there was a third thing that was not given by the law, That was the indwelling of the Holy Ghost, for as the apostle Paul says, "If life could have been given by the law," it would not have been necessary for Jesus Christ to come, and to die. They were in the spirit of bondage, in the spirit of little children who were now under tutors and governors; but unto all who believe in Jesus there is given the Holy Ghost as the indwelling spirit and comforter Therefore in them is fulfilled the righteousness of the law. who walk not after the flesh, but after the Spirit. And to conclude, what applies to the law in order to obtain righteousness or the knowledge of God, or the possession of the Holy Ghost, applies to everything else in connection with Israel; for what the law could not do in that it was weakened through the flesh, God Himself must do. Where is the land which God gave unto Abraham, Isaac, and Jacob? Is it not trodden down under foot of the Gentiles? And has not God promised it to them, and has not God given to them this law on purpose that they might enjoy the land, and He would make it a fruitful and lovely land, where every man could sit under his own fig-tree, and rejoice in the bounty of the Lord his God? They have not got it. Why have they not got it? What the law could not do, in that it was weakened through the flesh, must be left to Jesus to accomplish. And so, as to the whole history of the Old Testament, you may write upon it that it is a failure, because it was weakened through the flesh. But you may write upon it that it is yea and amen in Christ Jesus, who is the Alpha and the Omega, the root and the offspring of David, the son of Abraham, and yet the I Am, before Abraham. Oh that the Lord would hasten the day when there will be no agnostics, but when "all flesh shall know that I am the Lord," when the glory transcendent of the new covenant will show us the faithfulness and grace of God manifested to Israel. Amen.

XVI - The Jewish Ordinances Shown to Reveal Vividly the Gospel

I must say at the beginning that I am obliged, very reluctantly, to give up my intention of speaking at present on the course of prophecy which had its starting-point in David, As there were so many points with regard to Moses, which I was not able to bring before you in the last lecture, I must limit myself to concluding the remarks which I made upon Moses and the dispensation that was entrusted to him.

The object of God's revealing Himself is worship. God reveals Himself to man in order that man may worship Him. God comes to man in order that man may come to God. God reveals Himself to us as a holy God. God reveals to us what man is, in order that He may show us the wonderful solution of this problem: — How there can be communion between God and man in the person of His own Son, who is God and man in one person, and who bringeth us unto the Father. He had chosen Israel to be His nation, a nation of priests. They were "holy unto the Lord." And yet, as in themselves they were full of sin, and under the sentence of death, He gave them the law in order to show that sin was exceedingly sinful, and that in His presence neither sin nor death was able to stand. And thus the whole life of the Israelite, from his birth to his death, was concluded under sin, and he was continually reminded, by the purifications and sacrifices which he had to offer, that all that was connected with himself and with his earthly life was polluted by sin, and required the grace of God and the propitiation of a mediator, in order that it might be no hindrance or obstacle to his having communion with God.

But although the whole nation was in that way "Holiness unto the Lord," yet it pleased God out of that nation to select for Himself one tribe, to be, as it were, the representative of the nation. Although everything that was said of the tribe of Levi, when Korah rebelled against their priority, may be said of all Israel: "On the morrow ye shall know who is mine, and who is holy, and whom I have chosen, that he may draw near unto God"; yet it was necessary that this special tribe should be to Israel a type and illustration of what was meant by holiness, and of what the purposes of God were concerning them. They stood before God, drawing near unto Him, and in this way representing the whole nation that was to be brought into His presence. It was they who offered the sacrifices and offerings unto the Lord; it was they who by incense showed that the prayers and supplications of the whole nation of Israel could only ascend unto God through holiness, and it was through them that the blessing of the Most High was pronounced upon His people. When we think of the priests and Levites as they were among Israel, we must look away altogether from the abuses which afterwards crept in among Israel, and, in a still worse way, into the mediaeval Church. In the first place, the priests that were in Israel had no political power. Their position, and the way in which they were sustained, precluded them from exercising any undue influence over the course of the nation. They were not like a priestly caste, as we find it among other nations, nor did they exert that influence which afterwards, in the days of our Lord, the hierarchy in Palestine exercised over the nation. Another thing to be remarked about them was this: they did not appoint themselves, nor did the people appoint them, but God appointed them. And it was they who were descended from Aaron, who belonged to the tribe of Levi, who by reason of their birth were appointed to represent the whole nation, and especially the first-born of the nation, unto God. Nor had they any power to develop the law. There was nothing in the form of tradition, there was nothing in the form of teaching and developing power given to them. On the contrary, it was their duty to guard the law, that nothing should be added to it, and that nothing should be taken away from it. And lastly — not as was the case in the mediaeval Church, and is still the case in the Church of Rome — was the relation between the individual conscience and God in any wi.se interfered with by the existence of the Levites and priesthood. They were not father confessors. It was the individual himself who, of his own accord and according to his own ability, confessed his sins and laid his hands upon the sacrifice. The priest in no wise interfered with the conscientious difficulties and with the soul troubles of the people that came to him. It was for him only to carry out the regulations which were laid down in the books of Moses, for it was deeply impressed upon Israel that although there were priests and Levites, yet it was only, so to speak, a sad necessity that led to this; and that the whole nation was a nation of priests unto the Lord.

But in this priesthood we find that there was one who was distinct above his brethren. He was called the "High-Priest," or, according to the original in one passage, the priest that is greater than his brethren, and upon whose head is the anointing oil. Although there was anointing connected with the induction of all the priests and Levites, yet it is most emphatically said of this one priest who is greater than his brethren, that the anointing oil was upon his head, or, in other words, that he was representative of Messiah. And it was the prerogative, and the prerogative of the high-priest alone, that on the day of atonement he was allowed to enter into the Holy of Holies, and there to apply the blood of propitiation unto the mercy-seat, or the lid which covered the ark of the covenant, thus showing that the whole glory of the priesthood and the whole glory of Israel consisted in this — that through atonement they were finally to be brought before the very face of the Most High, there to be accepted by Him, and regarded with His good pleasure. And here is a remarkable point, which shows the imperfection of mere individual types, all of which have to be combined, in order to give us an approximate idea of the fulness that is in Christ. Sacrifices and offerings and all the services which were offered unto the Lord on behalf of His people were not sufficient to effect communion between God and them. It was necessary that there should be a person who represented Israel before God, and here comes in again that idea which at first sight appears so strange to us, but which runs through all the dealings of God with man — the idea of a federal representative, of one who represents a multitude. So Adam represented the whole human race, and so Aaron represented the whole nation of Israel. When God is pleased with Aaron, He is pleased with the whole nation. This man Aaron is in the sight of God, Israel. Upon his forehead is written, "Holiness unto the Lord." And not merely does he represent Israel in that he brings the blood of propitiation into the Holy of Holies, but all Israel's holy things are full of defilement and pollution; their prayers, their sacrifices, their offerings, their services, would altogether be in vain, unless there was this one man to bring them before the Lord, and to make intercession on behalf of them, and on behalf of the sins of their holy things. What a wonderful thing it is, then, that although all Israel was holy unto the Lord, because God had chosen them to be His, and that although the first-born of Israel belonged unto the Lord, instead of whom stood the priests and the Levites; and although there were sacrifices of every kind and description, all showing forth the various aspects

171

of our being brought near to God, yet in this one man stood all Israel. The forgiveness of their sins, the acceptance of their offerings, their justification, and their sanctification were all vested in this one man.

There is another idea connected with the priesthood, and especially with the high-priest, which is of great importance, and it is this: God is holy, and that which cannot stand before a holy God is twofold — namely, sin and death. Sin and everything pertaining to it, death and everything leading up to it: these two are excluded from the presence of God; for God is the living One, and God is of purer eyes than to behold iniquity; and both these ideas are included in that which includes everything, namely, that God is holy, or God is God. Therefore the priest was never allowed to come into contact with death. He was the representative of life. Death did not exist for him, in so far as he was a priest. And this is the beautiful symbol and sign which God gave to Israel, that Aaron's rod budded and brought forth blossoms and almonds; for what we want is righteousness, and what we want is life; and the law, because it is weakened by the flesh, can neither give us righteousness, nor can it give us life. But there is righteousness, and there is life, not in any sacrifices, not in any services, though they also adumbrate Jesus Christ, but in a person — in the great priest — in Jesus Christ, who is called the priest after the power of an endless life. There is only one other point, and I must pass on from these holy persons. As representatives of the nation and as the types of our Saviour Jesus, they had to bring the blessings of God to His people. God alone can bless us, and the blessing of God includes everything that God, in His sovereignty and in His covenant love, intends to give to His people. And that remarkable blessing that the sons of Aaron pronounced upon the congregation of Israel is a summary of all God's teachings and of all God's promises. The doctrine of the blessed Trinity can be clearly seen in it by us, and, to a certain extent, must have been understood by the children of Israel, who continually heard that benediction, and rested in it. God, in so far as He is incomprehensible and infinite, the hidden source of all blessing and of all preservation, is the Father. The Father hath blessed us with all spiritual blessings in heavenly places, and it is the Father also who keeps us holy. "Father, keep through thine own name those whom thou hast given Me." And everything that can be seen of God is manifested in the Son, who is the countenance of God. Therefore the second part of the blessing proceeds: "The Lord make his face shine upon thee, and be gracious unto thee" in that manifestation of himself which is in Christ Jesus. But all that is in God, incomprehensible and hidden, and all that is in God, manifested and through propitiation purchased for us, cannot be appropriated, unless it be by the power of the Holy Ghost. Therefore we have here God again, Jehovah lifting up the light of His countenance, and so applying it to the mind and conscience that we may have peace. This was the wonderful benediction which the sons of Aaron, in God's name, pronounced upon the people, and this is the only trace that I can discover in the Old Testament of anything like a fixed form, that was to be used in the services of God. The prayers of the people, the prayers of the priests, the intercession of the high-priest, were not trammelled by any fixed form of words, but were expressed as the Spirit gave them utterance. Thus they poured out the desires of their hearts before the Lord. But what God wished to give to His people — the covenant, revelation and blessings of His infinite love — was given to the people by the words chosen by the Holy Ghost, to be to Israel a never-ending and inexhaustible source of strength and of consolation.

As there were holy men set apart, although all Israel was holy, so there was a place set apart, in which God and His people were to meet, where God manifested His glory, where He bestowed upon Israel the blessings of forgiveness, acceptance, and all that was necessary for their spiritual life, and where God also enabled Israel of His own to give back to Him again. The gifts which He bestows are changed into gifts which Israel offers again unto the Lord.

You know from reading the whole Old Testament that Israel never entertained any superstitious idea that God could not be worshipped everywhere. "From the utmost corner of the land will I cry unto Thee." Wherever God manifests Himself, there is holy ground. When the manifestation of God is at an end, the holiness of the ground is also at an end. But quite in consistency with this idea, God wished to show to Israel that there was only one mode of worshipping Him, and wished also to pre-figure that great meeting-place, where God and His people will be united together for ever, in Christ Jesus our Saviour. It is impossible for me to say more than what may just serve to remind you of this wonderful tabernacle, which is explained to some extent in the epistle to the Hebrews, but which every Christian, more or less, through the light of the New Testament teaching, is able to explain to himself Thirteen chapters are devoted to the description of the tabernacle, whereas scarcely two chapters are devoted to the narration of the creation of the world. For this purpose was the whole world prepared — that God and His people should be united together, and that there should be glory to God, through the pardon and sanctification of a people whom He has chosen unto Himself In the outer court, where the people were allowed to come, we have Christ manifested, as our substitution and our atonement. There stood the brazen altar, upon which the sacrifices were brought into the holy place, where the priests served. There was the candlestick with seven branches. There was the table with the twelve loaves of the hallowed bread. There was the golden altar of incense. In the Holy of Holies there was always darkness, but there was the ark of the covenant, for everything was based upon the covenant which was made with Abraham, Isaac, and Jacob. And as the great treasure and jewel of that covenant — inside the ark — there was the law of God; and since Israel was a transgressor of the law of God, there was the mercy-seat, or the lid, which was sprinkled with the blood. And since in Israel, as afterwards in the Church, there was to be shown, to the powers and principalities the wonderful depth of the love of God, and the end and purpose of all creation, there were the cherubim, as the representatives of God's creative glory, who desired to look into this mystery. The light which was in the holy place was in reality the manifestation of that light which could not be seen on account of its great brightness, and that light is none other but Christ; and at the same time that light is also in believers, who in Christ Jesus are light unto the Lord, even as Israel in Jehovah was a light unto the Gentiles. The bread which was upon the table in one aspect was the bread which God gave unto the twelve tribes; it was the bread which came down from heaven, in which the countenance of God was manifested. But on the other hand, it was also the bread which the twelve tribes offered unto God, working for bread which should not perish, bringing forth that which in the sight of God was regarded as the true bread, and thus satisfied Him, because it was the life of His people. And so was the golden altar of incense a representation of the prayer that is acceptable to God— both the prayer of Christ and the prayer of all who are Christ's, who only in Him and with Him are able to offer up their petitions to the Father. The difficulty of explaining the tabernacle is this, that God in His wonderful wisdom has combined so many things by this one illustration; for the primary fulfilment is in Christ, who was the tabernacle. "The Word was made flesh, and tabernacled among us." "Destroy the temple, and I will build is again; this spake he of his body." And in this temple there were two things that there were in the tabernacle the glory of God revealing Himself, and Jesus in His humanity giving to God all that man can give to God, that is well pleasing to the Father. And if even this application already contains such a number of elements and aspects that we can only profitably meditate, so to speak, superficially on them, the riches and abundance of the teaching of the tabernacle appear still more, when we go on to say that the fulfilment of the tabernacle is not in Christ alone, but that it is in Christ in union with His people — that in Christ both God and man meet, God showing Himself to us, and God giving in Christ all that we need, light and bread and the power of prayer, after having been reconciled to us by the blood of Chri.st, and we offering up to God in Christ all the offerings that are pleasing to Him, and being a light before God, and showing to God that the purposes of His grace are fulfilled in us, through the indwelling of the Spirit. And so everything in this tabernacle was intended to teach; for it was not as sanctuaries of other nations, built according to the ingenuity and wisdom of man, but it was built according to the pattern which God showed to Moses in the Mount. Moses was only carrying out the idea of God, and all the men that were engaged in preparing the tabernacle were fitted and sustained by the Holy Ghost, in doing this great work. So there is nothing in this tabernacle that does not teach us. Even in the metal that is used — where brass is used and where gold is used — there is always a spiritual meaning. And so with even the colours which occur, and the order in which the colours occur; for they are always in the same order. There is the blue, and there is the purple, and there is the scarlet, and the white, the white either before the three or after the three, but always in this order; the Holy Ghost by all this symbolising what is reality and substance in Christ Jesus.

I hasten on to the third holy thing represented — holy times. Here we must notice the times which are represented by the number seven — the seventh day, the seventh month of the year, which was the beginning of the civil year, the seventh year, and the seven times seventh year, or the fiftieth. And in all these festivals the same idea is represented, namely, that, notwithstanding that this world is under sin, and under the chastening government of God, it is the wish of God that in all our affliction, and in all our trouble, and in all our labour, we should always return to Him and find in Him our rest and our joy; and therefore the burden and the toil are ameliorated, the deeds are cancelled and released. The property in the fiftieth year returns to the original owner, God showing to us in all things, that although we are here upon earth, and although we are a sinful and fallen people, yet, being His people, the number that characterises us is not six but seven; for six without the seven is a dreadful number, as is shown by that mystical number in the book of Revelation — six hundred and sixty-six. But ours is the seventh, because we are holy unto the Lord, and even here have a foretaste of the coming glory. And Israel specially as a nation was to show forth that glorious millennium which we are all awaiting, when upon the earth there shall be the beauty of the Lord, and all things shall rejoice before Him, and be prosperous through His presence.

Then we have the other festivals all based upon the passover, which is the beginning of the year, the passover of which we find in the Bible seven celebrations recorded, the last being that at which our blessed Saviour brake the bread and gave to His disciples. There is one aspect of the passover which is often overlooked, and that is the resurrection of our blessed Saviour, when the sheaf, as the beginning of the harvest, was waved towards heaven on the first day after the Sabbath, or on the first day of the week, which is Christ the first-fruits rising from the dead, after having been the Paschal Lamb. And so, seven weeks after that, there was the feast, when the harvest had been completed; for God combined the works of grace with the manifestations of His goodness in nature; and specially as Israel was an agricultural nation, all the blessings of God in nature and the events of the natural year were to be connected with the events of divine grace and redemption. And then we have the two loaves, that is the conclusion of the harvest, and the realization of the harvest in Israel being holy unto the Lord, afterwards fulfilled in Pentecost, when the hundred and twenty were filled with the Holy Ghost. This is the fulfilment, as the resurrection of Jesus is the fulfilment of the waving of the sheaf. And then there was the feast of tabernacles, which looked forward to the future, when Israel should rejoice before the Lord, reminding of the days in the wilderness, that they might always be humble before Him, but delivered from all their troubles; and the day of atonement, upon which the whole communion of Israel with God rested from year to year.

And now I need not say more than a few words about the fulfilment and the substance of all this to us. Among Christians there are no priests, because all are priests. All Christians are holy unto the Lord. They are a royal priesthood. They are all of them priests to offer up sacrifices unto the Lord. Those who are appointed to be stewards of the mysteries of God, and shepherds of the congregations, have many names assigned to them in the New Testament epistles, but never is the word "priest" applied to them, because it would have been quite unintelligible both to them and their congregations, and a contradiction of everything that they had been taught; for the priesthood of our blessed Lord and Saviour Jesus Christ is not after the order of Aaron, but after the order of Melchizedek, and all who belong to Jesus, are holy in Him. To quote the words of a recent writer in Germany on the question of holiness: "It was only when the Jewish Christian branch of the Church had, so to speak, disappeared, that not knowing the Old Testament in the original, but only from the Septuagint version, the deterioration in the view of people with regard to holiness commenced and rapidly developed;" for the idea of holiness, as I have often had occasion to remark, is a twofold one, The first, the fundamental, the primary idea, is that which God in His election separates unto Himself. The second idea, which is merely derivative, although special and precious, is the idea of purity — that what He has separated unto Himself is to consider itself separated from sin, and from the world, and from all ungodliness. But as in those days they had chiefly to do with the gross sins and vices of the pagans, which had come into the Christian Church, so they left out the primary idea of holiness, and laid more stress upon the secondary idea of holiness, that is purity. Precious as this idea is, to present this separate from the primary idea brings us back into the flesh and to the law, and to that which is in contradistinction to all the doctrines of grace. And so it came to pass that people spoke about a very holy man. Could you imagine the apostle Paul or the apostle John saying "very holy"? They could not say it. The expression "very holy" is an absurdity, for in holiness there is no degree. We are separated unto God by Himself. There are degrees of our faithfulness; there are degrees of our diligence; there are degrees of our attainments; but in holiness there is no gradation. Likewise is it an utterly unbiblical idea to speak of "Saint" Paul or "Saint" John, as if the other believers were not saints. Likewise are there no holy places any more: "Where two or three are gathered together in my name I will be in the midst of them" while they are gathered together; but when they are not gathered together there is nothing in the place whatever. The only holy place that we have is the heavenly sanctuary, where Christ is at the right hand of God. And as there are no holy places, so are there likewise no holy seasons. There is one day which we commemorate, the day on which our blessed Lord rose from the dead; and that, not merely in contrast with the day of the Sabbath which the synagogue observes, but also as a kind of preliminary to it, so that both the ideas of the creation and of the redemption are combined in this. But how imperfect all this symbolism is, is evident, because there are so many things that have to be combined. The first sign of the imperfection of it all, is that there are so many things. It is broken up into fragments, and we know that in reality it could not be so; it must be one. And the second sign of its imperfection is this, that even the priests and the high-priest had to offer up sacrifices for themselves to appear before God. How glorious is that perfection which is given to us in Christ Jesus, who is the tabernacle, who is the priest, in whom there is everything that God taught His people, condescending in His great mercy to their weakness.

Let me add now a few words upon the law which God gave to Israel as a nation — the national law. He was their king. The first time that holiness is mentioned in the Bible is in the song of Moses after redemption: "Glorious in holiness, who is like unto Thee?" The first time that the kingship of Jehovah is mentioned is in that same song. In your translation it says, "Jehovah shall reign"; the Hebrew is, "Jehovah shall be king for ever and for ever." This law which God gave to Moses, political and civil, or whatever you like to call it, is wonderful, when we contrast it with all other legislation. Plato, the great philosopher, wrote a kind of poem of what the State should be — the ideal that he had of a State; but, in the first place, this was all a work of imagination, and secondly, even as a work of imagination, his ideas of a State are such as cannot for a single moment be compared with the divine idea of a State. He only regarded what appeared to him the prosperity of the Commonwealth. The value of the individual soul, the sanctity of the family life — these were mysteries to him which he was not able to fathom. But oh how different is that law which God gave to His people. He Himself, in the strictest sense of the word, was their king. Law emanates from Him; and everything that He has commanded, even though it refers to minute detail of our daily life, has upon it the impression, "I am holy." Parents, governors, magistrates are not representatives of the family or of the nation; they are the representatives of God, and in that respect they are, so to speak, combined with God. The greatest justice is to be observed. The judge is to take no bribe. He is to consider all alike, as in the sight of God. And the idea of purity pervades the whole law of Moses, even to an extent we are not able to appreciate, because the distinction that is made with regard, for instance, to food and the many regulations that are made in connection with the various events of life, must all have a symbolical meaning; but this we can understand — they mean that Israel is to be separate unto the Lord in everything — for the multiplicity of duties, relationships, and occupations which God has put us into, do not contradict our being "holy unto the Lord"; but God Himself must show us how they are to be used and enjoyed as in His presence, and as in communion with Him. And the next question as to the law is this: Where is the centre of gravity in the commonwealth? It was a blasphemous saying of the French king, "I am the State"; nor is it right to say that the masses are the State. The centre of Israel was Jehovah. All was to Him, and for Him; and the king upon his throne, and the governors and rulers, and all the people were living for one another, because they were living unto God. The idea of a State, of a Commonwealth, and all the problems that are connected with it — most deeply interesting and affecting as they are when we consider the condition of the world — finds its grand solution here, if we would only study it and lay it to heart. The poorest among the Jews considered himself a nobleman. The Jews kept their genealogies. They were a nation of brethren. The twelve tribes were, as it were, twelve brotherhoods, and before Jehovah they were all united. Moses said, anticipating that there would be a king in Israel, that the king was not to lift up his heart above his brethren; nor did God ever wish or command that in Israel there should be great accumulation of wealth and of property. He Himself made provision against this. Poor there should always be in the land, but not that abject poverty which we behold in those countries that call themselves Christian. The law was a law of kindness and of mercy, under which the poor, the lonely, the stranger, the blind and the weak, and the widow and the orphan were to be considered; for "I am the Lord." The cattle were to have rest on the Sabbath day, and the owners were to see that they were not overburdened. And not merely was it a law of kindness, but it was a law of generosity. In what other legislation do you ever find such a provision made as this— that when we see an enemy in distress or peril, we are not to look away, but are to go to his assistance? How wonderfully generous were all the provisions made with regard to the poor; what generosity was to be shown to them in the seventh year, and in the fiftieth year, and at the harvest times. And this law was a law which had always before itself an idea — not an ascetic idea, but an idea of joy and gladness — that Israel was to rejoice before the Lord their God in all the occupations which He had given them, and in all the blessings with which He had surrounded them, in a land that was to be fertile, as long as they were under the blessing of God, and in a land that was to be desolate so soon as they departed from God; for even the land was in sympathy with Jehovah, as it is still in sympathy with Him. On this very earth of ours, and from the very fields and plants and trees there shall be a response when man, who is the priest of the whole creation of God, shall be really such a priest in the presence of the Most High. But now we know that the law could not accomplish this, in that it was weak through the flesh. Let me remind you of the principle I announced, which I think is the key by which to understand properly the whole Old Testament, This Mosaic law was a mere intermediate parenthetical dispensation; and it was not merely with reference to the individual sinner's righteousness and life that the law was feeble, but also as to the life of the nation. With regard to the national position of Israel, and even with regard to Israel having a tenure of the land of Canaan, the law failed, in that it was weakened through the flesh. The law made nothing perfect. The law was only to excite in Israel the great desire after Him, in whom all the promises of God are Yea and Amen, and to prepare and educate Israel for His advent.

And now let us, for a few moments, look upon Moses, who was the mediator. God does all. "Of Him and to Him are all things;" but God uses man as His instrument. He made the covenant with Abraham; He redeemed Israel by Moses; He afterwards elected David to be the beginning of the kingdom, and upon these men and their faith, so to speak, depended the continuance of God's dealings with Israel. So we must learn to combine the two aspects — that all things are of God, and that the very beginning of our faith is the gift of God; and at the same time the other aspect — that Abraham, Moses, David, the apostles, were pillars; and the pillar has to bear a weight, and if the pillar gives way, that which is based upon it will also give way. Therefore there was a great weight upon Abraham, and upon Moses, and upon David, and upon the apostles. We are built upon the foundation of the apostles, Jesus Christ being the head corner-stone. How wonderful was that man, Moses, whom God chose to be the mediator of the old covenant God chose him; God watched over his infancy. How marvellous was his protection. How marvellous was the providence which brought Moses into the house of Pharaoh, and still kept up his connection with his own family, in which Jehovah was known and worshipped. How marvellous was that choice which Moses made. He who was the only Hebrew who could, if he wished, forget his nation, and their bondage, and degradation, preferred the reproach of Him of whom Abraham, Isaac, and Jacob had testified, to all that Egypt was able to offer to him. How marvellous was it afterwards, in order that Moses might learn to distinguish between nature and grace, between flesh and the spirit, that his own zeal and enthusiasm for his nation came to nothing. And then for forty years there was a time of quiet and isolation, when in the wilderness he was a shepherd, and there God prepared him for becoming afterwards the shepherd of the nation. How marvellous was the appearing, in the burning bush, of God, or rather of Christ, the angel of the covenant, who said to him, "I am the God of Abraham, Isaac, and Jacob." God had to make him willing, for now he was not willing to go, and to be His messenger, and now He learned the lesson, "When I am weak, then am I Strong." God did everything, but all went through the trembling heart of Moses. By faith, he led Israel out of Egypt; by faith, when he was at the Red Sea, he was, crying unto the Lord, although he uttered not a single word, for the whole burden of the nation rested upon him. He it was to whom God gave the law, and God saw in Moses the whole nation. It is most touching to see how the whole nation of Israel was bound up in that one man — Moses. When God was not pleased with Israel, He said to Moses, "*Thy* people, whom *thou* hast brought up out of Egypt;" and Moses complained to God and said, "Have I begotten them? Am I their father? Am I their mother? Am I to bear and nourish them?" Moses was full of zeal for the glory of God. He forgot self completely. "What will the nation say if thou, who hast brought them out of Egypt, dost not consummate thy work and thy purposes?" Very touching is the intercession of Abraham for Sodom and Gomorrah; but there we are in a different region. Abraham appeals to God as the God of heaven and earth, who will do what is right. Abraham is touched with a feeling of pity and compassion for the inhabitants of these cities; Abraham thinks it would not be according to justice that destruction should come upon them, if there were a few righteous men. All this is very noble, is very much according to the mind of God, and shows a heart full of faith and full of love. But still higher was the position of Moses. He alone knew God; he alone knew Israel. When he was before God, it was only Israel; when he was with Israel, it was only God. When God was going to destroy Israel, and He offered to make Moses a great nation, Moses was willing to be anathema, that Israel might be saved. Never did any one rise to such a height — a height which it is almost impossible to contemplate without bewilderment — but that dear apostle Paul, who was willing to be anathema on account of Israel, his kinsmen according to the flesh. Jesus Christ Himself is the great Intercessor, who was not merely willing to die for us, but who was actually made sin for us, and a curse for us, in order that we might be brought to God. And this Moses, as the servant of God, was faithful in all God's house. He was prophet, priest, and king in Israel. To him was revealed the glory of God. To him were shown the mysteries of the kingdom, in the pattern on the Mount. His patience, his meekness, his love, his tenderness, his fortitude, his zeal; there seems no single attribute in the character of the man of God, that was wanting in him; and therefore it is difficult to speak of any excelling virtue in Moses, because he seems to have possessed all virtues. And yet you know that Moses also failed, and, strange to say, he failed just in the faithful representing of the mercy of God, the sovereignty and the grace of God, which is full of tenderness and of kindness; when he did not sanctify God before the people; when he did not show them the entire forgiveness of God; that notwithstanding all their obstinacy and rebelliousness, God was not merely about to supply them with water, but was going to give it to them, without rebuking them, or reproaching them. This was the sin of Moses — that he did not sanctify God before the nation. How can we sanctify God? What can we do? It is by not doing anything that we sanctify God. It is just by leaving the name of God as it is, that we sanctify God; and there it was that Moses failed. And so the book of Numbers is full of sadness and melancholy, and would end altogether in darkness if it were not for the book of Deuteronomy, in which Moses appears as the prophet, seeing into the far distance, showing to us, in the first place, the spirituality of the law that it is love to God and love to man, and then showing that God would never forsake Israel, but that after all their backsliding, and after all their apostasy, and after all the punishments which would come upon them, God would again have mercy upon them, and bring them home to Himself, and the prayer would at last be fulfilled: Oh that they were wise, and had a heart to obey my commandments.

The chief promise which God gave to Israel, in which there is advance upon the promises given in the book of Genesis, is the promise through Moses, that a prophet like unto himself God should raise up to the nation from among their brethren; and the adherence to this prophet was to be the essential condition of a person belonging to the people of God. To belong to this prophet was to belong to God; to reject this prophet was to reject God.

Now let me say a few words on the death of Moses. The last words on record uttered by the lips of Moses, are words of blessing, even as our Saviour, before He was lifted up to heaven, blessed His disciples: "Happy art thou, O Israel"; and then, although Moses was still strong, his eye full of brightness, and his natural strength not abated, he died. He died not in the course of nature, but as an expression of the displeasure of God on account of his sin, and also because it was not possible that Moses, who represented the law, should lead Israel into the promised land. Here we see how no human type was able to combine all that is in Christ. We must take Moses and Joshua together to complete this type. But God, before Moses died, showed to him, no doubt in a miraculous way, from the top of Mount Nebo, all the land which He was about to give to His people. Then there was a remarkable thing; Moses, who was the man of God, Moses, with whom God spoke as a friend speaks to his friend, must die; and therein was a most solemn lesson to himself and to all Israel. It was the dispensation of death, and he also, as a transgressor, must die. But it did not seem good to the heavenly wisdom that the shadow of death should be beheld on that countenance, which at one time was so radiant with the glory of God that Israel was not able to look upon it; and therefore it was that God Himself buried Moses. And many centuries after, we behold on the Mount of Transfiguration this same Moses, who represents the past and the law, and Elijah, who represents the prophets and the future, appearing to our Saviour Jesus Christ, and their conversation was about the death which Jesus should accomplish at Jerusalem. And then the disciples, after having beheld Moses and Elijah, beheld Jesus, and Jesus only; and the promise and prediction which Moses had given — "A prophet like unto me shall the Lord thy God raise up from among thy brethren," was now ratified by the voice which came from the excellent glory, and said, "Hear him." So it is that Moses leads us to Christ, in order that afterwards we should see Christ only.

There is a twofold application of this, with which I must conclude.

The first is with regard to the Jews. During this whole present dispensation, although it is their great pride and delight to say, "We are the disciples of Moses," Moses is buried, and they know not where he is. So was the law utterly unintelligible to Saul of Tarsus, and he thought that he had kept the law, and that he had a righteousness of his own, not understanding that the law was spiritual, and that neither righteousness nor life came by the law; but when Jesus appeared to him, then Saul of Tarsus not merely saw Jesus, but he saw also Moses. He understood then what was the real glory of Moses

— to lead us to the Saviour; and therefore he says that Israel, when they read the law, are not able to understand it, because there is a veil upon their hearts, but that when Israel shall turn to the Lord — he does not say "if," as if there were uncertainty — it is a mere question of time; *whenever* Israel shall turn to the Lord, then the veil shall be taken away from their hearts, and they shall not merely see Jesus, but they shall understand how it was the Lord who buried Moses, and that this Moses lives, because he testified of Christ.

And the second application is to ourselves. It was the sign of a sincere Israelite, who loved the law of Moses, that, being convinced of his guilt and of the weakness of the flesh, he longed after the Messiah, and after the promise of the Father, the Holy Ghost; and it is a sign of our sincerity, who profess to have received Jesus and the Holy Ghost, that we delight ourselves in the law, and that the righteousness of the law is fulfilled in us, who walk not after the flesh, but after the Spirit.

www.ingramcontent.com/pod-product-compliance
Lightning Source LLC
Chambersburg PA
CBHW031957040426
42448CB00006B/395